HARRIS ROSEN

THE REAL EMINEM

Revelations of an American Original

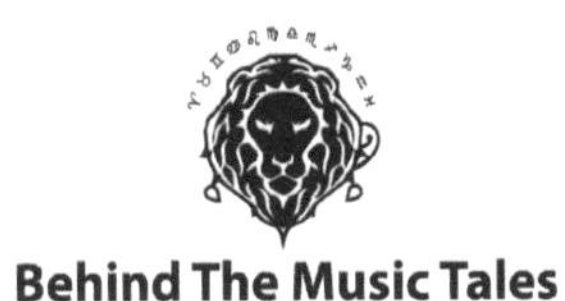

Behind The Music Tales

Behind the Music Tales Books

N.W.A: The Aftermath
The Real Destiny's Child: The Writing's On The Wall
New York State of Mind 1.0
The Reasonings of Buju Banton, Bounty Killer & Sizzla
Magnolia: Home of the Soldiers
The Real 213
The Real MC Eiht: Geah!
P. Diddy 1999: The Keys to Success & Not Giving A Fuck
The Real Daft Punk

First published by Peace! Carving 2019

First Edition

ISBN: 978-1-988956-18-3 (black and white paperback)
ISBN: 978-1-988956-17-6 (full-colour hardcover)
ISBN: 978-1-988956-16-9 (ePub)

Cover, Photo Shoot &Warped Tour Photos
by Ron Boudreau

Downtown Detroit, True Masters & Hash Bash Photos by
Matt Sonzala

This book was professionally typeset on Reedsy.
Find out more at reedsy.com

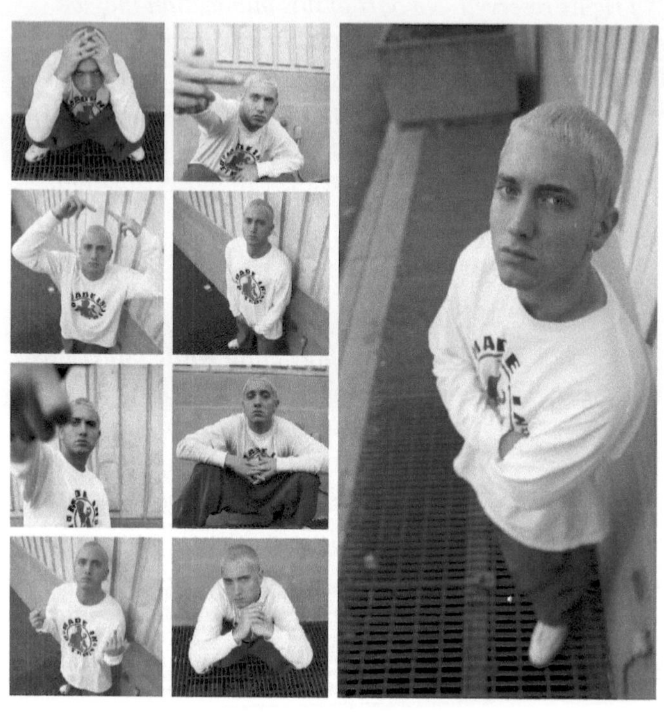

April 10, 1999 Toronto, Canada by Ron Boudreau

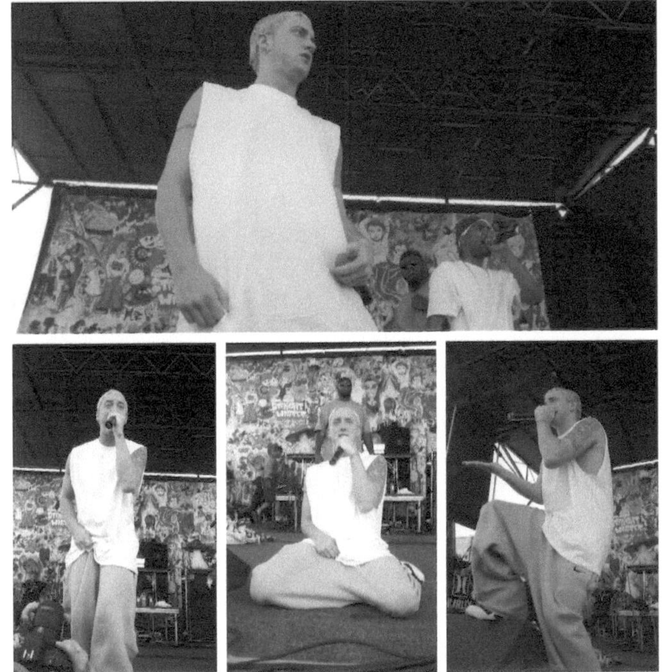

Warped Tour, July 24, 1999 Toronto, Canada by Ron Boudreau

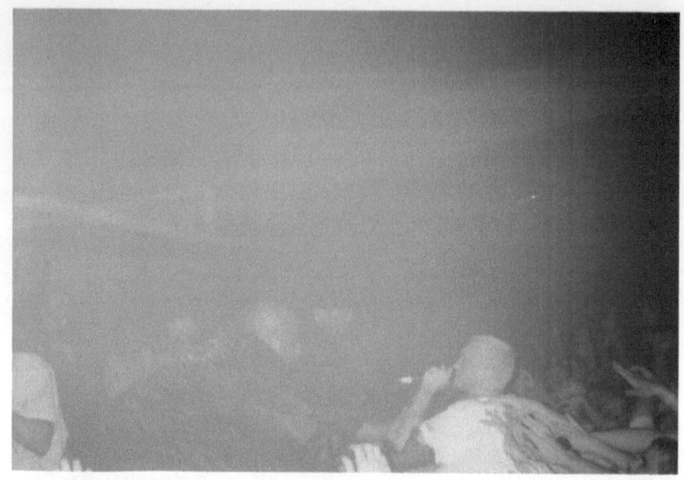

True Masters Homecoming Rave, April 3, 1999 Detroit, Michigan by Matt Sonzala

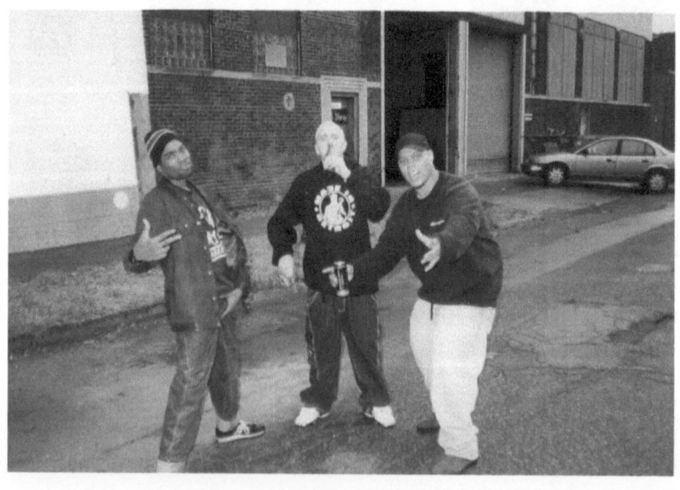

Big Proof, Eminem & DJ Head @ Mack & Bellevue, Detroit, Michigan, April 3, 1999 by Matt Sonzala

TO LOUIS, RANA, ELLEN & FAN

FOR ALL THEIR LOVE

&

THE MEMORY OF

DANIEL COHEN & RICHARD LIGHTSTONE

I am a sick fuck. I am a sick-minded fuck. I've got an imagination that's out this world.

Eminem

Contents

Preface

It is challenging to comprehend the moral sense of the past twenty years. No person, place or material is unaffected by time. The ravages of generations exceptionally cruel to Eminem. His continuing influence on two generations of Hip-Hop, Rap, and Pop Culture is incalculable. Tremendous achievements cleaved by immediate family, the death of his best friend, mental illness and drug addiction. The strength and fortitude to endure the stuff of legend.

THE REAL EMINEM like Eminem himself, holds nothing back. An unfiltered testament, *THE REAL EMINEM* presents Slim at the pivotal point of his life over two exclusive 1999 interviews and an exclusive 2001 interview with D12. Initially released in 2015 as *Broke City Trash Rapper, THE REAL EMINEM* is now illustrated by 90 original, 1999 photographs published here for the first time, and an additional 17 000 words.

The three interviews featured here present an intimate, unaltered, direct connection with Eminem at the exact point as his ascension to stardom. Others may have spoken with and interviewed him during this crucial period; however, this questioning brought deep-seated, definite reactions.

I met Proof at the Maurice Malone booth in February 1998

during the MAGIC Las Vegas apparel trade show. The biannual gathering the world's largest fashion marketplace, where clothing brands showed upcoming seasons of their line and accessories to independent one-stop stores and national chains. The Canadian distributor, Tyfoon International, advertised the brand in my magazine and I stopped by the booth where I was greeted by Proof, who worked in their Detroit showroom.

"The Enfant Terrible" of Hip-Hop fashion, Maurice Mal-one's Mojeans denim creations were instrumental in setting the path for 90's urban fashion shipping over $15 000 000 of product per year. Malone is also the founder of the legendary Hip-Hop Shop that proved integral to the growth of Eminem as an artist. I showed Proof a few issues of the magazine, and he asked if I had heard of Eminem. He declared his name-check on "Just Don't Give A Fuck" and reached into his pocket to produce the matching photo ID of DeShaun Dupree Holton. We spoke for twenty minutes and reconnected at the August 1998 edition of *MAGIC Las Vegas* for an early evening drink.

As the Publisher of Canada's largest national magazine that featured Hip-Hop, I always received the first option to interview artists. As a result, I was awarded the opportunity to become the first Canadian media to interview Eminem. The first interview featured in this book the dawn of April 4, 1999, inside a downtown Detroit City asbestos filled warehouse at the intersection of the notorious Mack Avenue and Bellevue. Eminem, Proof, DJ Head and crew set to perform at the *True Masters* Rave.

The second interview happened one week later over lunch

with Eminem and Proof, up here in Toronto, Canada, on the afternoon of April 10, 1999. The site designated as the three-star Primrose Hotel. Now the *Parkside Student Residence of Ryerson University*, at the corner of Carlton and Jarvis. The same day Proof pulled me aside and whispered a request for Molly. The quest for Room 911 revealed inside this book.

The third interview transpired with Dirty Dozen, D12 members Proof, Kuniva, Bizarre and Swifty McVay on May 30, 2001. Three weeks before the release of the Hardcore Hip-Hop, Horrorcore offensive, *Devil's Night*. Inside the Birmingham, Michigan, Four-Star Townsend Hotel northwest of Detroit.

Unknown to me at the time, further connecting Eminem and me is the gift and curse of ADHD. Eminem's battles with mental health the stuff of legend. Straight from the dome, unresolved, honest psychological back and forth anger, joy and pain. Inner demon experiences of personality faults and tendencies. Voluminous exhibitions of restlessness, inability to focus, scattered thoughts, short temper, hyper-focus, depression, isolation, perfectionism, and acting crazy. Indeed, validation of the method to the madness of my often misunderstood, filterless, direct line of questioning. Likely, the primary reason he connected with Joyner Lucas to record "Lucky You" for *Kamikaze* and the title-track of Lucas's *ADHD* album.

I began to consider a hardcover version of *The Real Eminem: Broke City Trash Rapper* in November 2017. The surprise release of *Kamikaze* earning best-selling Hip-Hop album of 2018, united by the 20th anniversary of *The Slim Shady LP* decided for me. *THE REAL EMINEM* came together between

December 2018 and May 2019. A huge grin on my face as I listened to the interview tapes again and hit rewind on every Eminem album in the CD player. The thoughts and emotions that led to seventeen thousand more words supreme.

The experience of going back twenty years grew when Ron Boudreau dug through decades of work to uncover over fifty unseen negatives from our exclusive cover photo shoot, live shots from *Warped Tour*, and a print of Slim, middle-finger extended, posing for Canada's platinum award presentation of *The Slim Shady LP*. The anticipation of releasing *THE REAL EMINEM* heightened by the reception to an early advance copy by contributor Matt Sonzala, who delivered 24 behind the scenes photographs of our trip to *Hash Bash* and hang with Eminem that are published here for the first time.

THE REAL EMINEM produces Eminem and D12, As Nasty As They Want To Be. Angry young men who lived for the day. Hungry and eager to prove themselves, middle-finger extended to the world.

Introduction

Commonly, the opportunity to interview breaking superstar artists in-person is limited. The fact that I was awarded the freedom to travel south of the border without the accompaniment of record label representation an anomaly, and I made the most of it. Forever up for an adventure, I called Matt Sonzala. We met two years earlier at *Canadian Music Week* up here in Toronto, Canada. An international promoter, in-depth inner-city scene reporter for *Murder Dog*, radio host and blogger, Matt followed the career of Eminem.

Eminem was set to perform at the *True Masters* rave. A brief stop on home turf on the heels of an intense, two-week overseas promotional journey. An eye-opening sprint through Europe consisting of live showcases and questions concerning his skin tone and the Spice Girl he wanted to impregnate. His first hometown Detroit show since being declared the hottest rapper in the game and selling over one million copies of his debut album in less than sixty days.

Matt and I shared a love of marijuana; therefore, it was imperative for us to meet the day before the interview in Ann Arbor, Michigan. Before the striking down of laws that governed the consumption of marijuana in public, many aspired to celebrate the herb and to promote its myriad of positive qualities. Matt and I compelled to participate in the festivities of the *28th Annual Hash Bash* on April 3, 1999. Ann Arbor, Michigan, University of Michigan Diag, the dedicated spot to pontificate and celebrate the proactive and positive reform of archaic marijuana laws with speeches, music, vendors, and consumption of cannabis.

The drive from Ann Arbor to downtown Detroit midday. Our arrival at the intersection of Mack and Bellevue, the location of the event, luckily at the same time as Eminem and his crew. Matt's casual photographs illustrate the easygoing character of Eminem and his crew looking to soundcheck. *True Masters*, promoted by BTM Productions on April 3, 1999, also featured DJ Magic Mike and DJ Rectangle "Tag Team" set with four turntables and two mics, U.S. Rave Godfather Frankie Bones, Da Ruckus, Paradime, Da Brigade, special guest Bizarre, Danny Tha Wild-child, DJ Mike Z, J-Money, Pakman, and Kandyman.

The entry line extended for a block, fifteen ravers wide past midnight as the music boomed from stacks of speakers sending electronic sound-waves to the axis of gyration. We paced the concrete and patiently waited to be ushered behind the scenes to His Majesty, Marshall Mathers III. Ultimately seated at the head of a large boardroom table. Proof and I exchanged a quick glance and mutual head nods as we sat for the interview and pressed record on our own tape decks. I added an on-loan video recorder to document the proceedings, and The tape may or may not reveal itself soon. Matt led the action with his superior Eminem knowledge.

Eminem kept it real and did not mince words. He spoke on his experiences coming up as an independent artist out of raw Detroit, addressed the 360 degrees flip of local media and radio, his roots in the Hip-Hop underground and how he viewed its community and the perception of him as a role model. However, with friends and crew present, and the responsibilities that exist whenever artists perform a hometown show, the interview came to an abrupt end when Slim stood up, declared *"I gotta piss like a motherfuckin' racehorse,"* and walked out at the thirteen-minute mark.

Fifteen minutes later, 1:45 a.m., Eminem took the stage in a "honky." t-shirt flanked by security, DJ Head, Proof and the Dirty Dozen. He launched into "Brain Damage," and then a freestyle of pure Detroit lyrics with Proof over Redman's "Pick It Up," and straight into Dr. Dre's "Nuthin' But A G Thang" and "Just Don't Give A Fuck." Proof addressed the crowd and called for hometown love. Then Eminem kicked it up a few notches as he glared at the gathered mass and declared he was *"going to attempt to drown myself and you can try this at home, you can be just like me* "and started into "Role Model."Detroit City star Royce Da 5'9 united with Eminem to form Bad Meets Evil and killed it with the classic "Scary Movies." More Redman love over the "I'm High" beat led into "Still Don't Give A Fuck." The classic "My Name Is" closed the short, high-energy set. Eminem offered up a gracious *"Thank you Detroit, I love you"* and exited the stage.

Indeed, Matt and I had witnessed a legendary show; still, Eminem's bowel movement made for the interview to scrape the surface and placed me in the awkward situation of having to produce a cover feature without sufficient material.

Luck on my side, Eminem was scheduled to perform his Canadian debut at The Opera House in Toronto the following weekend on April 10, 1999. I placed a few calls to Universal Music Canada and secured time for a photo shoot and follow-up interview. The intent was for Matt to complete the cover feature story interview on the phone. Sadly, the plan snuffed out in its tracks when Universal Music Canada demanded that I sit with Eminem and Proof over lunch. Reasoning that there is no point for an artist available in-person to do a phone interview. Unfortunately, I had to call Matt in Chicago to relay the bad news and upset him.

The redeeming factor of free lunch perked me up, and I sat with Eminem and Proof inside the hotel restaurant. Proof ordered a steak, Eminem a club sandwich with no bacon. The three-star service drove Slim to ask the waitress for napkins and silverware and blurt - *"This lady's crazy, man. We didn't get no silverware, little girl."* Then, when the sandwich was served, he took a bite, tasted swine and became angry.

"I asked for no bacon on the club, they put bacon on the fucking -"

"I know, and they just gave me my steak knife."

"What's up?"

Between familiarity with me from the Detroit interview the week before and my past talks with Proof, it made for a relaxed, calm and open thirty-five-minute conversation. The playful duo riffed back and forth. Eminem spoke from the heart and described essential events and incidents that led him to where he stood in the Rap game. Proof added first-hand insight and commentary as he egged on his best friend. Music as therapy; the baby momma drama that led Slim to dye his hair and tattoo his belly on the same day; the state of underground Hip-Hop; white rapper stereotypes, and the legacy of Eminem were detailed.

Eminem toured for the remainder of the year and brought the ruckus everywhere he touched down. In higher demand each and every day, his legion of fanatical disciples spread across the globe and likely beyond into the Universe. The *Slim Shady LP* the recipient of the 2000 Grammy Award for Best Rap Album.

The Marshall Mathers LP arrived on May 23, 2000, and satiated 1.78 million young Americans its week of release as it entered the Billboard Top 200 chart at #1. The brouhaha of Slim's feats was no longer undetected. His words punched international heft, and the moral majority diligently worked behind the scenes to bar his movements. Eminem, middle finger extended, laughed all the way to the bank and doubled up on accolades as *The Marshall Mathers LP* earned the 2001 Grammy Award for Best Rap Album. The brightest star in the Universe in the thick of open hostilities with ICP, Cage, Everlast, Fred Durst, DJ Lethal, and Dilated Peoples at the same time! No fucks are given to Durst, despite his stature as acting Interscope Records, Senior Vice President.

Hotter than sliced bread, the Spring of 2001 was ripe to launch Shady Records and put money in his crew's pockets. D12's *Devil's Night* the incendiary deed of saying and acting ignorant as men can get. D12 sailed high on the charts with the leadoff, pro-drug single "Purple Pills" in constant rotation masquerading under the guise of "Purple Hills" on radio and video shows. Eminem perpetually big money for *Universal Music Canada,* the regional distribution arm of Interscope Records spared no expense. A private plane was chartered to shuttle a select crew of print, television and radio media to interview the Dirty Dozen. The caveat of Mr. Mathers occupied filming *8 Mile* and unavailable to participate.

Instantaneously, I booked Photographer Steven Carty. Innately, not one to be left out when he smelled an opportunity, the Fashion Editor did whatever he could to be included, and through sheer persuasion and backroom tactics finagled an official invite and seat on the plane. The coordinates of D12, the upscale suburb of Birmingham, Michigan's Townsend Hotel. The date of the same day inbound and outbound flights and a media blitz, May 30, 2001. Three weeks before the release of *Devil's Night.* Our party arrived amid afternoon tea service and were instructed to sit and wait for designated media outlet times in the lounge area adjacent to a set of elevators. Time passed by the clink of each round of Heineken served up by the friendly waitress who befriended us and revealed her criminal record past for selling drugs and watching guests stroll into and out of the elevators.

Respect for how far D12 had risen since their days as solo artists and battle rappers inside the Hip-Hop Shop on the west-side of Detroit when we collectively spotted individual members of U2 approach the set of elevators. The upwardly mobile status of D12 illustrated by the presence of the superstar group in the same hotel. U2 nested onsite, set to perform a sold-out show inside The *Palace of Auburn Hills* on the *Elevation Tour*. Together, we observed drummer, Larry Mullen Jr. and his trainer, bassist Adam Clayton, and guitarist The Edge, who declined casual photo requests. Eventually summoned to the suite of D12 and directed to the bedroom, where Proof and Kuniva held court for the first part of the interview. Then shuffled to the central area of the suite to face Bizarre and Swifty McVay. The conversations an exact perceptive of the crew's "Just Don't Give A Fuck" mindset and attitude at the crux of Eminem's evolution.

D12 straight and to the point unequivocally cultivated the message of *Devil's Night*. The message behind the madness of the controversial X-rated lyrical assault declared. They emphatically stated the desire to spoil kids and ruin their lives. Additionaly spoke on coming up from the gutters of Detroit City alongside Eminem. They also granted insight into the hidden track "Girls," as they unmasked the source of martyrdom and beef that rallied against them and its particular, secret reaction. Its original title and diss songs focused on former *Anger Management Tour* mate Fred Durst of Limp Bizkit also included.

The quartet assembled together in the central area of the suite to complete the conversation as my time came to an end. The Fashion Editor stepped into action, and placed t-shirts branded with the name of his Toronto store on D12 and patted himself on the back. Photographer Steven Carty unluckily left with minimal location options to shoot the quartet of Dirty Dozen members, strained to capture them in the stairwell.

THE REAL EMINEM is essential for those seeking to know the actual state of mind and the thought process of Eminem and D12 in the period their music captured the hearts and minds of a new breed of Hip-Hop for the first time. The original photo shoots, live, and rare behind the scenes photographs make it the complete package.

Harris Rosen

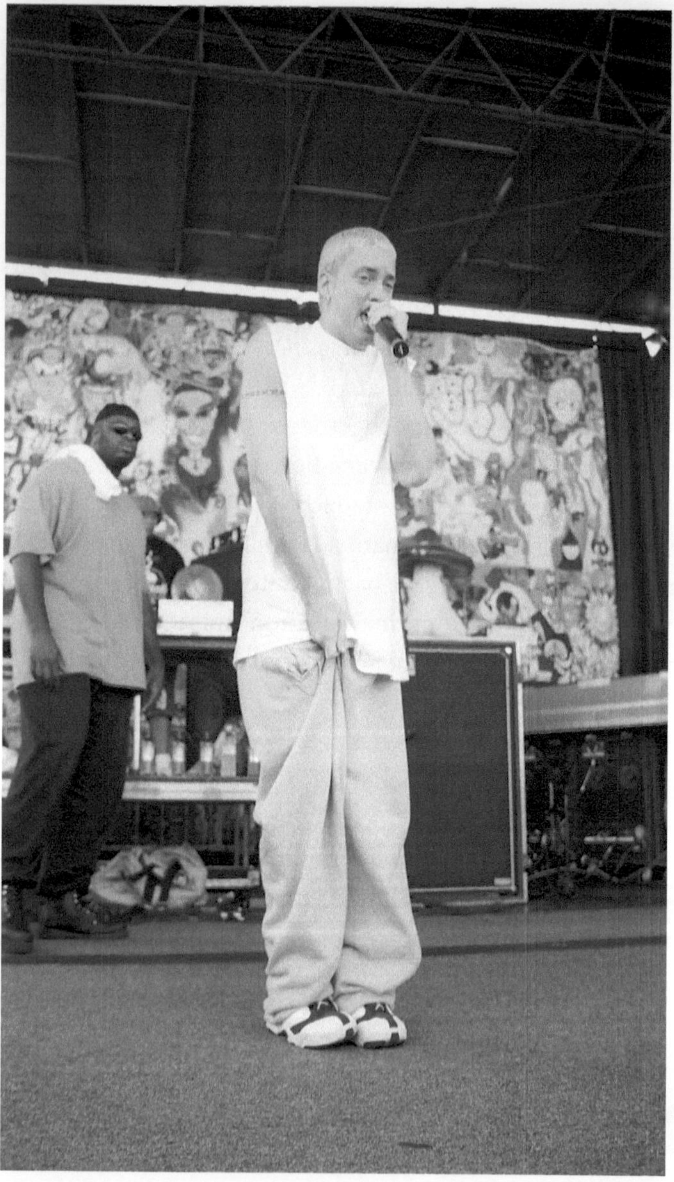

Hi, kids, do you like violence?

Harris Rosen

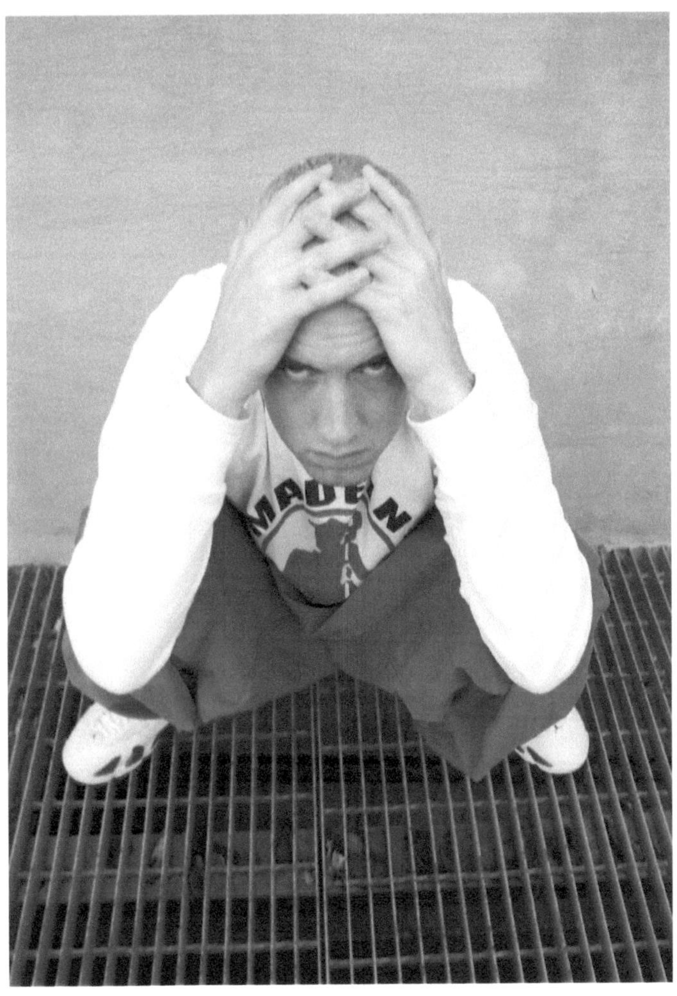

Friends are people that you think are your friends
But they really your enemies with secret identities

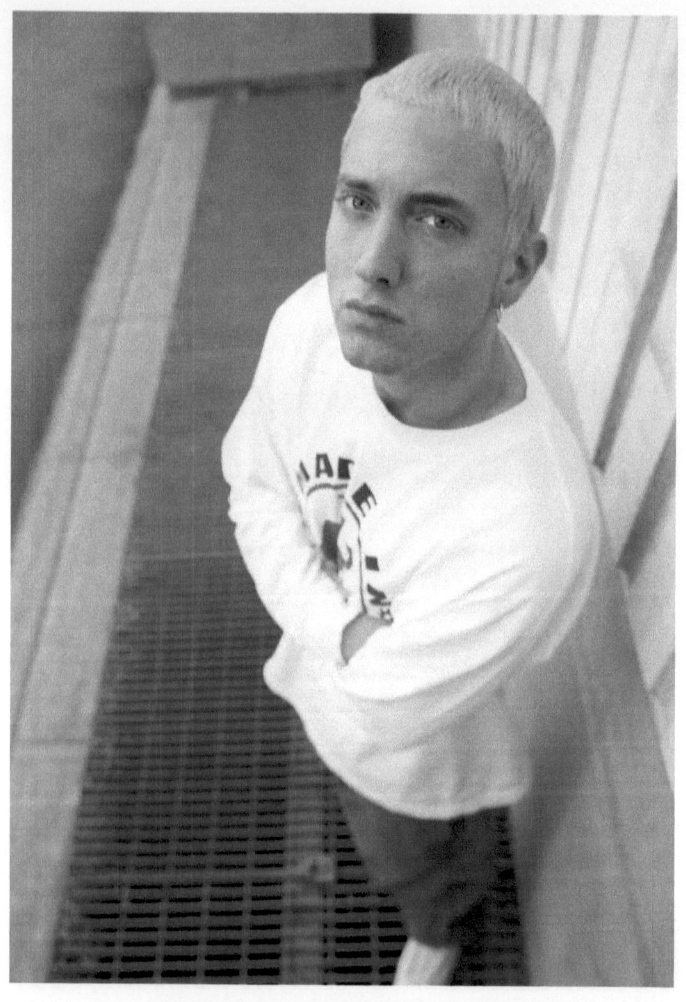

To be the Sad Man Behind Blue Eyes

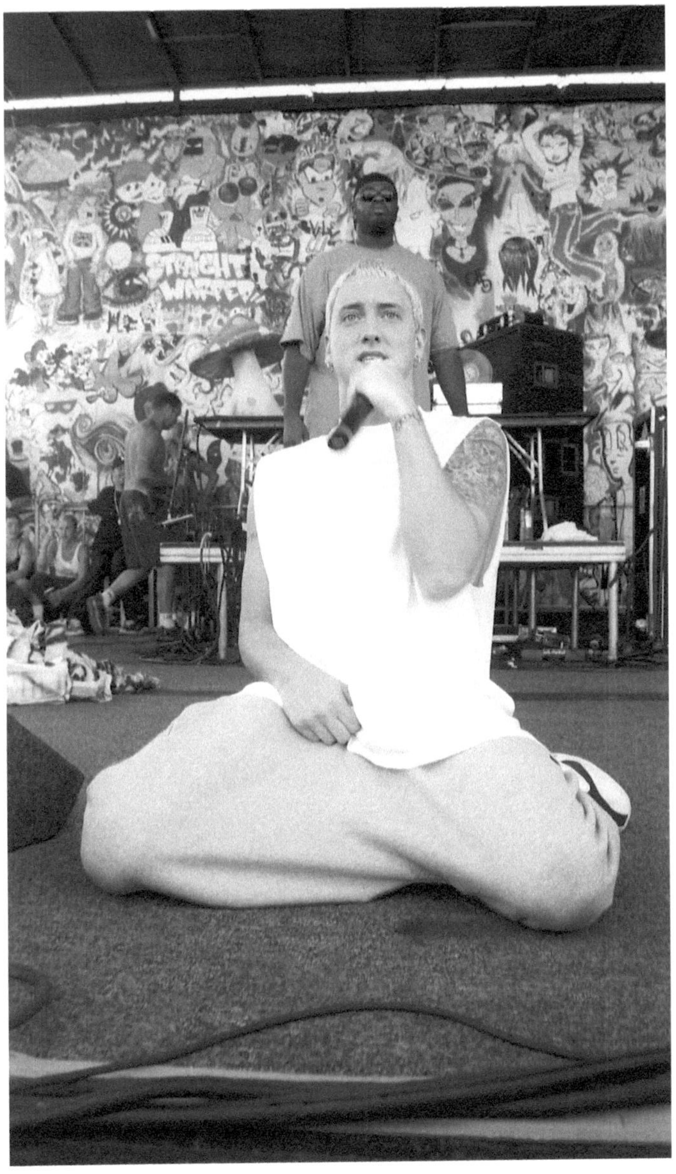

I'm low down and dirty but not ashamed.

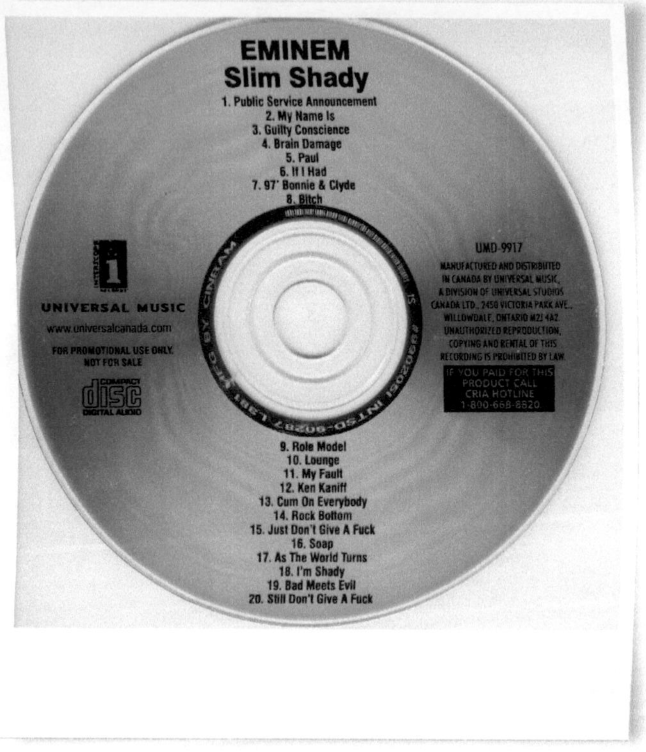

Universal Music Canada Slim Shady Advance CD

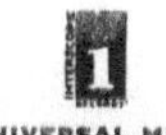

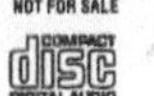

Universal Music Canada Slim Shady Advance CD

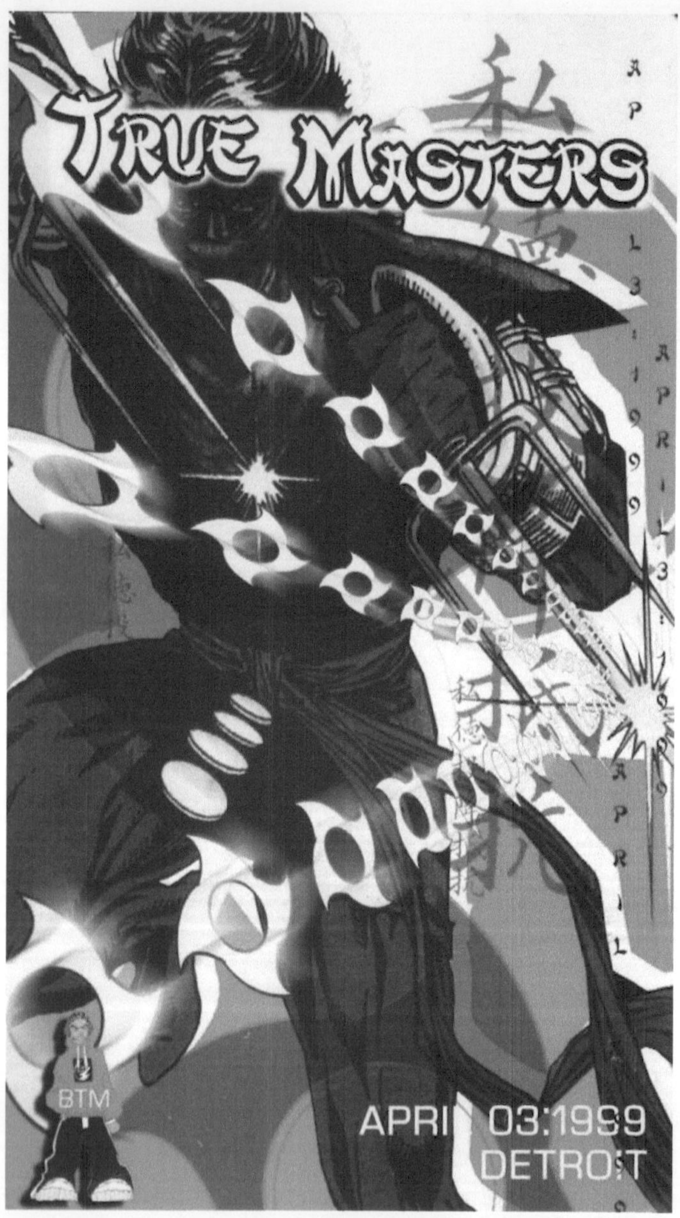

True Masters flyer

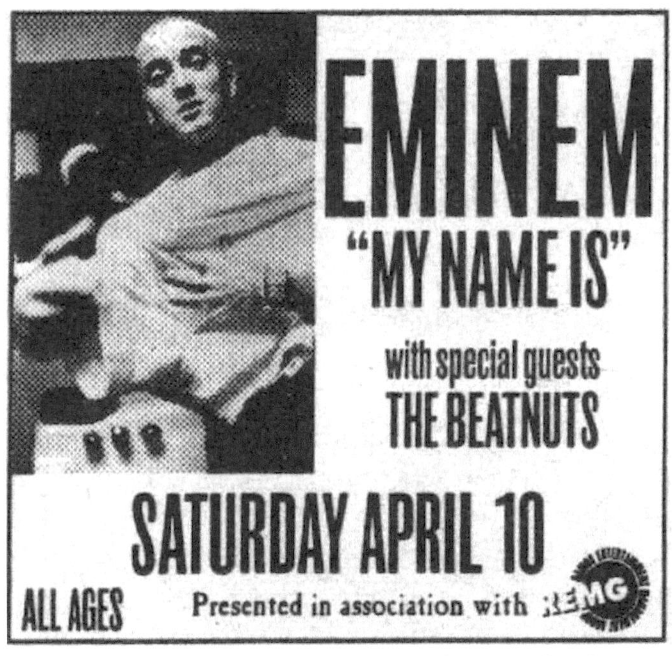

The Opera House show ad courtesy of Daniel Tate/The Flyer Vault

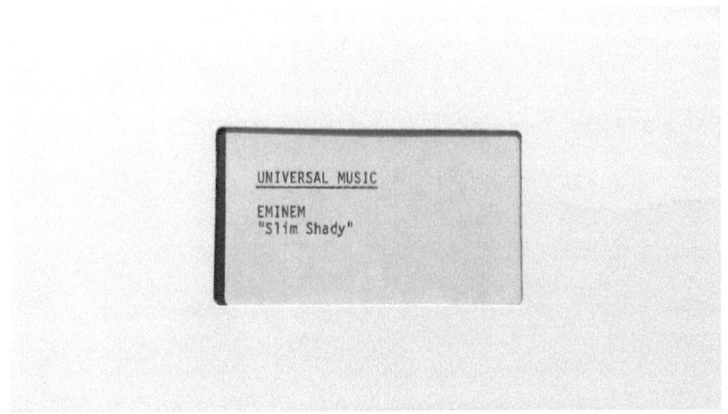

What do you know about VHS?

I

DETROIT ROCK CITY

I grew up on the east-side of Detroit, man. And shit was not good, shit was not good.
- Eminem

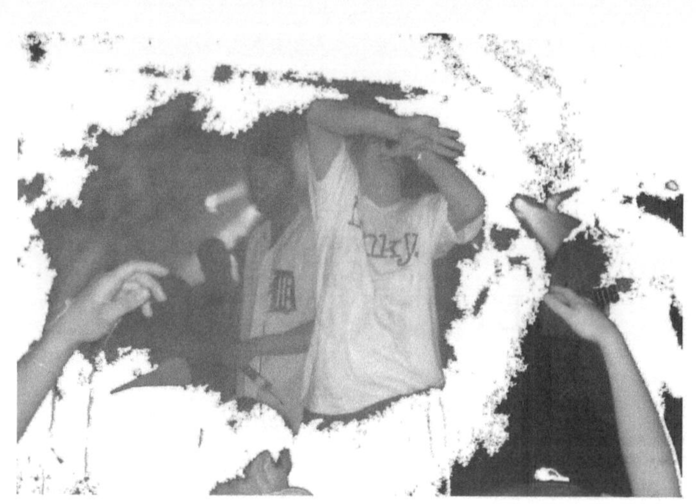

Murder City, U.S.A.

Driving the mean streets of downtown Detroit to connect with Eminem, we came to face Mack Avenue. Images of Detroit City's seedy underbelly: cutthroats, drug addicts, drunks, pimp's, ho's, thieves, robbers, gangs and cops on the take. The dirty Jazz, Funk, Punk, Grunge, Heroin Blues of Big Chief's *Mack Avenue Skullgame Original Soundtrack* racing through our minds.

The location of Eminem's homecoming rave site on the corner of Mack and Bellevue. The asbestos filled warehouse of the evening's event an intimate snapshot of days past. Previously a booming and vibrant commercial district of factories; turned desolate wasteland. It is alleged one-third of parked cars were broken into at another rave in the same venue later that year.

Once the fourth largest city in the United States of America, Detroit City had become a forgotten industrial wasteland of abandoned factories and deserted streets. The discarded consequence of the declining auto industry, job losses, suburbanisation, industrial restructuring, and an alarmingly high rate of crime.

After the end of World War I in 1918, the east side of

Mack Avenue housed an important constituency that became known as the Black Bottom. The district one of few open to housing African Americans fleeing Jim Crow laws of enforced racial segregation in the Southern United States. An economically isolated, bustling city within a city rife with African American prosperity and poverty through the 40s. The district tore down and bulldozed consequent of post-World War II The Detroit Plan blueprint and the *Federal Housing Act of 1949.* Uniformly drafted by the all-white city government in the name of slum clearance and urban renewal. The voices of tens of thousands ignored as they were dislocated without input or permission and the path cleared for private housing, large public housing projects, and the modernist residential district development of Lafayette Park. The act dubbed "Negro removal" by its critics.

Inflamed by unemployment and underemployment, absolute poverty, racism and racial segregation, and a lack of educational opportunities and school funding, racial tension spread like a disease. Until, inevitably, the scars of high-level police brutality toppled the cycle of oppression and led to violent rebellion. The Detroit Riots escalated over five hot summer days, July 23-July 28, 1967; 33 African Americans and 10 white people were killed, 342 injured, 7000 National Guard and U.S. Army troops called into service, 2509 stores burned or looted, and 388 families displaced or homeless.

The gasoline crisis of 1973 and 1979, and the subsequent demand for fuel-efficient vehicles made for even more cutbacks and plant shutdowns. The residual effects of high-unemployment and inadequate public transit forced suburbanisation and departure from the State for employment. Consequently, the upended population balance generated a reduced tax base and lower property values. The development of Detroit in a constant state of flux worsened by its abandoned districts pervaded by catastrophic levels of poverty and crime. Deserted buildings left to the drug trade, illicit activities, and arson. The stage set for violent gangs and narcotic traffic on all corners of the city. Young Boys, Black Mafia Family, and other syndicates thrived and opened franchises in other cities and out of the State. Detroit branded "Murder City" in the '80s for its notorious criminal enterprises. FBI crime statistics pronounced Detroit City as the "most dangerous city in America" with greater than 2700 violent crimes per 100 000 people in the peak year of 1991. International travel warnings to avoid the City were established by multiple countries

The redevelopment of the downtown core with the construction of One Detroit Center, now known as Ally Detroit Center, and a renewed focus on immigration served to influence revitalisation of the district. The desire to seek downtown housing heightened in 1999, by an influx of young professionals and the imminent opening of the MGM Grand Detroit, MotorCity Casino-Hotel, and Greektown Casino-Hotel at the time of the interview.

* * *

Eminem and Proof exuded a deep love and deference for Detroit. Did Detroit City return the respect? When "My Name Is" discharged on January 25, 1999, the high calibre skills of Eminem satiated with the blessing of Dr. Dre opened up the Rap and Hip-Hop skies to legions of new kids. The redneck, trash rap tales of *The Slim Shady LP* a grievous paradox of the music industry that shocked the world with its lyrical criminal assaults.

On the international promotional grind to indulge media, fans, and spread the right word, Eminem and Proof travelled overseas to Europe for the last two weeks of March 1999 and induced mass hysteria. Highly rated amongst underground rap backpackers glued to the Internet is one matter; still, this was something new. Europe reinforced an ingrained belief international superstar status was likely in the immediate future.

By the first weekend of April 1999, *The Slim Shady LP* earned platinum status for sales of over one million copies. The tables turned, Eminem and Proof finally sat in the driver seat. No murders were committed; however, when certain men are pushed not even pussy is a sweeter joy than revenge.

Back on home base in Detroit, Eminem and Proof barely had time to digest the epiphany. April and May were booked entirely, and offers were flying in at a record pace. The road out of hood life illuminated. The performance of April 3, 1999, billed as the "Homecoming Rave"signified a farewell to life as they knew it. Forwards ever, backwards never.

2

The Homecoming

Detroit, Michigan

April 4, 1999

Matt Sonzala: I've been following you for a long time. You talk about hating going on in Detroit. How have the tables turned, not necessarily since you signed? Since Eminem has become a household name and blown up?

Eminem: The tables are like a 360, not for like no Detroit radio stations, shit like that, certain ones that I don't give any more press too. I just told this station I don't want them to play my shit because they never supported me, ever, and don't show me, fake love, now that I got on. That was my whole argument, you know. They don't - They never supported Detroit Hip-Hop. There was a couple of groups that got favouritism shown towards them and shit, and I'm not going to mention those groups either, but, you know. It was just some bullshit politics, dog. But now, now it's like a fucking 360. I was trying to - I couldn't give my tapes out before, you know. Now all the sudden, Bam! Motherfuckers is buying my shit.

Matt Sonzala: In the city before all this happened, in Detroit. What kind of adversity did you face?

Eminem: Just bullshit, just bullshit. Local record stores wouldn't put my shit on the shelf, just fucking bullshit, you know.? Yo, I've been battling, I was battling, I was fucking - had albums out, you know what I'm saying? I was on the scene; nobody was trying to fucking - nobody was trying to hear me. Now all of a sudden motherfuckers is trying to hear me.

Matt Sonzala: How does that feel?

Eminem: I mean, how do you think it feels?

Matt Sonzala: It feels good, I'm sure.

Eminem: Right, right. It feels good but it's kind of, you know? I don't know, it's like a good and a shitty feeling all at the same time, like I felt like motherfuckers could have did more to help me out, you know? Before I fucking - before I blew. Fuck it now; it's all said and done. I ain't - Yo, I ain't mad at motherfuckers. I just, you know, certain people that got power in the city should - should keep their ear to the street more. I will say that.

Matt Sonzala: It's not just this city though, it's every city, as far as the industry.

HR: A lot of people have labelled you a white trash rapper from Detroit.

Eminem: Yeah, what about it?

HR: *What's your take on that? Do you care? Do you have a response?*

Eminem: I am. I am. I'm a white trash rapper from Detroit. I'm not afraid to admit I'm white trash, you know? I fucking - Yo, I never knew my father. My family was fucking broke. I spoke on it, you know what I'm saying? I'm a trashy kid, you know, growing up and shit. I ain't scared to admit that shit.

Matt Sonzala: That's one thing that people don't understand about you. There's a big misunderstanding about Detroit 'cause this is one of the rawest cities in the fucking world.

Eminem: Yeah, no doubt.

Matt Sonzala: In this country, Detroit is raw.

Eminem: Yeah, no doubt, no doubt. Who you tellin'? I grew up on the east-side of Detroit, man.

You know, and shit was not good, shit was not good.

HR: *Sum up Detroit. What's your take on Detroit?*

Eminem: What's my take on Detroit? I love Detroit. I love Detroit; it's a hard city to come up in but - I mean, some people shitted on me, some people didn't. Some people showed love. It's a crazy type of thing, so, you know. I'm not bitter at all at Detroit. I love the city, you know? I'm going to live here and settle down and shit. I'm going to live in this city. I'm not moving out of this fucking city. I might; I don't know, but - I love Detroit like I said. It's where I'm from, and I'm just trying to give back to the city.

3

Libras

Toronto, Ontario

April 10, 1999

Someone who booked you produced the Rave. I assume you did not choose a homecoming show in a venue like that.

Eminem: Nah. Yeah, that was somebody who just wanted to do the show. It was a rave though. I thought it was cool, but the only thing that I didn't like about it was that I didn't have room to move for shit, you know what I'm saying? That shit was - Yo, I was slipping and falling down. Shit was all muddy and fucking - That shit was a nasty ass show, that shit was crazy.

Growing up in Detroit there is a lot of Techno, and House music.

Eminem: I never really got into that shit, I never did. I don't like Techno. I don't like Techno music. If it's on at like a party or something, you know what I'm saying? I ain't paying attention to the music anyways. I'm looking for the bitches; you know what I'm saying? I'm not - you know? I don't get into that shit. I know Techno is fucking huge in Detroit though.

Detroit seems to be blowing up now, or at least your crew is blowing up now. You're blowing up, Proof has his thing starting to happen, Royce's shit is on fire. Why is it all shining on you guys now?

Proof: Because we're talented and we're Libras.

Libras?

Proof: [Laughing]. That's some made up shit.

Eminem: I feel like all I did was work hard, did my shit, and got on, and then put Royce on. Now I'm trying to help put Proof on, you know what I'm saying? So, all I'm doing is giving back to the motherfuckers that gave to me, you know what I'm saying? And that I see true talent in. Everybody else that wasn't fucking down with me and didn't fucking support me and shit can eat a mother-fucking dick. Fuck these motherfuckers walking up to me, *'Yo, I got a tape. Listen to it.'* Bitch, you wasn't trying to hear my mother-fucking tape when I was trying to give it out! You know what I'm saying? Don't fucking come up to me with a tape, motherfucker!

He's right, but that's how life is.

Proof: [Laughing] He got emotional.

Eminem: No, but it's true.

4

The Black Bottom

Birmingham, Michigan

May 30, 2001

Give me a story. The best or craziest thing that ever happened to you on Mack Avenue?

Kuniva: Mack Avenue?

Yeah.

Kuniva: Nothing crazy has happened to me on Mack Avenue because I stay the fuck away from there. I stay the fuck away from Mack and B-Way.

Proof: But that's a good question because -

Kuniva: It's fucked up there.

Proof: If something happens to you over there you

deserve it to happen because something always happens over there. It's like, you a dumb motherfucker when you get caught up over there.

Kuniva: My mother was dumb. She went there a couple of months ago. She was dumb, she knows it too. She stopped on Mack to get some cigarettes on her way to work, like 6 o'clock in the morning all by herself. She stopped at a gas station to get some cigarettes. Somebody threw a jack through her back window, took her purse, her cell phone, all kinds of shit like that, and just took off with her shit at 6 o'clock in the morning! But, you know, broke people - I mean, crackheads, get up early. If they sleep at all, you know what I'm saying? So, she was asking for the shit. So, I could tell you her story. That's what happened, but as far as the story of mine, I stay the fuck away from Mack. Unless you stay over there and the people who stay over there stay the fuck away from Mack.

Proof: Right.

Kuniva: You're dead! Get the fuck away from there. If you ever find yourself there, that's the last place. That's where they are going to find you.

Didn't Eminem play a rave right off Mack a couple of years ago?

Proof: Mack does this, once you get - It's crazy because when you went - Oh no, that wasn't Mack.

Yeah, it was. It was right off Mack.

Proof: That was 94. It was off by the 94 Freeway. Mack is in that area but that ain't the Mack we're talking about because Mack when you go so far it gets pretty. There's one section of Mack on the east-side, as a matter of fact, it used to be called the *Black Bottom.* That's what it used to be called. That's like the roughest area in Detroit history, that's how it goes. But that Rave - Oh yeah, hold up. It was around the corner from Mack.

We were talking to Proof and Kuniva about tales that happened to them or associates on Mack Avenue.

Bizarre: What the fuck? You don't live on Mack Avenue.

Swifty McVay: Mack Avenue - Hey man, I know I deal with the barber shop on Mack and B-Way.

Bizarre: Shut the fuck up, man.

Unison: (Laughs)

Swifty McVay: Made a whole bunch of new friends, you know. Hey man, I ain't got nothing to say about Mack that -

Bizarre: I'm a Mack.

Swifty McVay: Me too. That's it.

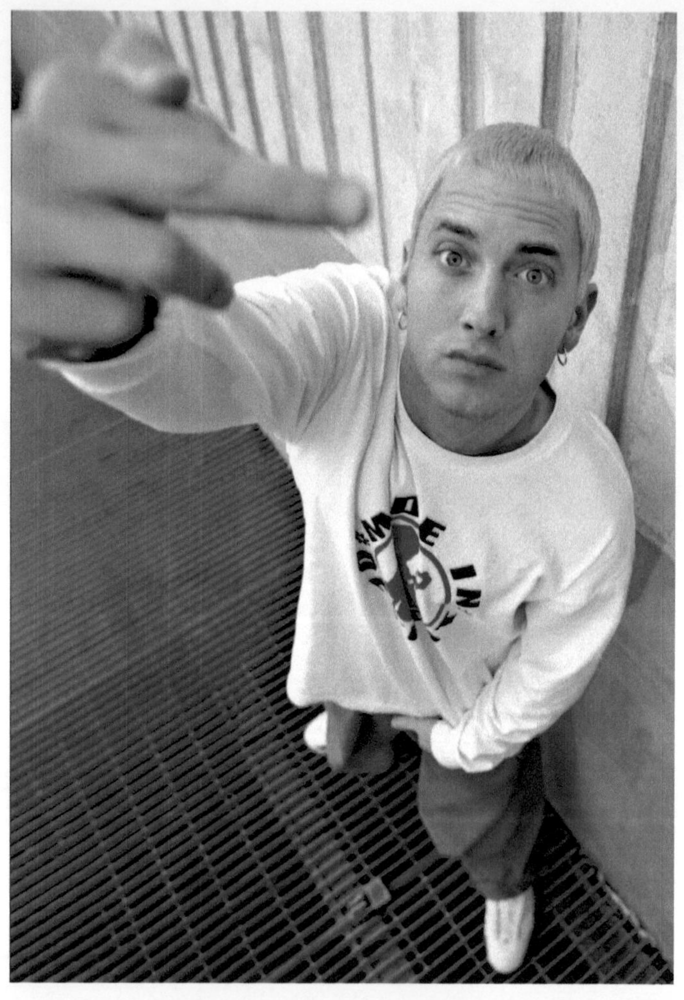

Fuck you! I won't do what you tell me!

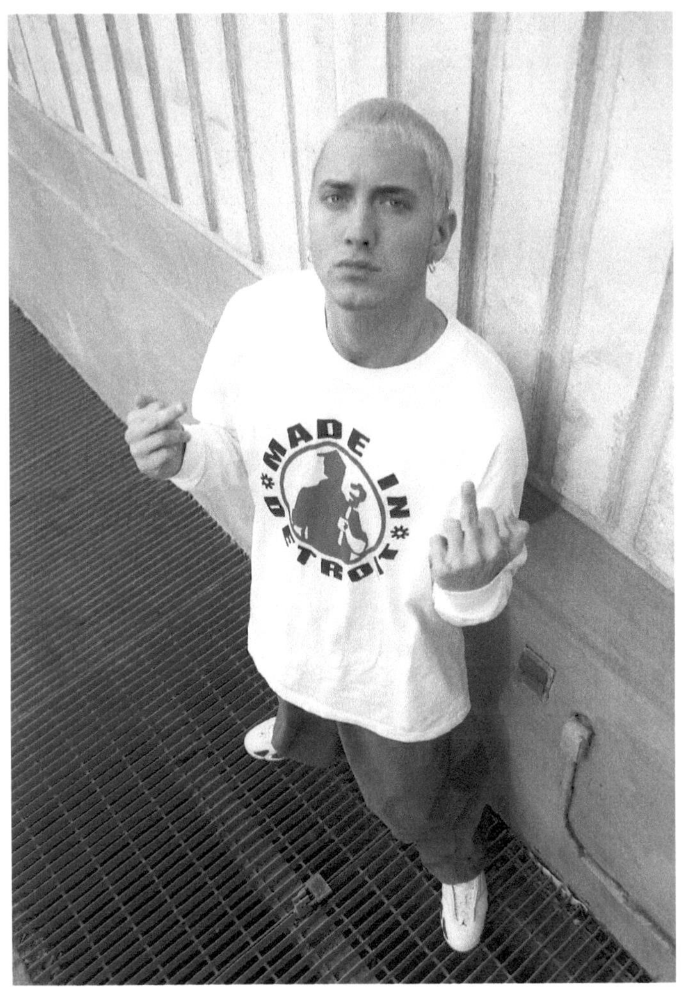

Made In Detroit

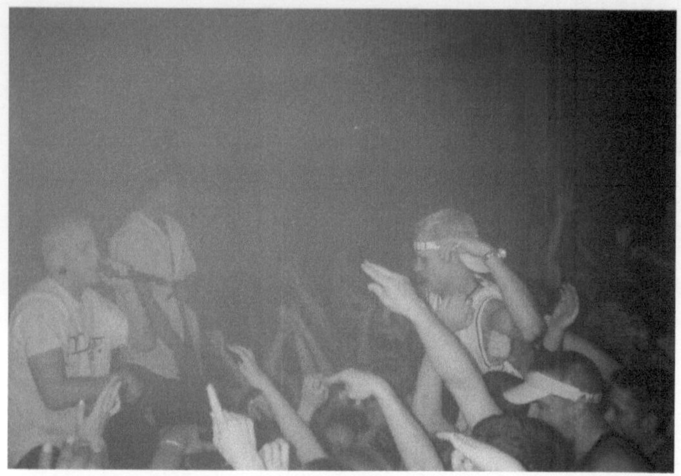

The origin of Stan?

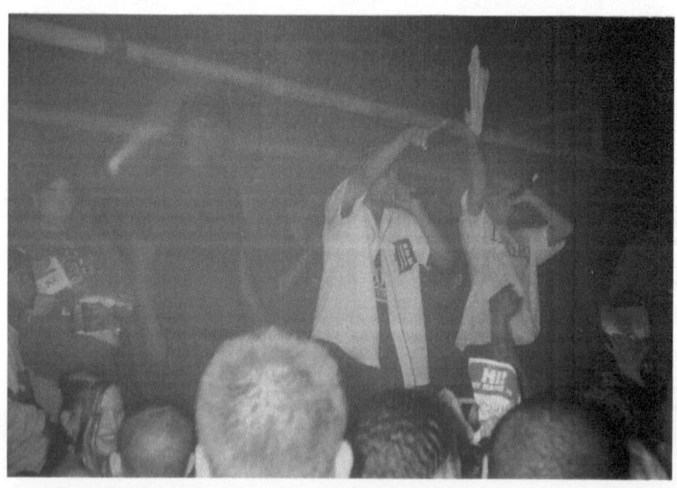

Up close and personal with Big Proof and Slim at True Masters

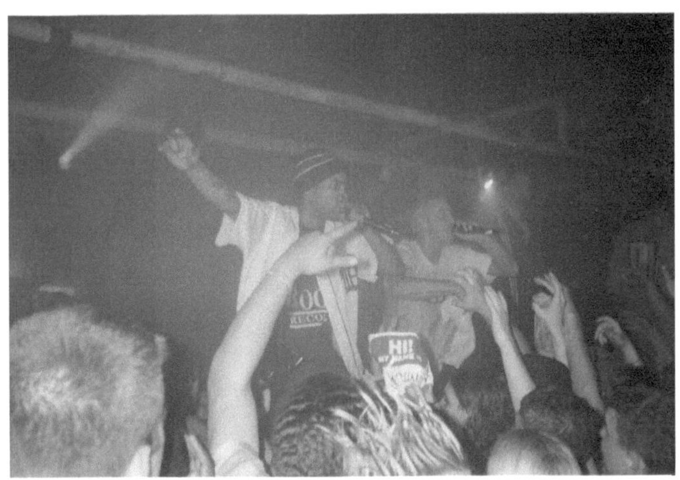

Detroit City to the max

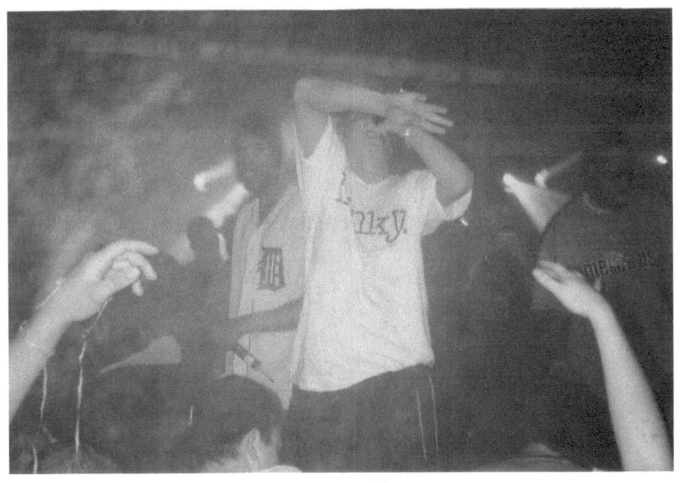

Deliver us to Evil

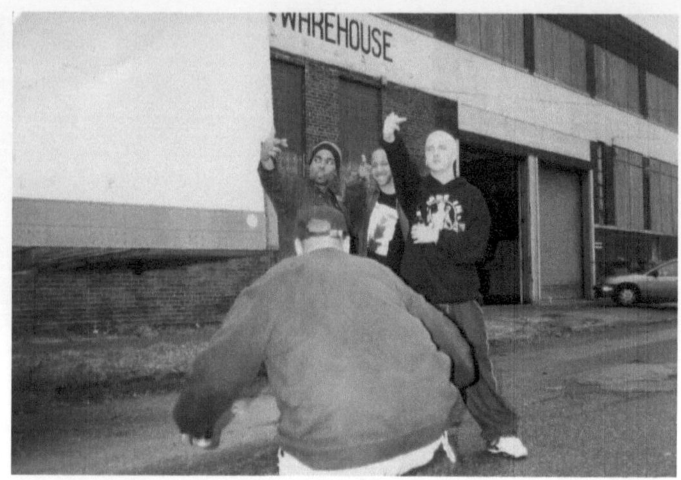

Big Proof, DJ Butter, Slim Shady & the back of DJ Head's head

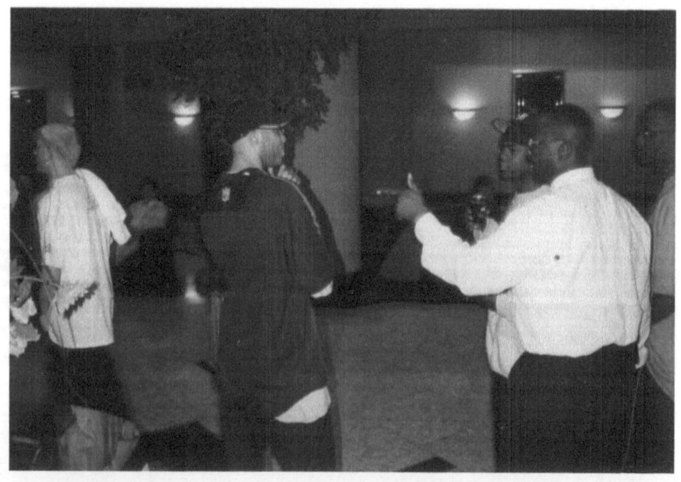

Slim x Royce da 5'9 x Detroit City Hotel Eviction

II

COMING UP

I keep a close circle, you know. Anybody else is just extra. Anybody else just trying to 'Yo! I do this! I make beats, and I do this and that and this and that.' It's just extra to me.
- Eminem

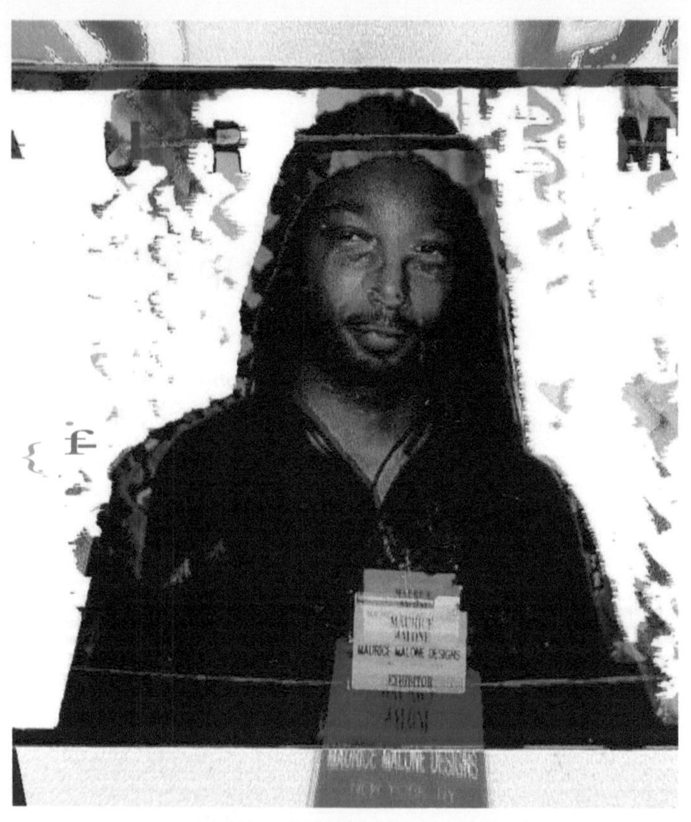
MAURICE MALONE DESIGNS
EXHIBITOR

5

7 Mile and Greenfield

having nothing to struggle against
they have nothing to struggle for
-Charles Bukowski, You Get So Alone at Times That it Just Makes Sense

Friends and rapping partners since their early teens, Eminem and Proof grew up living below the poverty line on the east-side of Motor City. Eminem as MC Double M and M &M, and Proof as Maximum. Dreams of becoming Rap stars sandwiched in-between the rigours of seemingly endless low paying, bottom feeder jobs, including Slim's days as a minimum wage cook at *Gilbert's Lodge*. Dramatically fired five days before Christmas and left with forty dollars to buy his daughter, Hailie her Christmas and birthday presents.

Life balanced as struggling independent artists. Each earned an individual reputation and notoriety within the industrial wasteland of Detroit's underground Hip-Hop scene as solo artists, in groups, and battle rap participants. Music exploited as an outlet only to regretfully observe the fruits of labour planted fade away to little fanfare. Elements of the trials and tribulations of the comeuppance documented in the 2002 motion picture *8 Mile*.

Time may have led many to become unaware of Eminem's early underground recordings. Songs and freestyles initially celebrated by a savvy group of pre-blogger tape traders. Subversive sessions that found their way to mixtapes and established his name on every critical Hip-Hop site. Indeed, Eminem is one of the first artists to advance from the world wide web.

* * *

Acknowledged as one of the Godfathers of urban apparel, Maurice Malone sewed his reputation as a master denim craftsman and apparel designer. His launch of the *Hip-Hop Shop* and its weekly Battle Rap sessions central to the rise and legend of Eminem. Malone's initial sideline as a DJ playing Rock, House and Techno. He journeyed to New York City to advance his couturier career in 1989, where he became engaged with the club scene. Enraptured by the raw energy communicated one night at *Powerhouse,* when KRS-One took over the mic with DJ Kid Capri behind the wheels of steel, he fell in love with Hip-Hop. When he decided to move back to Detroit to grow his business, he felt obliged to bring the same live energy to the D.

The first *Rhythm Kitchen* party at a 200 square foot spot on Grand River with less than 30 people in attendance. A homage to NYC's *Soul Kitchen,* its midnight freestyle session the high point of the night. The night relocated to the larger

Stanley's Other Place Chinese Restaurant where Malone DJ'd and worked the door. Then cut, sewed and printed t-shirts during the day to prepare for the Wednesday night jam. One group featured each week. Paul Bunyan, AKA Paul Rosenberg, took the stage with his crew the second week. Proof an early customer who bought a hoodie and befriended Malone. News of the night spread to the suburbs by the D's largest newspaper, *The Detroit News,* and soon after Malone opened the *Hip-Hop Shop* on 7 Mile.

Every Saturday, the clothes and t-shirts moved from the centre of the floor between 5:00 p.m. and 7:00 p.m. to make way for the contest as featured in the *8 Mile* movie. Proof managed and hosted the night, drawing names out of a hat to match up the battles. The victor moved on to the next round until the final two combatants. Indeed, Proof won every time. Yet, he never faced off against Eminem. The best-friends refused to enter the competition on the same week.

The night maintained by Maurice Malone until he and his partner, Jerome Mongom, relocated to Williamsburg, NY, in 1995. A solid decade before it became the tight pant and moustache mecca of irony inhabited by hipsters.

* * *

Eminem spoke on the Internet; the *Hip-Hop Shop;* the trust factor; and clarified circulated rumours that arose as he broke. Swifty McVay and Bizarre discussed meeting up at the *Hip-Hop Shop,* where they witnessed a young and hungry Eminem demolish all comers with his ferocious freestyle skills; and provided essential behind the scenes tales on the roots of the Dirty Dozen, D12.

6

I Learned That In Life

Detroit, Michigan,

April 4, 1999

Matt Sonzala: One thing interesting about you is you're one of the first Rap artists that did - maybe not personally or perhaps it wasn't intentional, the Internet. It was a big part or at least something in your blowing up and coming up.

Eminem: Yeah, yeah. No doubt, especially through the underground.

Matt Sonzala: For sure, through the underground, that whole scene, the Internet. I've heard your tapes and stu before that. There's a lot of sites that are dedicated to you or have been, and you're one of the first rappers to utilise it. There is the word, whether you did it or not.

Eminem: I didn't do that shit. I don't - I have never touched a computer in my life.

Matt Sonzala: Never? You didn't check out what was being said on the Internet leading up to your release?

> Eminem: Very seldom, sometimes. I mean, every now and then I do.

Matt Sonzala: 'Cause almost half of the Hip-Hop sites are dedicated to Eminem.

> *Eminem: That's crazy.*

HR: What's this whole Web (Entertainment) thing? Break it down. Are you tied to them? Are you having problems getting other publishing deals, like I'm hearing, because you're bound to them?

> Eminem: Oh, no, and that's personal business anyway. I couldn't share that with you. I'm, you know? I couldn't even begin, I couldn't even share it with you. That's classified shit, you know?

Matt Sonzala: You came up in Detroit. I have to ask, were you ever a Metalhead?

> Eminem: Hell no!

Matt Sonzala: Never? Not even as a youngster coming up?

> Eminem: Nah, I said no!

HR: One time I heard a rumour you were down with the Duck Down camp.

Eminem: Um - I mean, I know 'em. I mean, to go as far as saying down with them, like rhyming with them or some shit like that? Nah.

Matt Sonzala: *Who in Detroit was in your corner coming up?*

Eminem: You see 'em around me in that room, in that room in there. That's who was around me.

Matt Sonzala: You keep 'em together.

Eminem: No doubt, no doubt. That's my people I grew up with, man. So, I'm fucking sticking with them, regardless.

Matt Sonzala: For the sake of printing all this. Break it down. Tell me the crew.

Eminem: Proof, Denaun Porter, Bizarre, Royce da 5'9. Um - The Brigade, you know? Who am I missing? Paul Bunyan, my Manager. He was there from the beginning. I keep the people. I don't keep - Anybody else is just extra to me. Anybody else is just a fucking extra. I see you on the street I'm like, you know? Give me play or whatever. Then, you know what I'm saying? I'll see you at Saint Andrews Hall or whatever. When I see you, I'll give you play, you know? Peace out, good-looking if you bought the album or whatever. I'm cool with you, but I can't do nothing for you. These are my people that I keep around me. I keep a close circle, you know?

Anybody else is just extra. Anybody else just trying to 'Yo! I do this. I make beats, and I do this and that and this and that.' It's just extra to me.

HR: How do you maintain trust?

Eminem: Just like I just said. It's pretty self-explanatory.

HR: That's it? Nobody else? You don't trust nobody else?

Eminem: Nope, not a fucking person! Not a fucking person. I learned that in life.

7

Battles

Toronto, Ontario
April 10, 1999

Is there a scene that you came up with? You, Royce, Proof? Did you come up together?

Eminem: Me and Proof came up together on the east-side. Yeah, me and Proof came up together. Royce stepped into the picture a little bit later; you know what I'm saying? I came up — Me and Proof actually both came up from like the fucking *Hip-Hop Shop* scene. 7 Mile and Greenfield on the west-side, you know what I'm saying? That's where me and Proof was notorious, especially Proof. In them couple of years that the *Hip-Hop Shop* was open. Proof was the shit! Everybody - you know?

Proof: Shut up! This man won all the battles.

Eminem: I won all the battles. I mean, the two battles that happened at the *Shop* and shit, but this motherfucker was battling everybody every day, you know what I'm saying? But we came up together and shit.

Proof: Actually, he taught me this shit. Fuck it. It was out there. It was out there. Fuck it.

8

One of the Few

Birmingham, Michigan

May 30, 2001

Where did all you guys meet up?

Swifty McVay: At the *Hip-Hop Shop*.

Maurice Malone's spot?

Swifty McVay: Yeah, Maurice Malone's spot on the west-side of Detroit, you know what I mean? He had open mic every Saturday in there from like 3 to 6, and all the MC's, all the producers, all the DJ's, everybody used to come up and meet up at that spot every Saturday. I'm talking about it's to the point where people didn't even buy clothes no more. They came up in there to see some entertainment.

Bizarre: It was like a battle once a month, you know

what I'm saying? And Eminem won like all of them and shit. That's how he got his rep 'cause Em - he was kind of quiet in the *Hip-Hop Shop* 'cause, you know? He had to work a lot, so he'd always come for the battle. The skinny white kid with his hat down, nobody, you know? Everybody underestimated him; he'd just come in ripping up shit and win the whole battle every time.

Swifty McVay: He'll come in, people be calling him out thinking like what he is going to do? What he going to do? But he ends up smashing them, you know what I'm saying? Like that.

Was D12 supposed to happen before he was doing his thing? Was that always the plan from back in the day, or did it come about recently?

Bizarre: Well, Proof, me and Proof started D12. Me and him was on our way to New York and shit. He was like - I didn't belong to a clique in Detroit, and he didn't belong to a clique either. So, he was like, '*Yo! We should start this clique, man. In Detroit, and call it the Dirty Dozen and do a thing.*' We're like it would be opposite of how a regular style is, on some crazy shit, you know? Then we got Eminem, said he was down with it, and then our lyrics came forward. We got who we wanted to do it.

One time we was at Saint Andrews and Em was like, '*How serious Y'all about this Dirty Dozen shit?*' We was like, '*Oh, we serious.*' '*I'll show you how serious*

I am.' Then he rolled up his arm; he had Slim Shady on his arm and shit. So, you know, we was like, *'Ah fuck, we got to come up with a name too.'* So that's why you got Eminem, Slim Shady, Bizarre, Proof, Derty Harry, you know what I'm saying.? So that's how the clique started. We made this pact; Em was like, *'Yo! You know what I'm saying? Whoever gets on first we come back and get each other, you know what I'm saying?'*

Just like every crew says.

Bizarre: Right, right.

If I'm on, I'm going to put you on, and with you guys, he put his money where his mouth is.

Swifty McVay: Exactly.

One of the few guys.

Bizarre: One of the few.

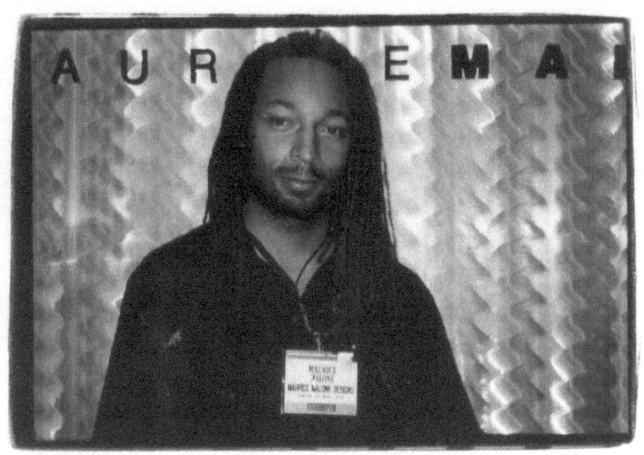

Maurice Malone @ MAGIC International, Las Vegas, Nevada, 1999

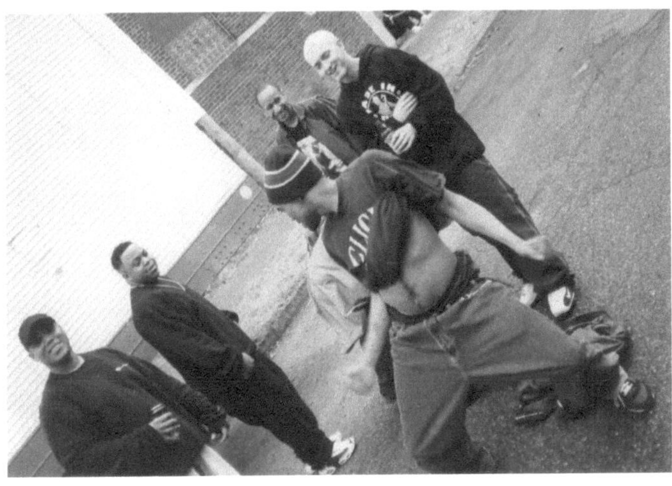

Beer and Smiles with DJ Head, Not Derrick Coleman, DJ Butter, Slim Shady & Big Proof

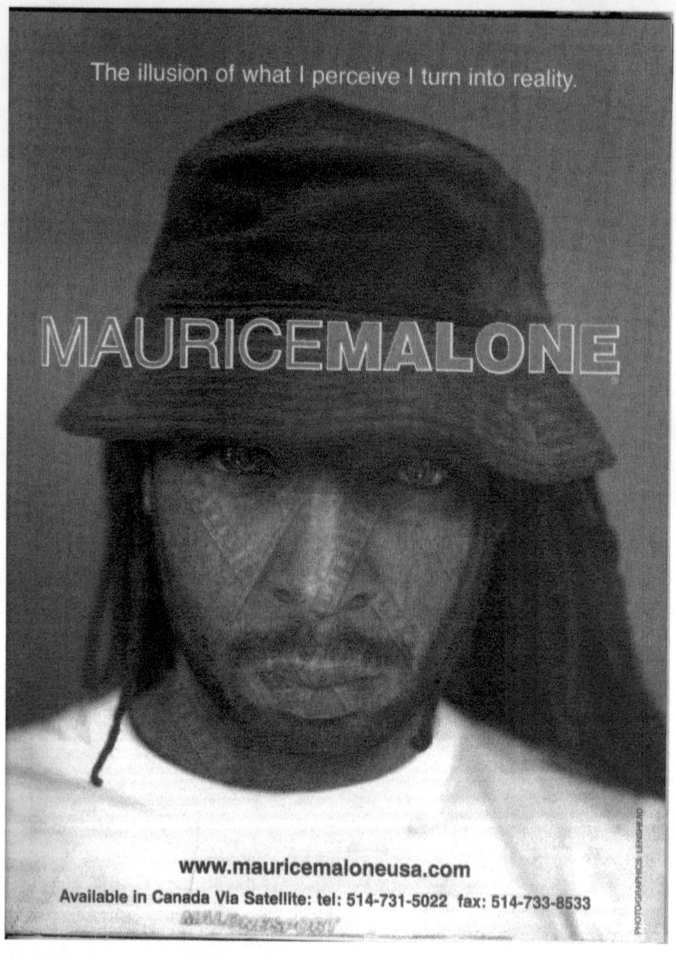

Laid back (with my mind on my denim and my denim on my mind)

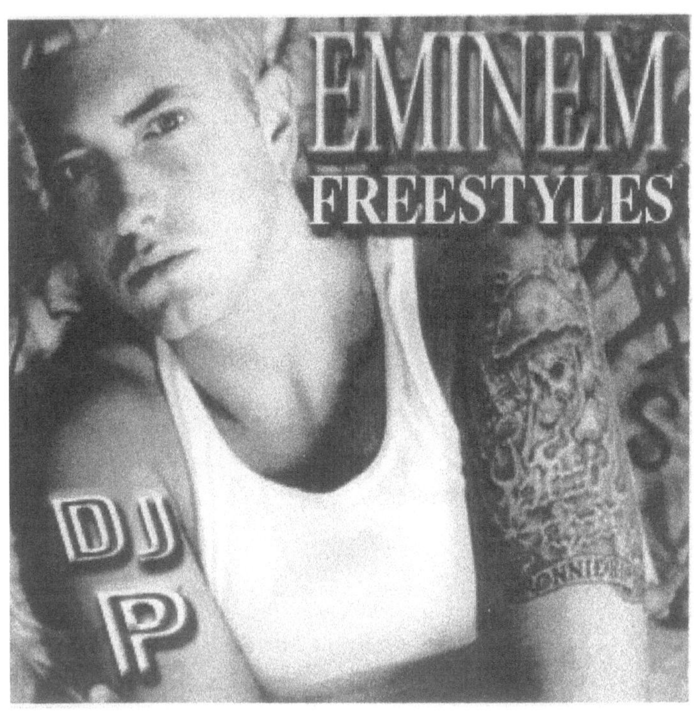

Double-Disc Fist-Pumpin' Freestyle Mania

DISK 1

1. Roll of Quarters / Born With a Set of Horns / Retared Kid Greg (3:06)
2. Just Rhymin With Proof (7:41)
3. I'm Cancerous (1:04)
4. Spit On Brandy & Mase (1:04)
5. Tube Socks Filled (10:56)
6. Trife Thieves - Feat. D12 (3:56)
7. All Grils Are Interns (:57)
8. Eminem & Aristotle & D12 Freestyle
9. Receiving A Call (:45)
10. Rapolympics Freestyles (4:10)
11. Off The Wall - Feat. Redman (3:55)
12. Our House - Feat. Limp Bizkit (4:40)
13. Hellbound - Feat. Masta ace (3:56)
14. Ryming Words (4:04)
15. Eminem with Sway & Tech (8:49)

DISK 2

1. Watch This (1:14)
2. Ice Grilling You (:58)
3. Eminem & Proof Freestyle for 16 Minutes (16:33)
4. Broke The Rubber (1:06)
5. Bust On The Mic - Feat. Ruckus (5:02)
6. Food Stamp (:23)
7. Original Bad Boy (:49)
8. Razor With Aids (1:52)
9. Releasing Anger - Feat. Scam (4:39)
10. Rhymes Galour (4:19)
11. Royce the 5'9 & Eminem Freestyle (5:47)
12. Shove a Gun In Your Grill (:46)
13. Kids (5:03)
14. Shovanistic Pig (1:48)
15. Shut Up and Pay Attention (1:17)
16. No One's iller - Feat. D12 (4:59)

Prime Movers

III

REST IN PIECES, KIM

Everybody wants to pass judgment on me for writing a song about killing my baby's mother, but nobody really knows what the fuck I go through with her.
- Eminem

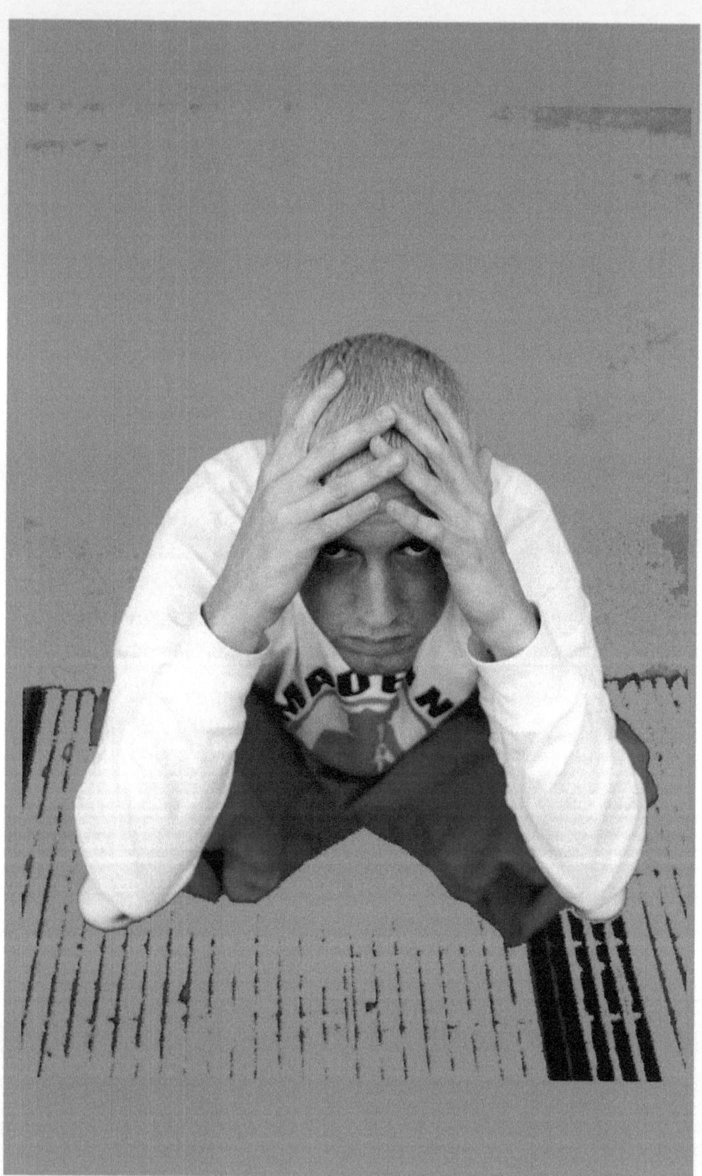

Chuck E. Cheese

The key song in Eminem's catalogue is "Just The Two Of Us." The harrowing abstract account of Eminem killing his baby mother, Kimberly Anne Scott. Perhaps eclipsing the indelible history of Bonnie Elizabeth Parker and Clyde Chestnut Barrow. The powerful song responsible for Dr. Dre exclaiming, *'Yo, I want this motherfucker!'* Retitled "97' Bonnie & Clyde" on *The Slim Shady LP*, its revision in deference to Tupac Shakur's implication of gun for a girlfriend on the *Makaveli* album. The audacious theme recreated by Danny Hastings on *The Slim Shady LP* cover.

The storied pairing of Marshall Bruce Mathers III and Kimberly Anne Scott dates back to a house party in 1989. Fifteen-years-old Marshall peacocking on a table rapping LL Cool J's "I'm Bad." Thirteen-years-old Kim in love at first sight.

Kim and her twin sister moved in with Marshall and his mother, Deborah. The perilous on and off love affair sired Hailie-Jade Scott-Mathers on Christmas Day 1995. The relation entails two marriages and an abundance of songs Yet, none as detrimental to the lives of Marshall Bruce Mathers III, Kimberly Anne Scott, and Hailie Jade Scott-Mathers, as

"Just The Two of Us."

The poverty-stricken challenges of white trash, trailer park life compounded by increased intense bitter battles inevitably exacted their toll. Kim awarded the upper hand by judicial decree ultimately withheld Hailie and made her unavailable to Marshall. Slim's mother, Deborah Nelson-Mathers conscripted to side against her son. Alone, with no father figure to consult, the Shakespearean act of betrayal at the hands of his own flesh and blood, sadly forced Eminem to be responsible for himself.

Those of you without children may fail to grasp the active signs of cruelty. Proof succinctly broke it down to its essence in the interview should you be of the ilk: *"Nobody sees the father's love for his daughter! Nobody sees the father's love for his daughter!"*

The psychological scars concurrently inflicted on Eminem's crucial developmental age, by his mother and baby mother, formed the base of his sensibility. The combination of these two women in his life compounded by the trials and tribulations of growing up poor on the east-side of Detroit; unequivocally led to escapism in the form of copious prescription drugs, and deep-rooted depression. Pits of love, hate, anger and devotion. Sleepless nights and permanent trauma of his lifeblood. The poor maternal lineage that instinctively laid waste to a boy and made him a man.

Eminem tuned in to his core and unloaded the darkened rational in short order, to free his psyche and indulge conscience. The piece de resistance of bringing the soul-crushing lyrics to a crescendo masked in deceit. An innocent request for permission to take Hailie to Chuck E. Cheese. In reality, the recording debut of Hailie on "Just The Two Of Us."

The elation and mood brought on by the accomplishment seemingly regarded as short-lived. The deed exploded back in his face when he proudly aired the song for Kim, self-betrayal served. A severe lack of tact and judgement that pierced the heart of the family and placed it into crisis mode.

The ultra-violence of Eminem rapping on killing his baby's mother and dumping her corpse. The exciting tale that mirrored his mental anguish and served to compel Dr. Dre to seek, sign and mentor him. The anathema of purity to his innumerable detractors.

It got real serious when Eminem and Proof opened up and spoke in graphic detail on what led to the creation of "Just The Two Of Us," and how deep it got behind the scenes with Kimberly Anne Scott.

10

That's Personal

Detroit, Michigan
April 4, 1999

How are relations with your baby mom now?

Eminem: Hmmm, personal. That's personal, that's personal.

11

A Page Out of History

Toronto, Ontario

April 10, 1999

"Just The Two of Us" *is a deep song.*

Eminem: It's a deep song. It's a fucking -

Proof: It's a deep song. Mostly misunderstood every time.

Break it down.

Eminem: People just don't understand how deep that song truly is because they don't know. Nobody knows. Everybody wants to pass judgment on me for writing a song about killing my baby's mother, but nobody knows what the fuck I go through with her. He knows, Proof knows. Motherfuckers that's close to me, that I grew up with and shit. They know what it fucking be. You know what I'm saying? But, a lot of times, motherfuckers they'll blame me, you know what I'm saying?

Proof: Nobody sees the father's love for his daughter! Nobody sees the father's love for his daughter!

Eminem: No doubt. My daughter was being kept from me at that time and like a lot of times. It's not necessarily as bad now, but before, my daughter was being kept from me a lot, you know what I'm saying? There was one point in time - I mean, honestly, I don't think you or nobody here could honestly say they've never at one point in time in their life felt like killing somebody. Somebody made them mad enough to fucking kill them. That shit has come from experience. So, I wanted to do it at that time, at that point in time.

I really wanted to fucking kill her, but I said to myself; instead of - I sat down with a pen one day, and DJ Head had this beat. It was a "Just The Two Of Us" (Bill Withers) sample and shit, and he flipped it some different way and shit. And I was listening to the beat, and I was like, *"just the two - "* and it just came to me like, concept. Like, I need to write about my daughter, and I need to write - You know what I'm saying? I was going through some shit where I was like I need to write about this bitch who's fucking with me! I just started la da-la da-la da, just writing and shit, you know?

It can't get more real than that.

Eminem: Nah. I mean, that's -

Proof: That's a page out of history for you.

Eminem: It is because a lot of people have children by fucked up mothers, you know what I'm saying? And fucked up girls, fucked up girlfriends. Oh shit! I said a lot of people have children by fucked up mothers. A lot of people have fucked up girls, you know what I'm saying? And they have kids with them, and they go through a lot of bullshit. They really feel the same way; they just don't say it, you know what I'm saying? And I figure like instead of me going out and doing that shit, let me write a song about it. My music is a way for me to fucking vent, to get shit off my chest. It's therapy for me. So, you know, I fucking got the shit off my chest. That's how I felt.

I heard you got a tattoo of that on your chest.

Eminem: On my stomach, on my fucking stomach. I got that shit like nine months ago when - Shit was worse like nine months ago than it ever was, and I was going through a lot of personal shit. That's when I dyed my fucking hair. I got the tattoo and dyed my hair the same day. Stripped all - I did it with peroxide, and it was all fucked up. My hair was all fucked up. It was like patchy and shit. I just wanted a new look, and I wanted a new fucking life.

I felt like my daughter's mother had finally sunk it with me, you know what I'm saying? It's like, Yo, that's it. So I just fucking went nuts, yo. I was on like three hits of ecstasy and fucking went crazy. I was up the whole night and then the whole next day and shit. I didn't sleep for like two days. Then the next morning at like 7 o'clock in the morning, I remember me and Royce was in a hotel, and I'm like, *"Yo! I'm going to get some fucking peroxide! I'm dying my shit! I'm going to get a tattoo!"* I woke him up and shit, and we fucking left and shit; early that morning and shit. I went and did all that shit in the same day.

What are current relations?

Eminem: Current relations? I'm going to keep that shit confidential, you know what I'm saying? I don't really care to speak on that shit. I speak on the past, but I can't speak on the present because I don't want to put my business or my daughter, or my daughter's mother's business out there, you know what I'm saying? The only thing I will say is it's an off-and-on relationship. It's always been that way. It's been that way for nine years; you know what I'm saying?

So, you're still hitting it?

Proof: Ahhhhhhhhhhhhhhh (Laughs)

Eminem: [Laughing] This guy!

Proof: [Laughing] Ahhh, you're amazing.

Eminem: I plead the fifth. I plead the fucking fifth.

And she's letting you after that song?

Eminem: Ha ha ha ha ha, this guy is nuts [Laughing]-i-ight.

Proof: I like that.

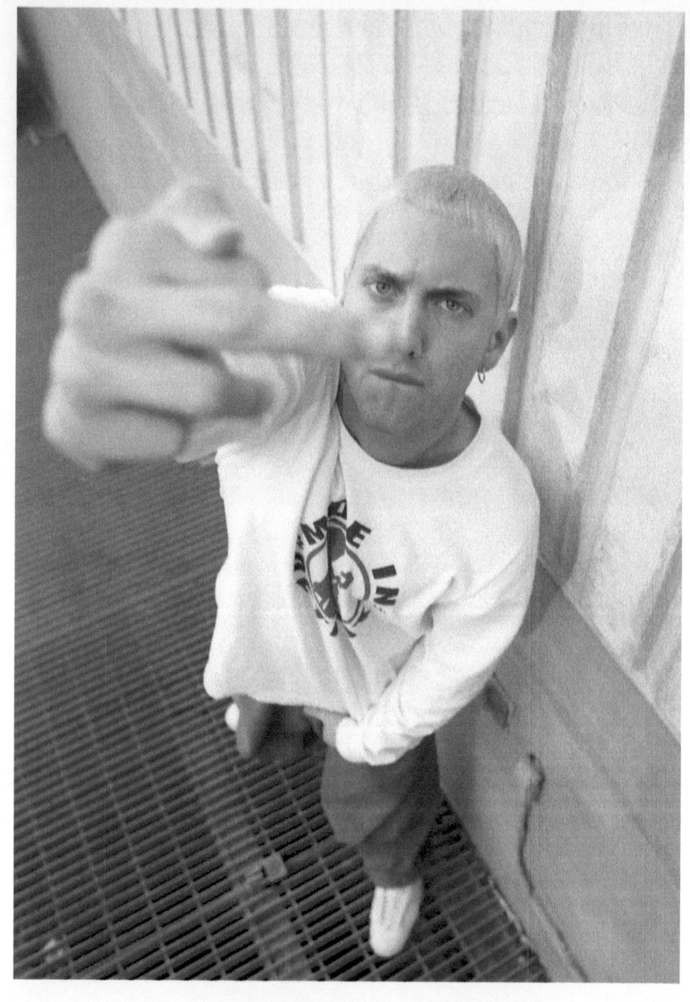

Take These Nuts and Shove It!

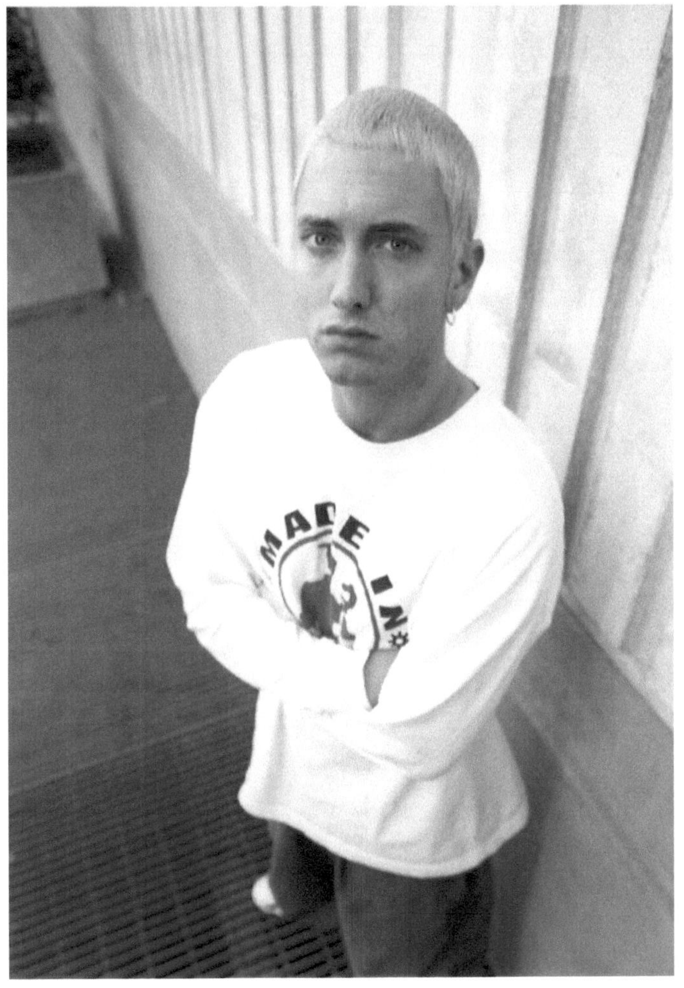

Young 'N Restless

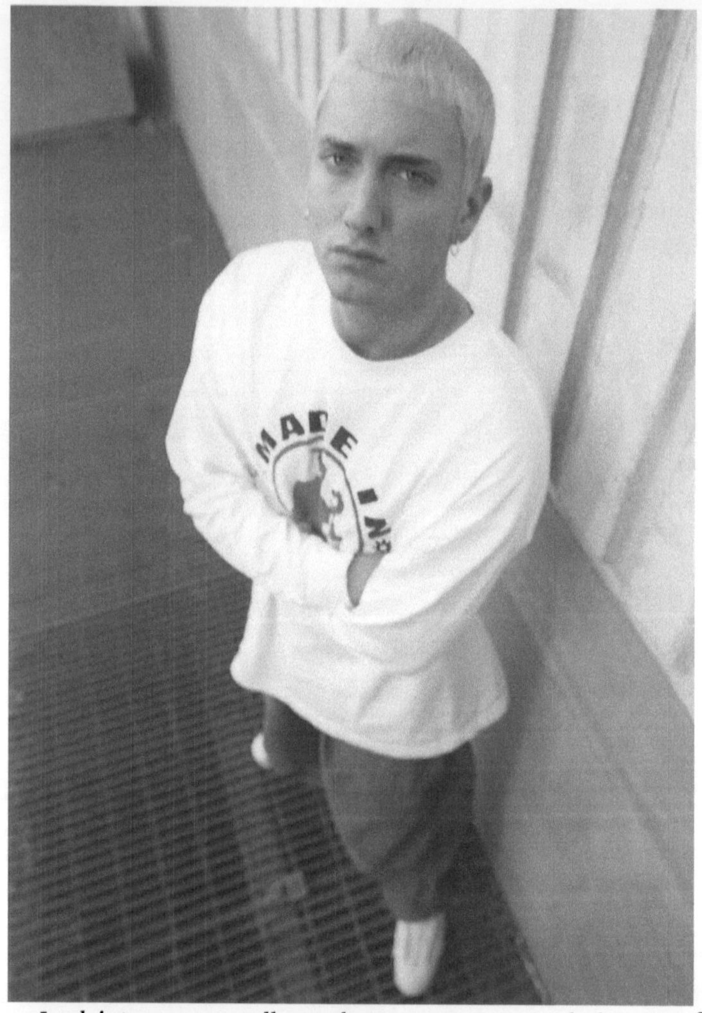

Look into my eyes, tell me what you see. Can you feel my pain? Am I your enemy?

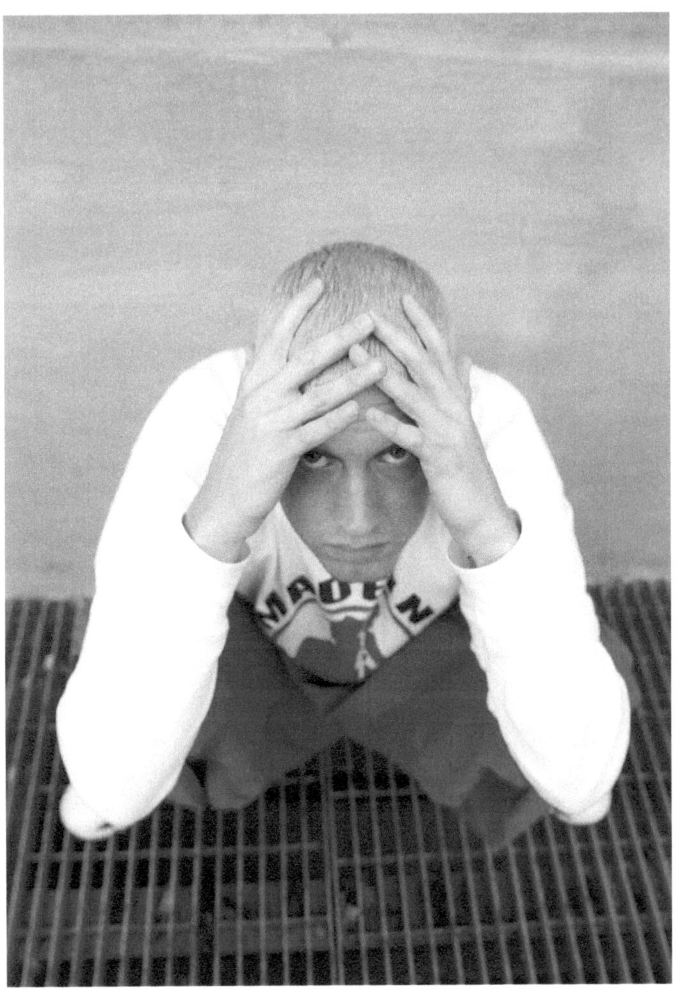

Big Proof, DJ Butter, Slim Shady & the back of DJ Head's head

IV

DR. DRE

These motherfuckers in the underground was wondering where Slim Shady went. What happened to Dre? Dre swallowed him up? Is he going to put him on the back burner?
- Eminem

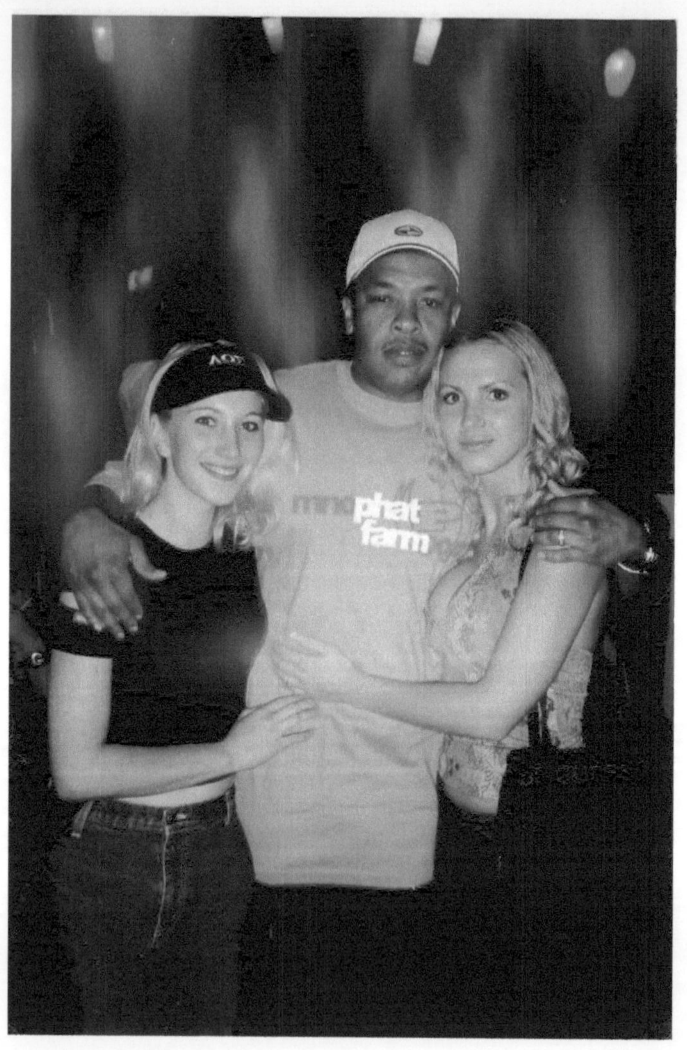
phat
farm

12

Find Him!

Dr. Dre played Q.B. for the drama-filled west coast Gangsta Rap revolution from 1986 through the summer of 1996. Toiling in the studio for Ruthless Records from 1986 -1991. The lone interest of crafting Gangsta Rap, Hip-Hop, and R&B for Eazy-E, J. J. Fad, Michel'le, The D.O.C., and N.W.A.

The fruits of his labour instrumental in Ruthless Records generating 10 million dollars per month. Regrettably jerked over by Eazy-E and Jerry Heller. The sordid emergence of Death Row Records pursued. The move from Ruthless Records expedited by antagonistic intimidation, violence and force.

Dr. Dre spoke on his caustic departure from Ruthless Records to Death Row Records in our summer 1996 interview, weeks before the untimely murder of Tupac Shakur. The story featured in my book *N.W.A.: The Aftermath (Exclusive Interviews with Dr. Dre, Ice Cube, Jerry Heller, Yella, and Westside Connection).*

> *"Actually, in the beginning, I wasn't running my business. I'm a young kid out of Compton. The only thing I was interested in was making Hip-Hop music. That's all. I had some people doing my business, which is a very big mistake, and I got jerked. Straight up. To be perfectly honest, I was getting two points for any production and a motherfucker could come off the street and get four. This is after I made a couple of platinum records and I went to Eazy with an ultimatum: 'Get rid of the fucking manager, Jerry Heller, or I'm leaving. Take a pick.' He chose to stay with Jerry Heller, and I bounced to Death Row."*

The production that emanated from the boards of Dr. Dre amplified to the nth degree. First perpetuated with the help of newcomer Snoop Doggy Dogg on the title track of the *Deep Cover* soundtrack on April 9, 1992. The debut Death Row Records release coming in the form of the "Nuthin' but a 'G' Thang" single on November 19, 1992. The release of *The Chronic* album on December 15, 1992, the detonation that turned the Art Form on its side. Death Row Records an overnight sensation. Prized solo releases by Snoop Doggy Dogg and Tha Dogg Pound, intensified by soundtracks that introduced the esteemed Warren G, Nate Dogg, and The Lady of Rage. The alarming pairing of Dr. Dre and his former N.W.A associate Ice Cube for the *Above The Rim* soundtrack immense.

With legions of eager fans eager to purchase new music, and the strong desire to earn as much as possible in a short period, the organisation designated alternate producers and artists to maintain a steady stream of releases. An assortment of hungry creatives gathered amongst a cadre of gang-bangers. The atmosphere of Death Row Record gradually acted out to resemble the wicked mentality of label co-founder Suge Knight with the Original Blood Family in command. A take no prisoners approach of cashing cheques and snapping necks, and not necessarily in that order. The chaos generated at the hands of vicious men engulfed the tenet of Hip-Hop, and a wave of deep-seated fear spread worldwide.

As a means to an end devised to control his destiny and escape a premature demise, Dr. Dre abdicated his title and abandoned the troops. The power move orchestrated with the intelligent backing and guidance of Jimmy Iovine. The P.G. version illustrated in HBO Films "four-part documentary event" *The Defiant Ones,* directed by Allen Hughes. Dr. Dre peeled back a few layers in our interview.

> *"Now, the Death Row whole incident is like this: I'm not comfortable. I wasn't comfortable, and it was time for me to bounce, and it wasn't just one thing. It was an accumulation of things. You got motherfuckers getting beat down for no reason; engineers and shit like that, and I ain't with that. I want to get down and make some music. I ain't trying to be no mother-fucking gangster, or fighting and all that; I want to make some music and have fun and party. I'm a fighter not - I mean, I'm a lover, not a fighter. Fuck all that!*
>
> *It was just - I can give you an example, and I've said this before. If you're at a party and you got to this party, and there are more people there that don't have your best interest in mind, or you not comfortable with those people being there. You're gonna leave the party and*

> *you gonna go home. Well, now I feel like I'm at home with the Aftermath."*

Characterised as a disgraceful indignity to Death Row Records, label despot Suge Knight supervised a non-stop salvo of deadly, tyrannical threats and words that boldly crossed the line. Amid the disorder circulated rumours questioned the sexuality of Dr. Dre; Daz went on the radio and stated that Dre stole his beats; and Tupac Shakur recorded "Toss It Up" featuring K-Ci and JoJo, Danny Boy and Aaron Hall.

> *"I left Death Row. Now, everybody, there is mad at me. So, 'Ok, fuck Dre! Let's talk some shit about him!' For one, Tupac did a whole song dissing me, right? One, Tupac never knew me. He never knew me! Tupac had never been to my house before, he doesn't even know where I live. We never even been in the same car together. The only thing we did was went in the studio together, made a song, did the video. That's it! So, how can he fucking diss me saying anything about me? That's all fucking hype. That's hype! Straight up."*

The dawn of Aftermath Entertainment coming opposite winds of violent oppression. Counting the venomous rancour of his *"friend"* Tupac Shakur within the setting. Dr. Dre endeavoured to cultivate and compose a hand-picked roster of artists. The label launch in the form of the Group Therapy - R.B.X., KRS-One, B-Real, and Nas - single, "East Coast/West Coast Killas" featuring Dr. Dre and Scarface, on November 14, 1996. The compilation album, *Dr. Dre Presents: The*

Aftermath followed two-weeks later on November 26, 1996.

A snapshot of where Dr. Dre projected the future to be, it showcased a new generation of Hip-Hop, and R&B artists sprinkled with appearances by R.B.X., Roger Troutman, and King T. Music that paled in comparison to what the world had come to expect from Dr. Dre. Its second single, the solo Dr. Dre song "Been There, Done That" depicted his exit from Gangsta Rap. Prima facie evidence the Death Row Records battery had exacted a pound of flesh.

Mixed-reaction to the compilation ended Dr. Dre's ten-year reign of domination and ensnared him in a period of confusion and anxiety. A self-imposed extended break from the limelight dedicated to rethinking his approach to Aftermath Entertainment ensued. A sparse production schedule occupied by co-producing superstar New York City-based group The Firm - Nas, Foxy Brown, AZ and Nature - with the Trackmasters, and intermittently seated behind the boards for work with B-Real, L.L. Cool J, Scarface, and E-A-Ski.

* * *

Marshall Mathers wrested control of his life from the shadows of obscurity through the dark, impassioned, moody menagerie of the *Slim Shady EP*. His heart and soul susceptible for all to hear, seemingly poised to climb the next rung of the ladder to success. A favoured participant in the second incarnation of the *National Rap Olympics*, he flew to Los Angeles in October 1997. Alas, the judges ruled in favour of the home team and awarded dynamic Project Blowed emcee Otherwize first-place, $500.00 and a Rolex, with Eminem, the runner-up.

In this tale of music history significance, two interns and the matrimonial leave of Interscope Records co-founder Jimmy Iovine's assistant proven to be integral. Nineteen-years-old Dean Geistlinger and Evan Bogart witnessed the *National Rap Olympics,* met with Eminem and Paul Rosenberg and parted ways with a cassette copy of the *Slim Shady EP*. Geistlinger passed the recording to Iovine and told him its something he can't pass up. Iovine played the cassette for Dr. Dre at his home, and Dr. Dre said 'Find him!' Supposedly, Eminem tracked down in Las Vegas where he had flown to show appreciation for a sizeable order of the *Slim Shady EP.*

Adversity breeds strength. Ask Dr. Dre and Eminem. The goal to impact the world within reach, again. The ardent supporters and hateful detractors of Dr. Dre and Eminem, notably those who gleefully snickered at them from afar, in the dark on what lay ahead. The entirety of 1998 consumed by the formulation of *The Slim Shady LP* and the follow-up to *The Chronic.* The good doctor refreshed and awash in confidence, motivated and diligently engaged behind the scenes to forge the career of Eminem, with Slim by his side to lend an ear and contribute to the development of *Chronic 2000.*

Suge Knight, the constant thorn in Dr. Dre's side tried his best to stop the momentum dead in its tracks. All-in, he exhorted his steeds to produce the double-disc compilation, *Suge Knight Represents: Chronic 2000.* Death Row Records leaving no stone unturned, hired Thomas Wlodarczyk, AKA Miilkbone. His single "Presenting Miilkbone" (Eminem Diss) featuring Naji, a response to Eminem's "Just Don't Give A Fuck," to ramp up awareness. Undeniably, the fruits of Knight's distasteful deed changed *Chronic 2000* to *2001.*

* * *

The conversations featured in *THE REAL EMINEM* occurred before the release of *2001*. Eminem spoke on the songs that turned Dr. Dre on and earned him his deal, the extended wait for *The Slim Shady LP*, his thoughts on the completed album, where Bad Meets Evil's "Scary Movies" fit in, and hinted at what lay ahead.

13

Chronic 2000

Detroit, Michigan

April 4, 1999

What are you doing on Chronic 2000?

Eminem: A lot, a lot. I participated a lot in that fucking album. I'm on there a few times, you know? I've done some writing, you know? Just being in there with Dre, just coming up with shit, you know?

How is your relationship with him?

Eminem: It's good, it's good.

Matt Sonzala: This might be a personal question but what was Dre's reaction to the Suge Knight Chronic 2000 coming out?

Eminem: Ah, that's - I can't say that.

14

The Bike

Toronto, Ontario

April 10, 1999

I heard you got your deal based on freestyling ability?

Eminem: Yeah? Nah, I don't think it was that. I don't think it was based on my freestyling ability. My name started getting known because of freestyling and battles and shit. I started getting a rep, but what got me the deal was the *Slim Shady EP*. That tape was what Dre heard and what Dre liked. Dre said his favourite songs on that EP was "Just Don't Give A Fuck," "Just The Two Of Us," and "If I Had." Those were his three favourite songs and shit. I think he said as soon as he heard "Just The Two Of Us" he was like, *'Yo! I want this motherfucker!'*

Are you happy with your album?

Eminem: I'm definitely happy with my album. I'm 100% happy with it. I feel like the true test is going to be my second album, you know what I'm saying? It's easy to come out and make your first album. All you're doing is setting the grounds. You're laying the foundation of how you're going to sound and how you want the world to see you and shit like that. The second album the true test is trying to maintain it.

Proof: Hell yeah.

Eminem: You know what I'm saying? It's easy to get on a bike and ride it, but you got to - Can you keep riding that bike without fucking falling off?

Is the second album going to be more Dre?

Eminem: Yeah, more Dre.

Proof: Gonna be more Shady.

Eminem: More Dre and more Shady. The second album is going to - If people are offended now by this album, the second album they're going to fucking - they gonna blow. They're going to hit the fucking ceiling, probably going to kill themselves. All these little uptight fucking critics. Fuck 'em.

Does that do anything to you? A friend told me he wrote a review and gave it a 7/10 and the owner of the paper put it down to a

5/10 just because he didn't like the album. Shit like that is going on, sheistiness all around.

Eminem: That's funny to me. I mean, I don't know, man. I'm not ego tripping but - I'm not ego tripping at all, but if motherfuckers don't like my shit — If they don't like my shit, is it because they think the album sucks or because they're offended? You know what I'm saying? People that get offended give that shit low reviews. I don't know, you tell it. It's like, motherfuckers are funny, man. Dissing my album and shit, whatever.

How come "Scary Movies" wasn't on the album? (The first Bad Meets Evil pairing of Eminem and Royce da 5"9 on Game Recordings.)

Eminem: That was done after the album was done.

For real?

Eminem: Yeah. Not long after. Maybe like a month after the album was done, but that was some shit — I felt like my album was taking too long to come out 'cause motherfuckers in the underground was wondering where Slim Shady went. What happened to Dre? Dre swallowed him up? Is he going to put him on the back burner?

Motherfuckers was asking. So, I wanted to do a side project, not only to get Royce out there, for people to hear Royce, but to let motherfuckers know Slim Shady is still here. I'm coming, you know? Plus, I was bored. I like to work, man. I like to write; I like to fucking do shit, you know what I'm saying? So, I wanted to put that shit out there and have a little extra buzz and shit.

What are you doing on Chronic 2000? You said you're all over it.

Eminem: Yeah, I'm on it a few times. I've been in the studio just helping write, helping, fucking whatever I can do. My input, making beats, anything. Whatever I can do, you know what I'm saying? I've been in there doing it. The album is fucking hot. I just wanted to return the favour to Dre for what he's done for me. I wanted to fucking just be there and whatever I could do, whatever input I could give. Because I got an ear for the shit. My ear, I'm not saying I'm fucking Dr. Dre. I ain't got Dre's ear, but I do have an ear for this shit, and I know what's hot and what's not. So, I just was just in there with him.

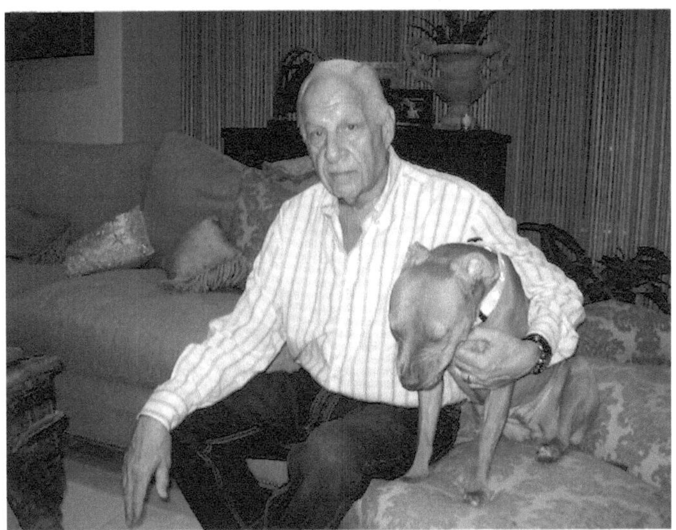

Inside the home of Jerry Heller, Calabasas, Ca October 22, 2006

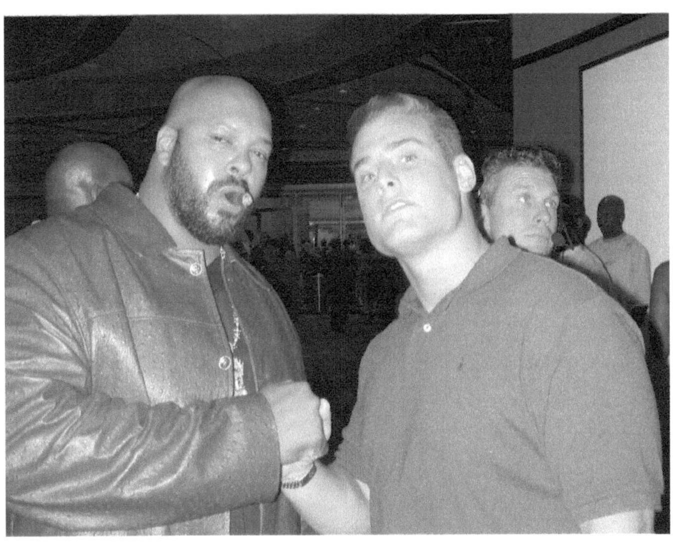

Suge Knight and Michael Etherington @ 2nd Annual BET Awards, Los Angeles, Ca June 25, 2002

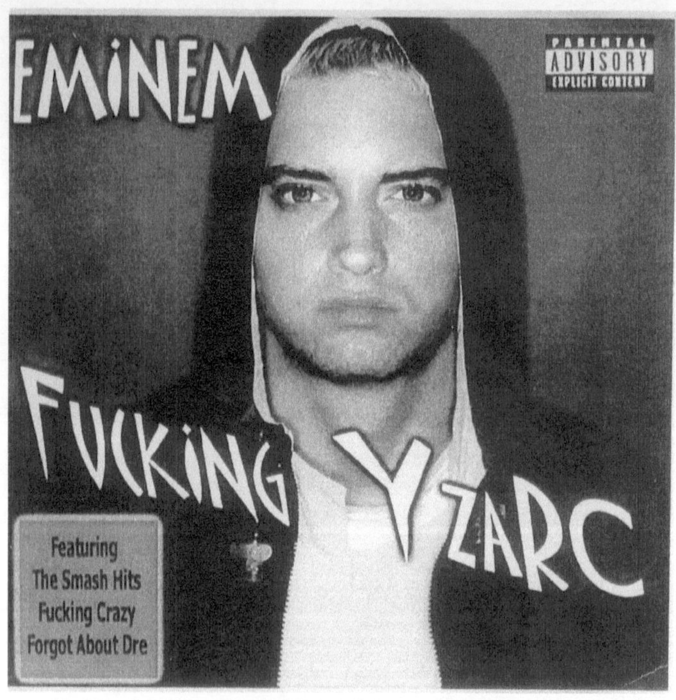

This mixtape is Fucking Yzarc

EMINEM FUCKING YZARC

1. FUCKING CRAZY
2. FORGOT ABOUT DRE
3. GREEN AND GOLD
4. THE SHOWDOWN
5. NOTHNG TO DO
6. WATCH DEES
7. 3 VERSES
8. GET U MAD
9. FUCK OFF
10. HUSTLES HARDCORE
11. THE ANTHEM
12. BUS A RYHME
13. FLYEST MATERIAL
14. MY NAME (KID ROCK)
15. 5 STAR GENERAL

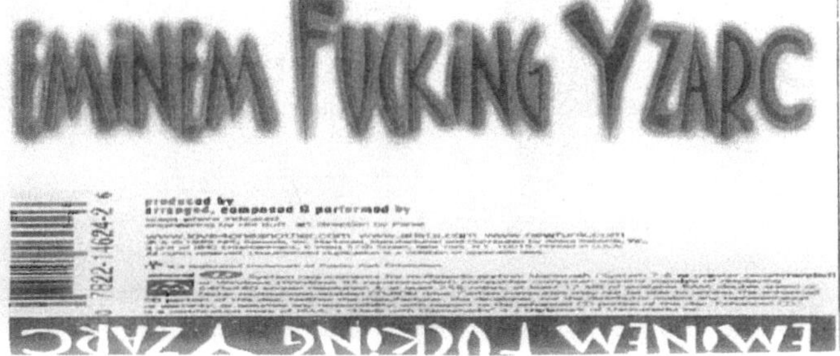

5 Star General

EAST COAST
WEST COAST
KILLAS

What do you know about street teams and stickers?

DR. DRE PRESENTS...
THE
AFTERMATH

AMPG04 202 B 16 ADULT
68.50 LVL200 AISLE 2 68.50
FARMCLUB.COM & THE SOURCE
202 DR.DRE / SNOOP DOGG
TM 5X UP IN SMOKE TOUR
B 16 THE MOLSON AMPHITHEATRE
MCA400A RAIN OR SHINE/R126007780
4JUL00 TUE JUL 4 2000 7:00PM

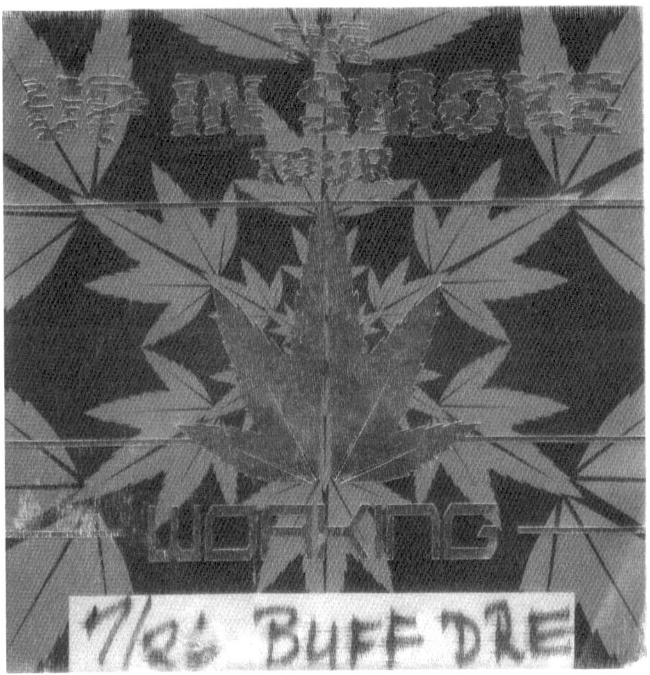

Working? No. We did bring a large box of Anchor Bar Suicide Wings and Nate Dogg loved them

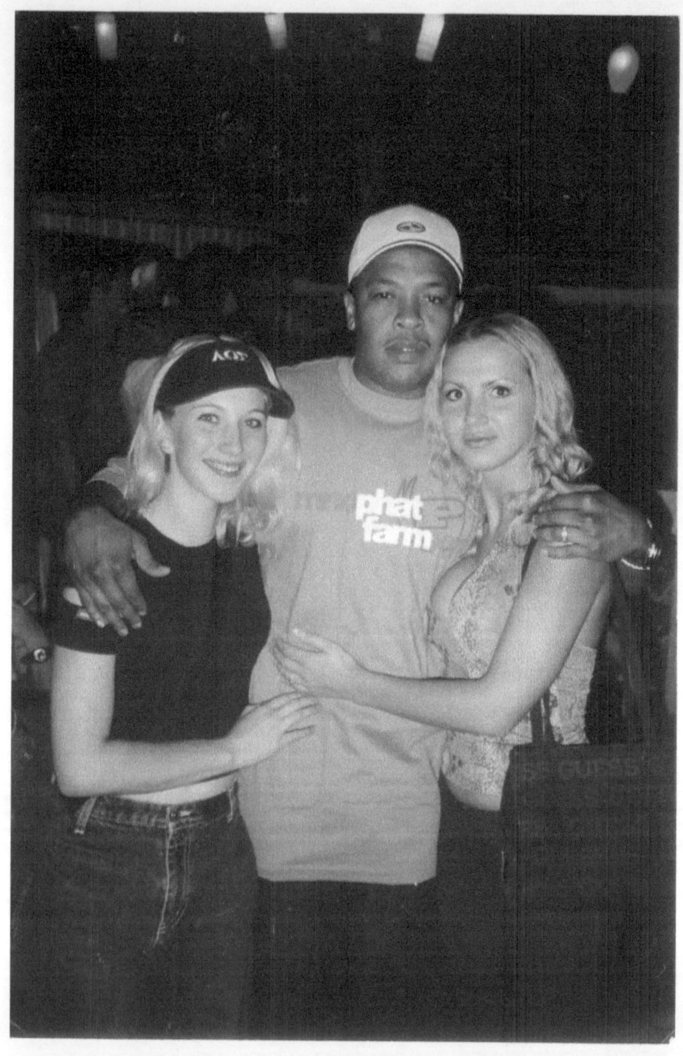

Post Up In Smoke show, Dr. Dre & DJ Jam lit up BamBoom in the pre-lit era Toronto, Canada, July 4, 2000

V

THE DARK DETROIT CITY CARNIVAL

They some hoe ass motherfuckers! They don't mean shit.
- Proof

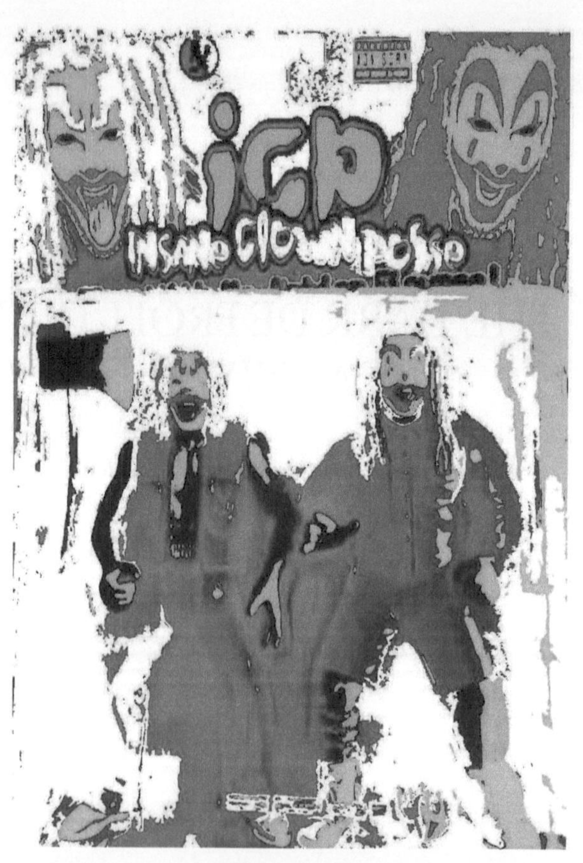
icp
Insane Clown Posse

15

'You Guys Comin' to My Release Party, or What?'

Through the course of his career, Eminem has had a beef with many artists and personalities. The war with Insane Clown Posse momentous.

The origin of the beef centred on the flyer for the *Slim Shady EP* release party at *Saint Andrews Hall* in Detroit, Michigan. It read *"Also an appearance by Esham, Kid Rock, and ICP ... maybe."* Eminem handed a flyer to Violent J. Violent J took offence and pressed Eminem. Slim said, *'It says 'maybe.' Maybe you will be there; I don't know. That's why I'm asking you right now. You guys comin' to my release party, or what?'* They cursed each other out, and it went downhill from there.

The bitter battles of diss songs, freestyles and bad words in the media, lasting twelve years. D12 allegedly entered the fray, chased ICP out of the club, and blasted their van with paintballs. The assault refuted by ICP. Eminem the first to bat when he launched three grenades at ICP over "Drastic Measures (Microphone Autopsy)." "'Till Hell Freezes Over" and "Get You Mad." ICP and Twizted hit back with "Slim

Anus." Unconfirmed rumours circulated that Eminem cried upon hearing it.

Whitey Don and I spoke with Violent J inside ICP's parked tour bus immediately following a sold show at Detroit's Cobo Hall - where we came close to being doused in Grape Faygo - on August 13, 1999. *Backyard Wrestling* and Juggalo icon, Mad Man Pondo by his side.

> *"Y' see, in Detroit, we had two albums and three EPs out before we even signed a record deal, so we was always on the Detroit music scene. And Eminem? I don't know where he came from. He was never on the Detroit scene, ever! I didn't know he existed. He dropped an EP about four months before he blew up, that was it. It was like he dropped an EP, next thing I hear on the streets that he signed with Aftermath, or whatever. Then he blew up - record time! He came out of nowhere!*
>
> *Then I started hearing from a lot of people that knew him. 'Cause when he first came out a lot of people were asking him "What's up? What do you think of Insane Clown Posse?" 'Cause we were the only ones really coming out of Detroit before him, and he was saying in a lot of interviews - "Fuck ICP!" - And we don't even know this kid. He was "Fuck them! They don't got no talent." And him runnin' his mouth like that could get a punk hurt.*
>
> *We had a radio show in Detroit, once a month. It was called the Juggalo Show, and we did a parody of his track "My Name Is," which turned out mad funny. We took on certain bars of his rap, and we went ahead and got one of our homies who sounded just like him, to*

re-rap it, called it "Slim Anus." It was mad funny, and we played that on our radio show. Finally, we got to the Howard Stern Show and played that - jokes! 'Cause Howard was even grillin' his ass when he interviewed him, asking him why he talks like a Black man. That guy's an idiot!"

Not one to let things lie, Slim clapped back and added fuel to the fire on *The Marshall Mathers LP* title track and "Ken Kaniff" skit. The consequences accelerated when ICP employee Douglas Dail insulted Eminem in the parking lot of a Royal Oak, Michigan, car audio shop on June 3, 2000. The short-tempered Marshall Mathers III charged with a felony for carrying a concealed weapon and a misdemeanour for taking it out in public to threaten Dail. Still angry the next day, June 4, 2000, Slim spotted his wife, Kim, kissing John Guerra outside a Warren, Michigan, club. Assault with a Dangerous Weapon added to the court docket for pistol whipping Guerra. The incident chronicled on *The Eminem Show* skit "The Kiss."

ICP, Blaze Ya Dead Homie and Twizted fed the monster with "Shittalkaz" on July 25, 2000. The first half of the *Bizaar Bizaar* double-album released October 31, 2000, counted three more anti-Slim songs - "Please Don't Hate Me," "Cherry Pie (I Need A Freak)," and "My Homie Baby Mama." All in the family, Dail's brother, ICP Road Manager William Dail, in a complete lack of judgment, stood accused of choking 23-years-old Eminem fan Thomas P. Goonan until he blacked out at the Omaha, Nebraska, ICP concert on May 8, 2001. Dail turned to savage when the Eminem t-shirt wearing Goonan tossed M&Ms and waved an Eminem flag at ICP as they performed. Upon Goonan being escorted from the venue, Dail grabbed him by the neck and threw him against the fence barricade. Charged with misdemeanour Assault and Battery, William Dail posted $1000.00 bail. ICP Manager and Psychopathic Records co-founder, Alex Abbiss, going on record saying, *"We encourage this type of activity."*

Eminem faced with five years incarceration for the Douglas Dail charges, got sentenced on June 28, 2001, to one-year probation, community service "impactful to young people," and $2360.00 in fines. The probation runs concurrently with the guilty plea to the weapons charge for the Guerra episode. Common conditions included counselling, bans on using alcohol and drugs and engaging in threatening and violent behaviour, and periodic drug testing. Mathers also required to seek approval from the Judge to travel out of Michigan. The prosecutors dropped Assault charges. William Dail pleaded guilty to a disorderly conduct charge and ordered to pay a $100.00 fine, July 31, 2001.

The unsettled display maintained over various onstage shenanigans. Eminem answered a mic'd phone and the voice on the other end said *"This is Violent J from ICP. Can I suck your dick?"* Juggalos dressed in clown makeup and ICP t-shirts once stood in front of the stage and caused Eminem to delay a show. Eminem dissed ICP on the *Up In Smoke Tour* stage by bringing out two blowup dolls in ICP face-paint. ICP duplicated the feat at a *Juggalo Gathering* with an Eminem blowup doll. The feud slowly ground to a halt over time. D12, minus Eminem, went bowling with ICP in 2005. ICP went on record in 2009 and stated that they liked the *Relapse* album. Eminem finally let go the same year with the claim he liked the ICP song "Miracles."

16

Ricky, Julian & Bubbles

Toronto, Ontario

April 10, 1999

I got your boy's CD last week, Butter.

Proof: DJ Butter?

Is that a representation of the Detroit scene?

Proof: He's cool. I like Butter. I got a lot of love for him.

Eminem: Butter supported. Butter fucking - Butter supported me. Butter was always putting my shit on his mixtapes, doing interviews.

So, it's more just a Detroit pride and mentality where you're coming?

Eminem: Yeah.

But your buddies, ICP -

Eminem: My buddies?

*Violent J and Shaggy2 Dope, or whatever the hell the guy's name is, with the Jerky Boys on their new album.**

Eminem: They have the Jerky Boys on their shit?

And Snoop.

Eminem: They got Snoop?!

On the album. I got it at home.

[1]Eminem: Get the fuck out!

I got it at home. But it sounds like — it's ridiculous. Snoop does his rhymes, does his nice flow, and then buddy comes on doing whatever he does. A lot of the lyrics from both of you are about shock value. Is that a Detroit thing or just coming from you?

Proof: Those birds are wack. When they put out their first CD, they weren't even rapping on the beat. Motherfucking Esahm helped them get on better in life. He helped they crowd; you know what I'm

---

1 **The fifth Insane Clown Posse album, Amazing Jeckel Brothers, was released on May 25, 1999. The fifth joker card, and arguably the pinnacle of the Dark Carnival decks.*

sayin'? We chased them motherfuckers at they own motherfucking autograph signing.

Eminem: Hell yeah!

Proof: They some hoe ass motherfuckers! They don't mean shit.

17

Eminem x Insane Clown Posse Diss Songs

1997

"Drastic Measures (Microphone Autopsy)" Indigenous Tribe featuring Eminem -**As of Light Into Darkness**

1999

"Get You Mad" Sway & King Tech featuring Eminem - **This or That,** June 15, 1999

2000

"'Till Hell Freezes Over" Eminem - **Detroit Underground**

"Slim Anus" - Insane Clown Posse **Psychopathics from Outer Space,** April 5, 2000 (Previewed in 1999 on the Howard Stern Show.)

"Marshall Mathers" - Eminem **The Marshall Mathers LP,**

May 23, 2000

"Ken Kani" (skit) - Eminem **The Marshall Mathers LP,** May 23, 2000

"Shittalkaz" Blaze Ya Dead Homie featuring Insane Clown Posse and Twizted

Blaze Ya Dead Homie, July 25, 2000

"Please Don't Hate Me" Insane Clown Posse - **Bizaar,** October 31, 2000

"Cherry Pie (I Need A Freak)" Insane Clown Posse **Bizaar** , October 31, 2000

"My Homie Baby Mama" Insane Clown Posse - **Bizaar,** October 31, 2000

2002

"Business" Eminem – **The Eminem Show,** May 26, 2002

"Ain't Nuttin' But A Bitch Thang" Insane Clown Posse - **The Pendulum,** August 20, 2002

2003

"Monkey See, Monkey Do" Eminem - **Straight from the Lab**, November 7, 2003

"Hard Times" Esham featuring Insane Clown Posse **Repentance**, November 18, 2003

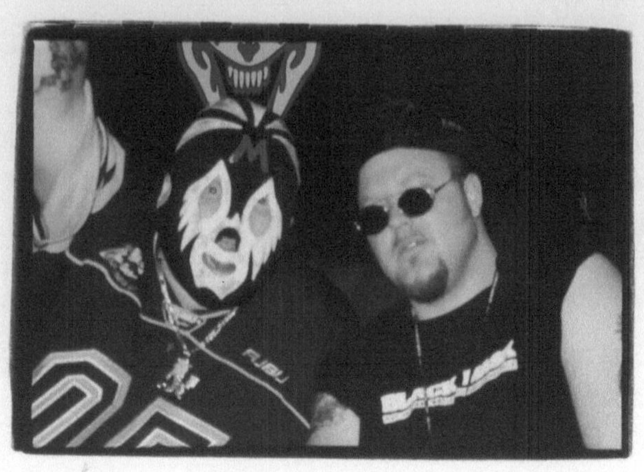

Violent J & Whitey Don on the ICP Tour Bus, Detroit, Michigan, August 13, 1999

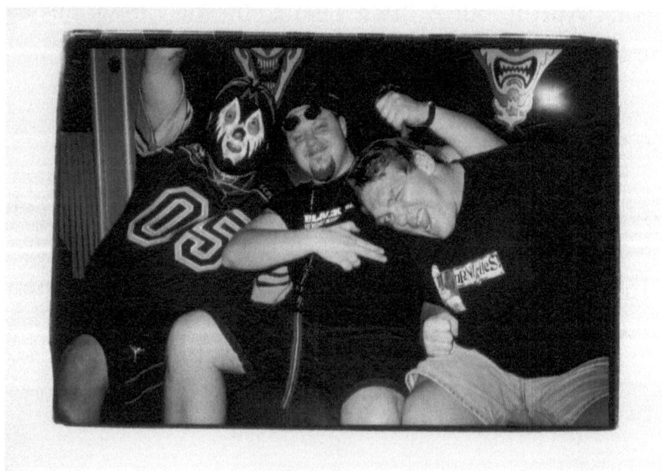

Violent J, Whitey Don & Mad Man Pondo!

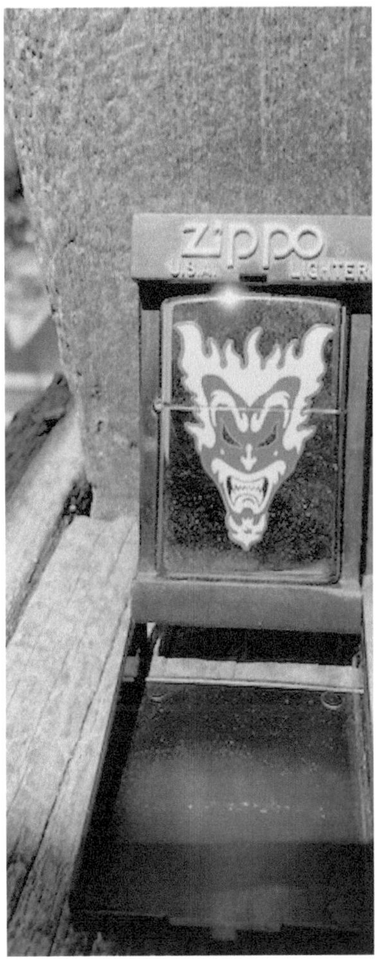
Zippo

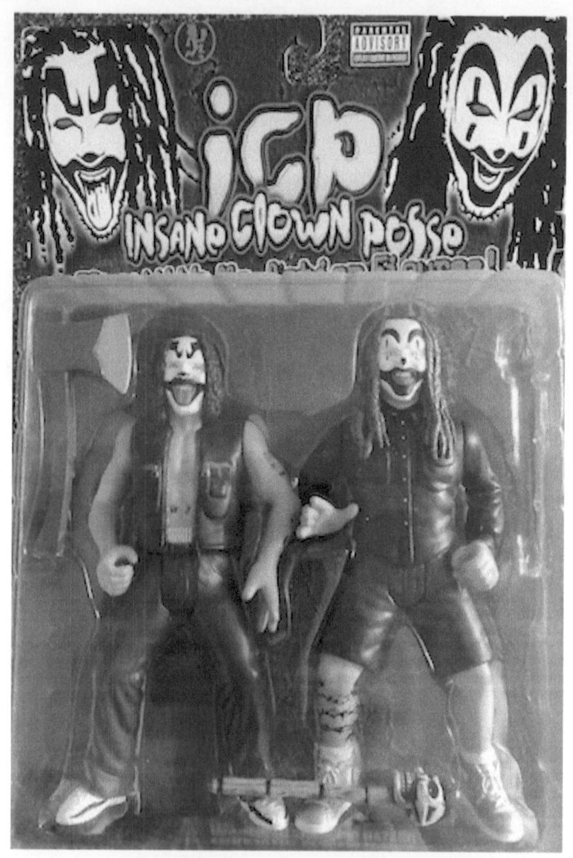

ICP Play With Me Action Figures, 1999

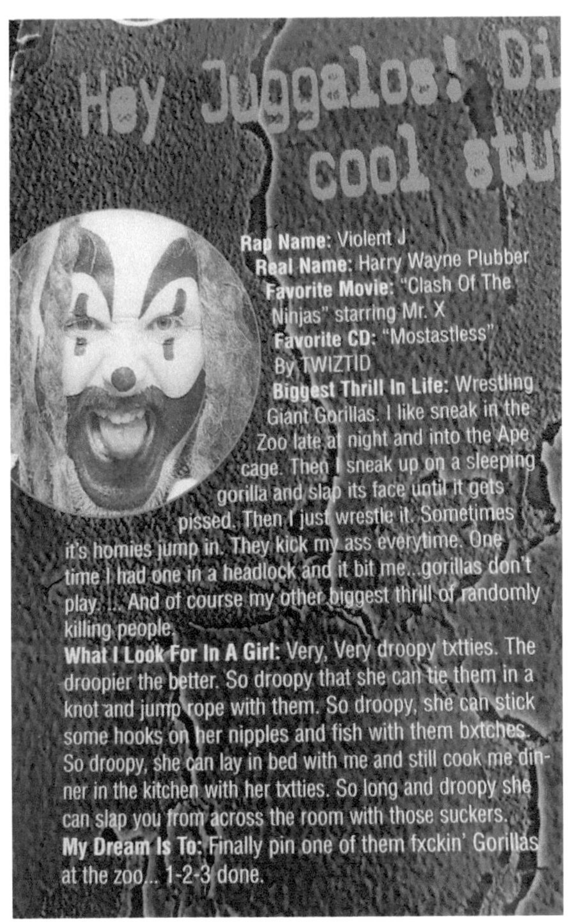

Hey Juggalos! Di
cool stu

Rap Name: Violent J
Real Name: Harry Wayne Plubber
Favorite Movie: "Clash Of The Ninjas" starring Mr. X
Favorite CD: "Mostastless" By TWIZTID
Biggest Thrill In Life: Wrestling Giant Gorillas. I like sneak in the Zoo late at night and into the Ape cage. Then I sneak up on a sleeping gorilla and slap its face until it gets pissed. Then I just wrestle it. Sometimes it's homies jump in. They kick my ass everytime. One time I had one in a headlock and it bit me...gorillas don't play. ... And of course my other biggest thrill of randomly killing people.
What I Look For In A Girl: Very, Very droopy txtties. The droopier the better. So droopy that she can tie them in a knot and jump rope with them. So droopy, she can stick some hooks on her nipples and fish with them bxtches. So droopy, she can lay in bed with me and still cook me dinner in the kitchen with her txtties. So long and droopy she can slap you from across the room with those suckers.
My Dream Is To: Finally pin one of them fxckin' Gorillas at the zoo... 1-2-3 done.

Inside the mind of Harry Wayne Plubber, 1999

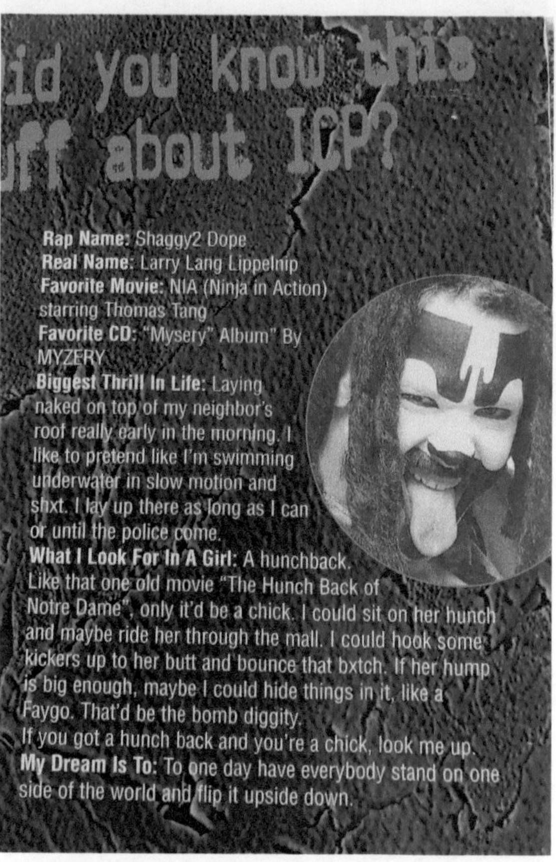

id you know this
uff about ICP?

Rap Name: Shaggy2 Dope
Real Name: Larry Lang Lippelnip
Favorite Movie: NIA (Ninja in Action) starring Thomas Tang
Favorite CD: "Mysery" Album" By MYZERY
Biggest Thrill In Life: Laying naked on top of my neighbor's roof really early in the morning. I like to pretend like I'm swimming underwater in slow motion and shxt. I lay up there as long as I can or until the police come.
What I Look For In A Girl: A hunchback. Like that one old movie "The Hunch Back of Notre Dame", only it'd be a chick. I could sit on her hunch and maybe ride her through the mall. I could hook some kickers up to her butt and bounce that bxtch. If her hump is big enough, maybe I could hide things in it, like a Faygo. That'd be the bomb diggity. If you got a hunch back and you're a chick, look me up.
My Dream Is To: To one day have everybody stand on one side of the world and flip it upside down.

Inside the mind of Larry Lang Lippelnip, 1999

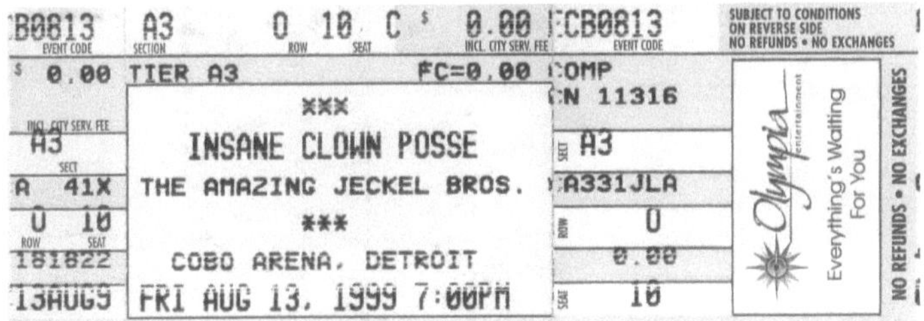

ICP live in The D!

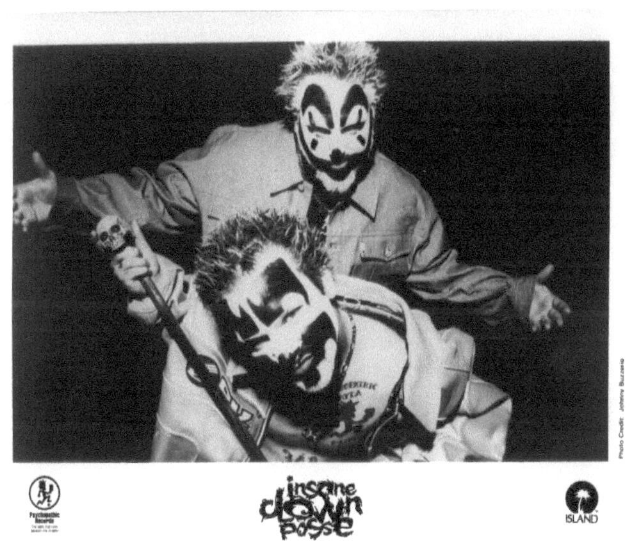

Say cheese?

VI

WHITE RAPPERS

I'm not dissing underground. I'm not dissing the underground at all. I'm just saying these motherfuckers are a bunch of fucking nobodies; people that don't have talent.
- Eminem

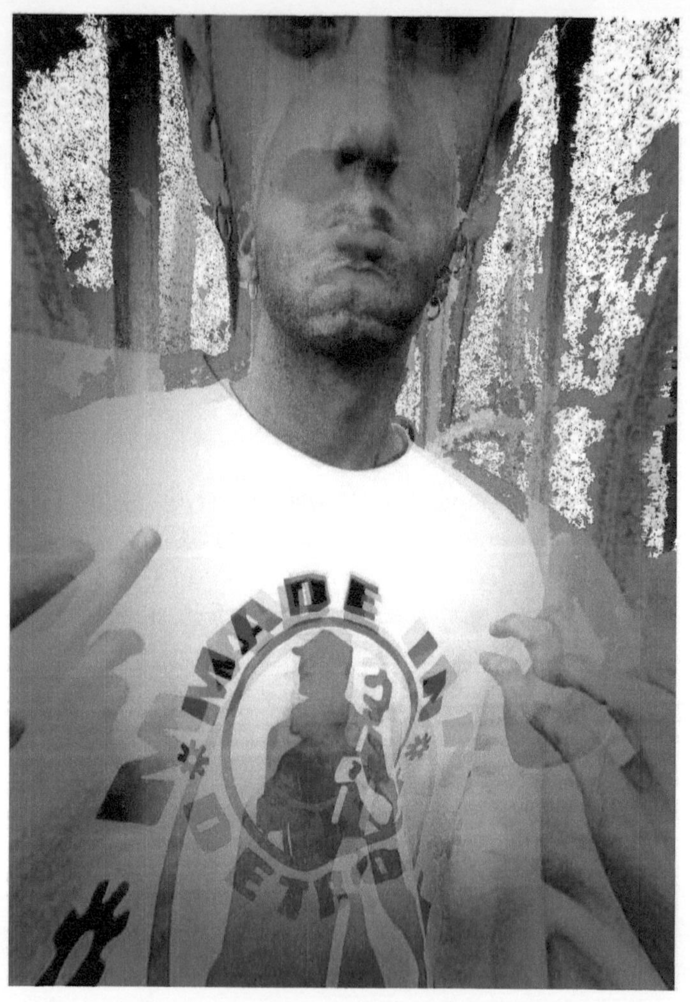
MADE IN

All In A Line

To struggle with anger is common for many who experience emotional wellness issues. Any perceived slight or annoyance, impatience or impulsivity can rapidly lead to cataclysmic outbursts that create long-term resistance. The psychological broadcast is necessary to emotionally and physically break free from the confines of the underground, to prove worthy of mainstream acceptance.

Once sadly lumped in with the burgeoning set of the white rapper's on the rise, the ingrained make-up of Eminem demanded all others be destroyed. The period between *Infinite* and the *Slim Shady EP* crucial to the story of Eminem. Though his freestyle and battle rap techniques were regaled within the underground, the lacklustre response to *Infinite* made it clear he had to change. Indeed, the future did not lay with tracks like "Searchin'." The most acclaimed emcee of his age, Eminem surveyed the landscape and compiled a list of potential challengers. Then, he put them all in a line. The first shot coming as a featured artist on Indigenous Tribe's "Drastic Measures (Microphone Autopsy)."

Like Eminem, Cage grew up a member of the lower-class. His father dishonourably discharged and expelled from the West German base he served as an MP for the use and sale of heroin. A bad man who often forced his son to assist in shooting him up. The bitter times constant throughout his teenage years. Removed from High-School and beaten by his step-father, he turned to an assortment of hard drugs and hallucinogens. Shipped overseas to an uncle stationed on a German military base, to have a year of sense systematically beaten into him. Hip-Hop as a means of salvation, Cage channelled his abundance of energy and became an underground force.

Pete Nice and DJ Richie Rich were the first to put him on. Cage paired with Benz on "Rich Bring 'Em Back" off the duo's 1993 *Dust to Dust* album. A short-lived deal with Colombia Records the same year unfulfilled, lost to inner demons and drug abuse. The spiral staircase rife with arrests for drug possession and fighting, Cage, faced with incarceration, entered a psychiatric facility for a two-week evaluation. Sixteen months and several suicide attempts later, it was back to life, back to reality. Bobbito Garcia's Fondle 'Em Records release of the acclaimed "Radiohead" b/w "Agent Orange" in 1997, pivotal. Cage renewed as an active underground force.

Eminem abandoned the rhythm of Nas and asserted his Detroit state of mind on the *Slim Shady EP*. Its dark, contemplative topics reflective of the life he led detailed in an ominous cadence. Sex, drugs, anxiety and violence out in the open for all to identify. Elitist-Purists tagged the work as derivative of Cage with several going on to label it a direct bite, and that included Cage. The inevitable consequent measures of scorn directed at each other by mixtape, freestyle and album cuts, and media sermons. "Just Don't Give A Fuck," is a fuck you to all who refused to rate Slim's calibre of skills.

Miilkbone, Everlast and Vanilla Ice the targets of his scorn. Miilkbone came up under the watchful eyes of Biz Markie and Cool V recording mixtapes twice a week in V's basement. A native of Perth Amboy, New Jersey, Naughty by Nature heard him, and he became an affiliate. Signed to Capitol Records in 1994, Miilkbone came with the club bangers "Wherez Da Party At?," and "Keep It Real," its instrumental a classic freestyle template. The anticipated June 1995 release of *Da Miilkrate* album dead in the water when Capitol shut down its urban department.

The disapproval of Miilkbone on "Just Don't Give A Fuck" without warning. Eminem's adoption by Dr. Dre presented an opportunity to clap back. Sure Knight and Company were on the offensive, entirely dedicated to bringing down Dr. Dre, and one of his producers had a connection to Death Row Records. "Presenting Miilkbone" featuring Naji formed the response. A cheque in his pocket for the task. The weight of Death Row Records completely behind the song as it became the lead single off their evil intention to undermine Dr. Dre's follow-up to *The Chronic, Suge Knight Represents: Chronic 2000.*

In consort with Dr. Dre, Eminem opted to not bring attention to the Death Row Records offering. Miilkbone denied the light, again, when he came at Eminem with "Dear Slim," in 2001, to bring attention to his *U Got Milk* album.

Eminem reflected on his roots in the underground trenches. Unequivocally distancing himself from the pack, he dissected underground Hip-Hop and lashed out at the white rapper stereotype. Proof added to the sentiment and argued the case of what set Eminem apart from other rappers, with a testimonial that fixed Slim amongst the all-time greats.

19

No Comment

Detroit Michigan,
April 4, 1999

What's your take on Miilkbone?

Eminem: No comment.

Matt Sonzala: No comment! Come on, man. What about the Clown Posse?

Eminem: Faggots.

20

Clowns

Toronto, Ontario

April 10, 1999

Now the album is out. Critically acclaimed, critically dismissed; the whole nine. It runs the entire gamut. All these jokers are popping up like Cage, all talking shit. ICP; all this fucking Miilkbone and all this shit. How are you dealing with all that?

Proof: They're all wack. Fuck 'em.

Eminem: Just ignore them. They're fucking clowns. They're little fucking underground Hip-Hop head clowns that fucking are jokes. Little fucking - little bitches. It's funny how all these little fucking white rappers want to compare themselves to me and shit just because I'm white. Miilkbone — I dissed Miilkbone initially, but truthfully, I wasn't even dissing him. I was dissing people comparing me to him; you know what I'm saying? I mentioned all the white rappers in a line and what I was talking about was stereotypes. I was talking about like stereotypically speaking, you know what I'm saying? I was talking about busting all the stereotypes and shit like that.

Proof: The only one he technically dissed was Vanilla Ice.

Eminem: Vanilla Ice. Yeah, that's it.

Proof: But he iced him.

Eminem: But now, if he wants to bring it, he can bring it, but he didn't. I heard his song, it's fucking garbage, and he didn't even bring it. So, it ain't even worth responding to.

I heard you guys were going to debut his song on your website.

Proof: That would be hot.

Eminem: I think Paul said that. We might do it. All the clowns, all the corny ass white rappers that diss Eminem, we'll make a website.

So, you're saying this, and you're dismissing all the underground Hip-Hop. I call them the Baboops. You deny all that but that's where you cut your teeth, and that's where you got your reputation, underground Hip-Hop.

Eminem: I'm not dissing the underground. I'm not

dissing the underground at all. I'm just saying these motherfuckers are a bunch of fucking nobodies; people that don't have talent. When you're in the underground, it's cool to come up from the underground, but if you don't got the talent to rise above that, you know what I'm sayin'? You're not going to go anywhere. These fucking clowns don't got the talent and got the fucking know-how and the skills to know how to use your talent.

When you know how to put words together, know how to utilise that shit. Don't fucking - you know what I'm saying? If you're an underground artist for a couple of years, a few years, and you end up keep doing it and doing it and doing it, and don't blow up. Then you obviously didn't fucking have what it took. If you're underground forever, then you got a fucking problem, you know what I'm saying?

It's very important to come from the underground, to come up from the underground. Motherfuckers knowing your name and you got the skill, and everybody's talking about you in the underground. Because Hip-Hoppers, the underground heads, they do appreciate true fucking Hip-Hop, you know what I'm saying? They love lyrics. They're all about lyrics, but you gotta be smart enough to know how to utilise that shit to take it above that shit. I don't know how I did it. I don't know, but I did it. I can't even explain my situation because I never thought I would be anything but an underground artist, you know?

I get sent a lot of tapes, and the beats are shit, and the guys can't flow, and they're talking shit, and it's just ridiculous. And the people who like it look like they would like it.

> *Eminem: Yup. Ha ha ha ha ha ha, that's funny.*
>
> *Proof: You know what though? You know what separates him a lot? A lot of them want to be the best white rapper, and that's never his goal. His goal is to be the best rapper.*
>
> *Eminem: Best rapper, period.*
>
> *Proof: Period. And when they do that, then that's why they seem underneath him. Because it's like what they responded to is nothing, you know what I'm saying?*

Yeah, I know. It's like, (the label) told me before: don't talk to you about being a white rapper. But I'm white, and I've been interviewing rappers for ten years. So, it's like the same but different, you know what I mean? It's Hip-Hop, it's not a colour thing.

> Proof: Right. If somebody asked me how does it feel to be a white rapper? They ask me that, right? I would look at them like, how the fuck am I supposed to know? And almost the same question. How does it feel to be a Black rapper? I don't know! I'm a mother-fucking Black rapper! I don't know how it feels to be - Now the question should be, how does it feel to be a Rapper? Period. Then their

lifestyle will reflect how does it feel to be a Rapper; you know what I'm saying?

Last week I spoke to you, and I was talking about a lot of people labelling you a white trash rapper, and you answered, I am a white trash Rapper from Detroit. I was toying with putting that on the cover.

Eminem: I am.

What do you think of that on the cover: I am a white trash rapper from Detroit?

Eminem: I don't give a fuck because people already - I'm a trash Rapper from Detroit, not just a white rapper or white trash rapper. I'm a fucking Trash Rapper from Broke City.

Proof: You know what's so funny about that shit? The reason I be hating they putting the white shit in there. It seems like they're trying to take away the art and the crown by keeping him the "White Rapper."

Eminem: Yup.

Proof: I mean, he can't be a great like Rakim? They gonna put him over there with Serch and the Beastie Boys, you know what I'm saying? He wants to be up there as one of the greats. When they say the Beastie Boys, they think that's one of the best groups of all time. They don't say the best white group of all time; you know what I'm saying? They make such a big deal out of that's all they want him to be, just a white rapper. It's wack.

Eminem: Yeah. I hate that shit, I've always hated that shit, man. I hate being put in a group. That's why I fucking took all the white rappers and put them in a line. I was saying don't fucking compare me to these motherfuckers because — I like Serch and Pete Nice, you know what I'm saying? They're fucking dope. I didn't diss them; I was using it metaphorically speaking. But don't compare me to them motherfuckers just because I'm white and they're white. We have nothing in common! I don't sound like them; they don't sound like me, you know?

21

Eminem x Cage Diss Songs

1997

Indigenous Tribe featuring Eminem "Drastic Measures (Microphone Autopsy)" - ***As of Light Into Darkness***

1999

Eminem - "Role Model" ***The Slim Shady LP***, February 23, 1999

Eminem -"Ken Kaniff" (Skit) ***The Slim Shady LP*** February 23, 1999

Tony Touch featuring Eminem (freestyle) ***Power Cypha 3: The Grand Finale***, 1999

Sway & King Tech featuring Eminem "Get You Mad" ***This or That***, June 15, 1999

DJ Eli & Shan Boogs featuring Cage - "And So Kiddies" ***Cloudkickers*** EP & Cage's - ***For Your Box***, October 28, 1999

Cage - "Bitch Lady" (snippet) ***For Your Box*** October 28,

1999

Cage - "4 Letter Word" ***For Your Box*** October 28, 1999

Cage - "Still Cage" freestyle ***For Your Box*** October 28, 1999

2002

Cage - "Escape to '88" ***Movies for the Blind,*** August 6, 2002

Cage - "A Crowd Killer" ***Movies for the Blind,*** August 6, 2002

Cage - "Pussy, Money and War" featuring Copywrite ***Movies for The Blind,*** August 6, 2002

2003

Cage - "Haterama" ***Weatherproof EP***, July 29, 2003

EMINEM X MIILKBONE DISS SONGS

Eminem - "Just Don't Give A Fuck" ***Slim Shady EP***, December 16, 1997

Miilkbone - "Presenting Miilkbone" ***Suge Knight Represents: Chronic 2000*** – April 30, 1999

Miilkbone - "Dear Slim" ***U Got Milk?*** - April 17, 2001

EMINEM X VANILLA ICE DISS SONGS

"MC Hammer VS. Vanilla Ice" Soul Intent (Eminem and Proof) - 1990

Eminem - "Just Don't Give A Fuck" ***Slim Shady EP***, December 16, 1997

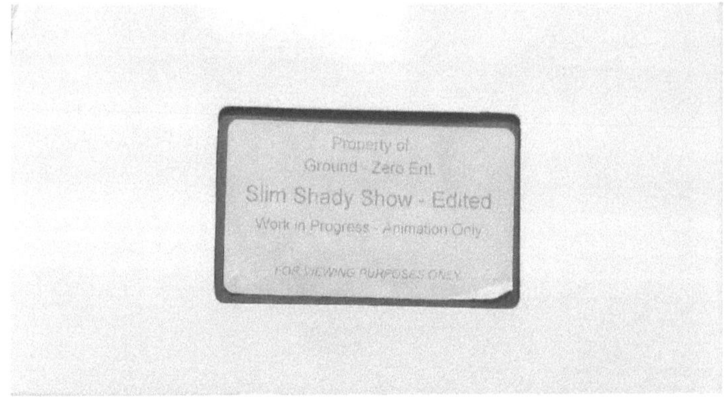

A preview of the short-lived 11 episode Slim Shady Show

Harris Rosen

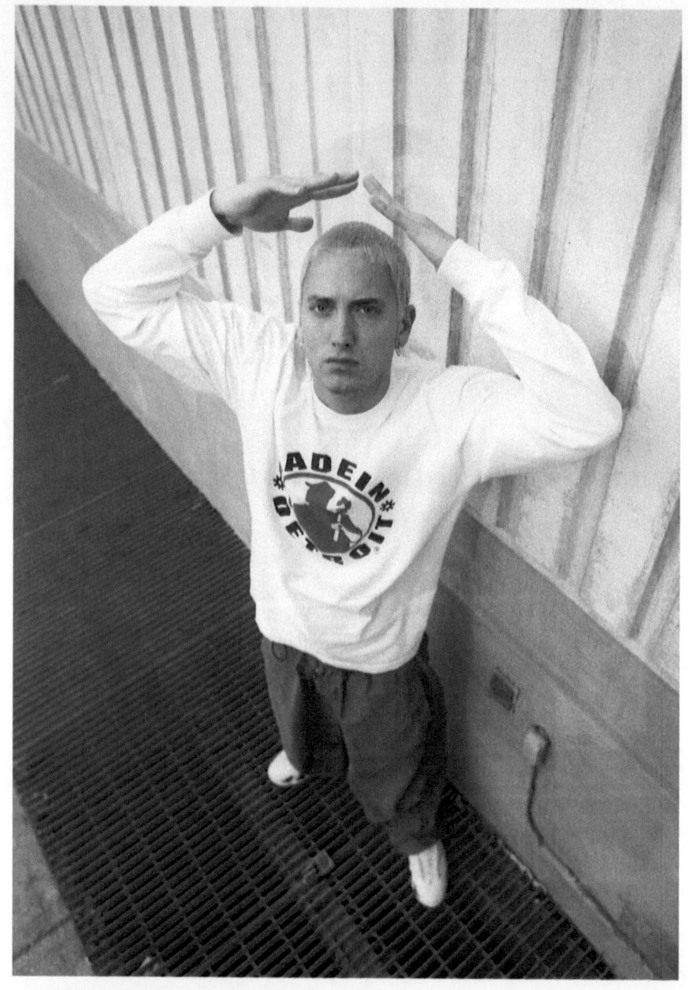

Raindrops Keep Fallin' on My Head minus Hal and Burt

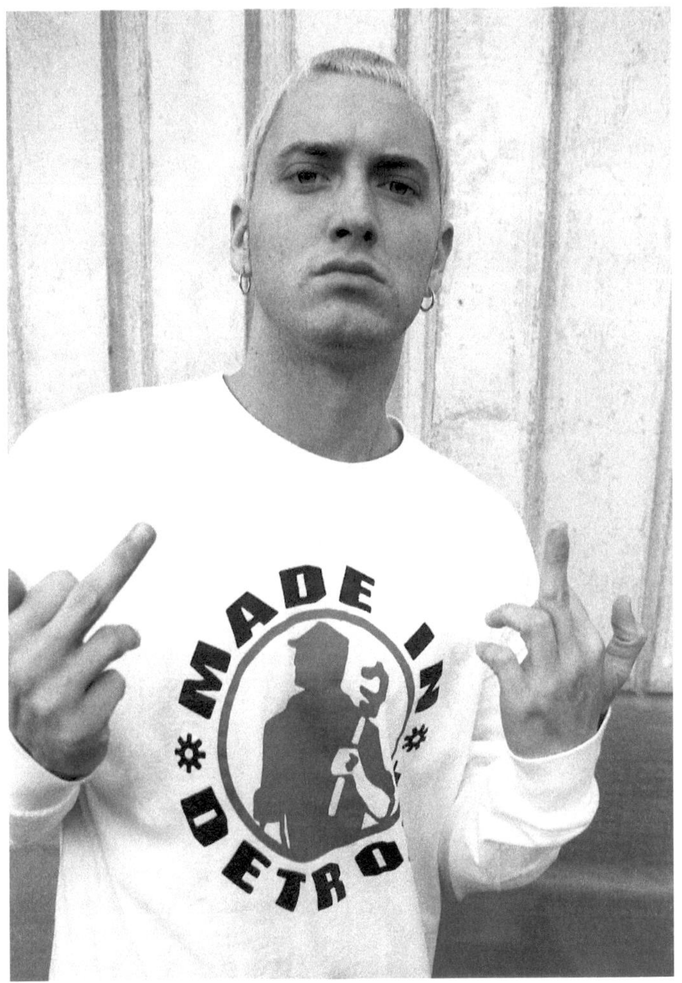

In a sentimental mood

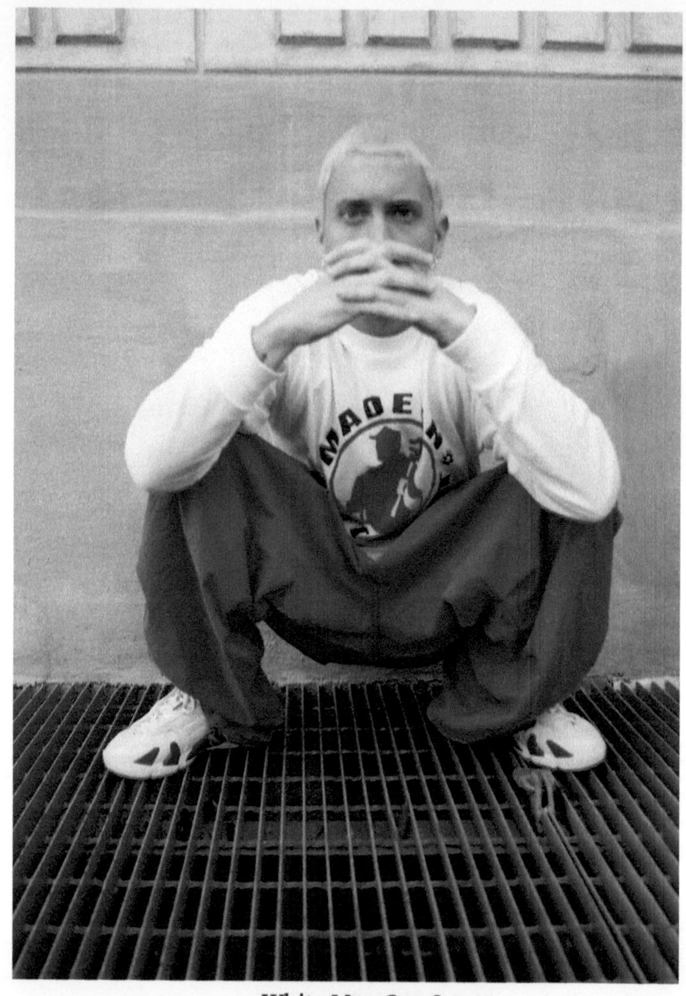

White Men Can Squat

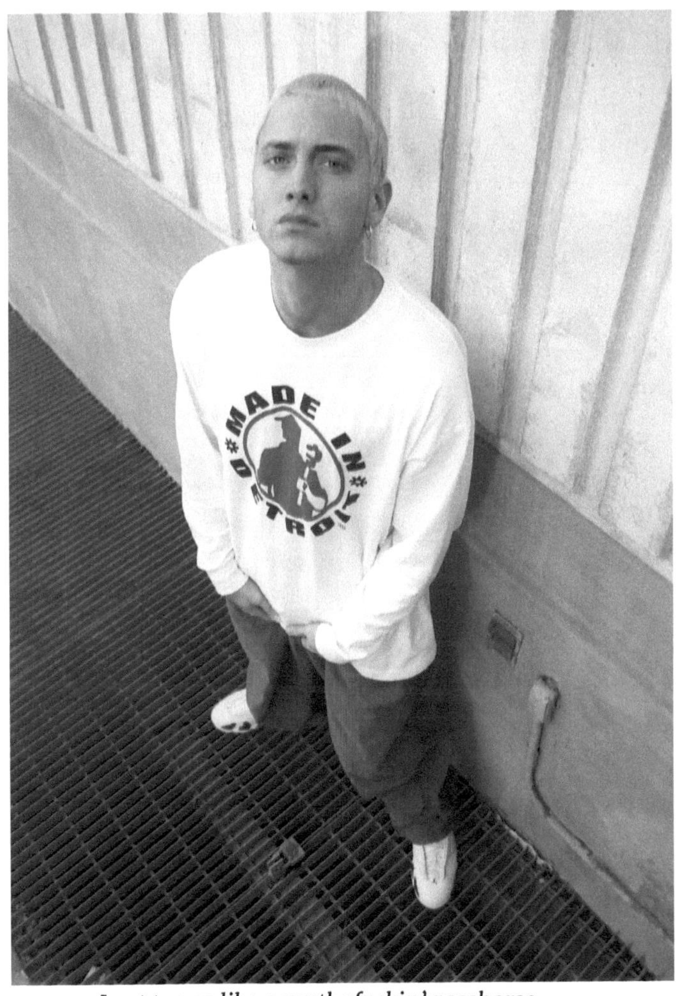

I got to pee like a muthafuckin' racehorse

Harris Rosen

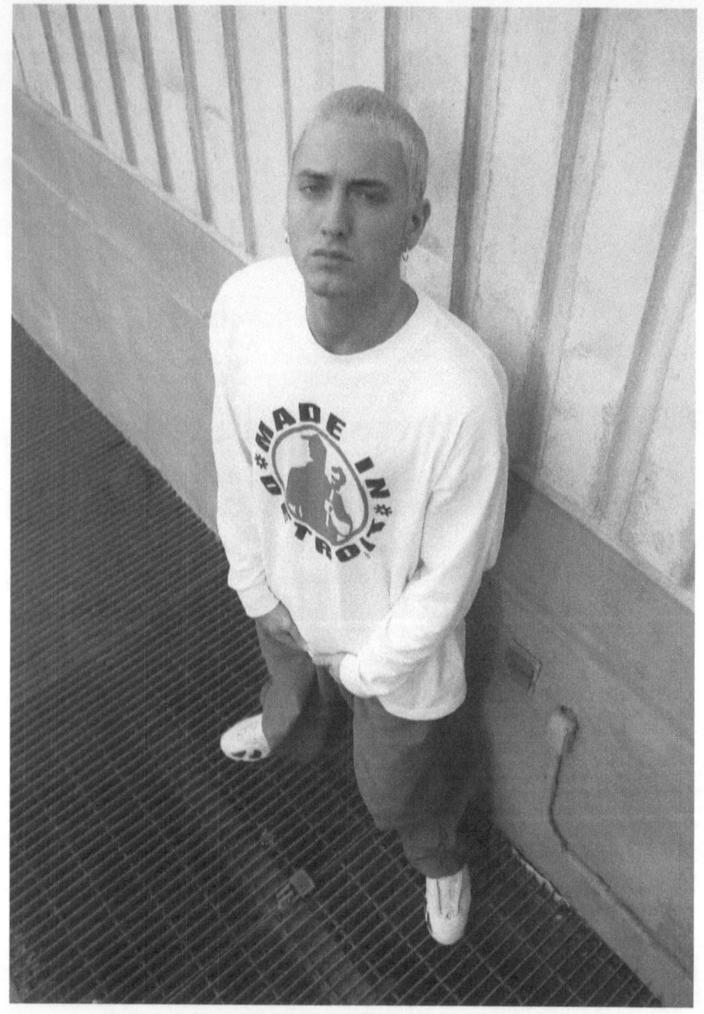

I'm so bored with the U.S.A. But what can I do?

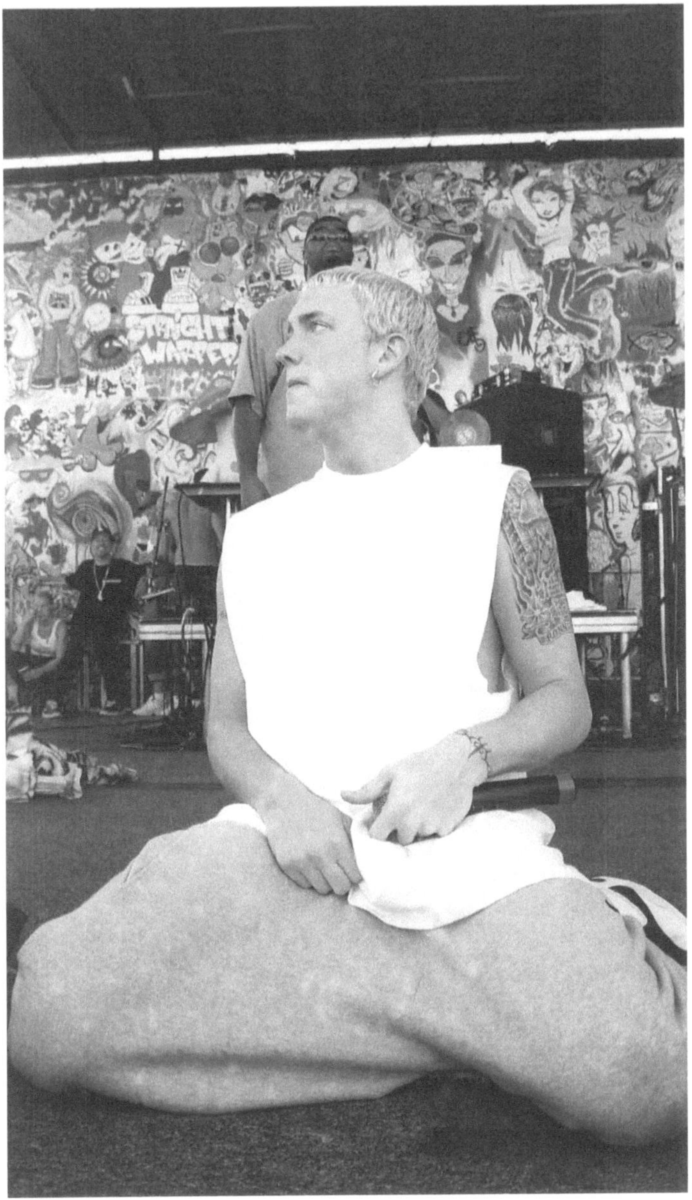

He's not a troublemaker, in fact, he's a trouble-breaker

VII

SEX, DRUGS & VIOLENCE

Motherfuckers just be too sensitive, man.
- Proof

PARENTAL ADVISORY EXPLICIT CONTENT
D12
$#!☆ ON YOU
www.D12online.com
DETROIT, WHAT

Criminal Code

As Eminem's energetic ascent to the sphere of global superstar status advanced, D12 stood in the wings and waited for their time to shine. *The Slim Shady LP* earned the Best Rap Album and Best Rap Solo Performance for "My Name Is" at the *42nd Annual Grammy Awards* on February 23, 2000. The exceptional success experienced by Eminem opened D12 up to a deluxe dimension.

Proof, Bizarre, Bugz, Eminem, Kon Artis, Kuniva, and Eye-Kyu had recorded *The Underground EP* in 1996, with it surfacing as a bootleg on March 2, 1997. The music and flow true to battle rap with heavy doses of Wu-Tang Clan influence. Eminem featured on four of the eleven tracks – "Chance to Advance," "Filthy," "Bring Our Boys," and "Take the Whole World With Me." By 1999, Swifty McVay joined the ranks, and affiliate Eye-Kyu moved on. Sadly, Bugz got murdered on May 21, 1999. Shot four times when a picnic water pistol fight escalated. Detroit City's earned reputation as "Murder City" is no joke.

The hugely anticipated *The Marshall Mathers LP* released on May 23, 2000, served to introduce D12 to the world, and produced the exceptional opportunity to become accepted by millions right away. Photos of the crew presented in the centrefold and a two-panel group shot of the booklet. Bizarre, the featured guest on "Amityville." Swifty McVay, Bizarre, Proof, Kuniva and Kon Artis represented on "Under The Influence." Eminem on the hook taunting his critics.

Eminem reached deep into his psyche to unleash demons of a misspent youth with honest, angry, concise raps that took on pretenders and offenders over bangers. The seductive maniacal ideas electrified with an intensity only a battle rapper can supply that forever sealed his legendary status. First week sales in the United States of America totalled 1.76 million. The fastest selling album by a solo artist until Adele's *25* in 2015.

As expected, the media and the virtuous maintained their anti-Slim stance, to collectively hit back and shut him down. The already high stakes raised with an advanced reply. Human rights groups and the United States Senate singled out the song "Kill You," and assailed Slim for *"promoting violence of the most degrading kind against women"* and effectively labelled him *"a Rap singer who advocates murder and rape."*

South of the border, up in Canada, Eminem fared no better. The inaugural *Anger Management Tour* of Eminem, Limp Bizkit, Papa Roach and Xzibit, booked for Toronto on October 26, 2000, Montreal, October 27, 2000, and Vancouver, November 15, 2000. The Province of Ontario Attorney-General, Jim Flaherty declared he was disgusted upon reading the lyrics and claimed Slim's songs *"advocate violence against women. Physical, graphic violence against women."* Liberal MPP Michael Bryant suggested charges could be laid under hate-law sections of the Criminal Code. Stating that any attempt to encourage violence against a specific group is illegal.

The House of Commons dutifully debated whether to permit Eminem to enter the country or to ban him outright. The federal Immigration Department dutifully investigated whether to ban or admit Eminem. Portions of "Kill You" read in the *Parliament of Canada.* Admiringly, free speech endured, and the Toronto and Montreal show proceeded. Unluckily, Vancouver cancelled, and the fans refunded hours before the show, due to "a reoccurrence of a throat condition" of Limp Bizkit vocalist Fred Durst.

As protectors of global realms stood at attention, lingered in the wings and prayed for his fall, Eminem laughed all the way to the bank as his concert ticket, and merchandise sales continued to skyrocket out of the stratosphere. *The Marshall Mathers LP* well on its way to the rare feat of Diamond sales status with over 8 million copies sold in the United States of America, in the seven months between its release and the close of 2000. Eminem lavished with the Grammy Award for Best Rap Album, Best Rap Solo Performance for "The Real Slim Shady," and Best Rap Performance for Duo or Group for *"Forgot About Dre"* with Dr. Dre at the *43rd Annual Grammy Awards* on February 21, 2001. The time ripe to launch Shady Records, and fulfil the promise and destiny due to his crew, D12.

Remember the Parents Music Resource Center? An elite group of "Washington Wives," spouses of Senators and the United States Secretary of the Treasury. "Porn-Rock" Senate Hearings with supporting and opposing witnesses. Record retailers directed to stock explicit covers under the counter. Pressure placed on television stations to boycott controversial songs and videos. Artist contracts of those deemed to perform violent or sexual songs and shows reassessed. The fruits of their labour the proven sales enhancing Parental Guidance: Explicit Lyrics sticker every self-serving artist desired.

Do you recall when Rick Rubin's Def American distributor, Geffen Records, and its manufacturer, Sony Digital Audio Disc Corporation, refused any association with *The Geto Boys* album? The incendiary Horrorcore raps of "Mind Of A Lunatic" and "Assassins" decreed "violent, sexist, racist and indecent." The label moved to Warner Bros.

Spitting in the face of principled, moral judgment, his name proudly attached as Executive Producer, Eminem mobilised D12 in the studio and set them loose without restriction into glory ride. The freedom to run wild, jump on and rock the mic over any beat of choice granted. Zero fucks are given, period. Secure in the knowledge the world would be tuned in. No topic off limits. The ambition to amp up the proven formula and controversial lyrical message of Eminem to the nth degree and shock the world. The results manifested in pure, no holds barred vulgarity for all to hear. *Devil's Night* expressly crafted to antagonise anyone and everyone in its path.

The album title is devilishly drawn from Detroit's infamous *Devil's Night*. The annual local custom that once marked All Hallow's Eve by soaping windows in the '30s that intensified over time to the degree Detroit City became labelled the "Arson capital of America." In 1984, a record 810 occupied drug houses and buildings set on fire by residents, with most left to burn by ignorant police. The City's first African American Mayor, Coleman Young, who served five-terms, on the record calling it *"a vision from Hell."*

The message of D12, why and how they embodied the

American dream and much more revealed here in the words of Proof, Kuniva, Bizarre and Swifty McVay.

23

The American Dream

Proof & Kuniva

Birmingham, Michigan

May 30, 2001

Break it down. What is D12 all about? What are you guys trying to put across? What positive and proactive message are you guys trying to put across?

Kuniva: The message we're trying to put across -

Proof: Is we want to destroy your kids, ruin their lives and fuck bitches in the ass. I don't think there's a general - Oh yeah, we do have a message, don't we?

Proof and Kuniva: We don't give a fuck about nothing at all.

Kuniva: Period.

Proof: The music part is important though.

I like that idea. You guys have been working on Devil's Night for a while. How did you cut down the lyrics? How did you come up with those lovely, powerful lyrics?

Proof: Alright.

Was it like getting cracked out and just dropping freestyle lyrics?

> Proof: That's basically what it was. We went to the studio and then either Denaun - (Denaun Porter, AKA Mr. Porter, Kon Artis, dEnAuN) - Kon Artis, he makes our beats or either Em; they worked on the track. Of course, you know the Dr. Dre tracks, but that's the primary difference between the new tunes and the tracks in the studio was whoever jumped on it, whoever don't don't, you know? It was that easy. I mean, of course when they come they going to spit something. Everybody was trying to spit something.

Are you concerned about being on this album, or you just don't give a fuck? It's like, you want to grind up the kids like the Pink Floyd movie grinding the children up at the end. Do shit like that, just like fuck the kids! Here's what you should do: shoot heroin and reh reh reh. It sounded like you guys got on the mic and said anything ignorant to piss people off and then just put it out.

Kuniva: We don't tell anybody to do what we do. We don't tell them that. We just tell them what we do. It's up to them whether they want to do some stupid shit. But we don't, you know - go out and be like, *'Yo, go do this and do that! And, if somebody asks you, tell them we said it!'* We don't do shit like that. It's just what the fuck we do, man. Whatever we do when we say it, then that's what it is. But we don't just tell people to do the shit, man. It just happens that they go out and do it.

Why do people take you at face value?

Kuniva: Like who? I mean, as far as like the little political groups and shit like that, probably *GLAAD - (Gay & Lesbian Alliance Against Defamation)* - and shit like that? Well, words affect people, I guess. Weak minded people. I mean, ain't nothing but fucking words, man.

Proof: Motherfuckers just be too sensitive, man.

Kuniva: For real.

Proof: Like, we callin' motherfuckers gay and a faggot get mad, you know what I'm saying? And it's like I told Vine - like, *'Yo, Vine, stick your dick in her mouth,'* right? And you tell a gay man, *'You like sticking your dick in his ass.'* They get offended; doot, dooty doo. We don't give a fuck, like, you know what I'm saying? It's like - I guess it's the coming out of the closet theory by being so shot in the dark now, the come out the closet thing. Now, since they out the closet now they don't want to talk about it, you know what I'm saying? It's like nobody's really - In Hip- Hop, you say fag just to be like, just to belittle a man. Like, *'You fag!'* You know what I'm saying?

To me, motherfuckers are too sensitive in this world, man. Somebody is talking about raping kids; they act like we invented it. Motherfuckers smoke crack! Motherfuckers take ecstasy; Motherfuckers do everything. We ain't invented one thing we say on the album. We talk about what the fuck we see.

Kuniva: It ain't like we called, like *'Who's all gay in the crowd?'* And somebody come up, like, raise your hand, and we come off stage, and we whip they ass. We don't do no shit like that, man. We just saying words. We not touching nobody. You ain't seen nothing about us going gay bashing, or they never caught us doing it, so we haven't done it.

To me, this album is the American dream; apple pie. It's sex, drugs, violence. Everything that Europeans and the world outside of America says about America.

Kuniva: It is what it is. We didn't make a formula and be like, *'Yo, let's make this song do this. We are going to go platinum if we do this and that.'* We just came up with what we came up with, and it's fucked up. That's how - That's what America is based on just about sex, drugs and violence. But we a product of our environment and that's what we - We just rap about what we know, not just an American thing, but it's a Detroit thing. We all rap about what we've been through and what we've seen and we just products of where we're from. So, that's how it just comes out. We don't have any formula for making those songs to piss people off; it's just what comes out our mouth.

Proof: Ewwww.

Kuniva: He just thought of something.

Proof: Really; sex, drugs and violence.

Kuniva: He just thought of a rhyme; he do this shit all the time.

Proof: 'Cause he said it, and it was fresh the way he said it because you be like:

The effects of bullets to die with
With sex and drugs and violence.

Kuniva: Oh yeah!

Proof: Ill, ill. Thanks, Harris.

24

A Burnt Up Apple Pie

Bizarre, Swifty McVay & Kuniva

Birmingham, Michigan

May 30, 2001

I listened to the album, and it's apple pie; America at its finest. It's what everybody thinks America is; the American dream. It's how everybody outside views America.

Swifty McVay: A burnt up apple pie that's been in that oven for a little bit too long.

Bizarre: Yeah! It's our brains, fucking fried. Nah, I ain't lace it, son. Simple, our album manages fucking controversy. It's saying what the fuck we want to say. There's no limit to the shit. We sayin' what people want to say but they too scared to say the shit. So, we done come out and say it. Our album is happening, man. Motherfuckers is getting raped; Grandmothers is getting fucked.

Swifty McVay: Y'all choose to do it. We choose to talk about it, you know?

What do you have to say about cats going around saying D12 sucks? They're running off the coattails of Eminem, and they got no skills, etc.?

Swifty McVay: Y'all fools just mad 'cuz you ain't got a deal: Local rappers talk too much!

Bizarre: Everybody is entitled to their own opinion, but we just show through the actions of the album. I don't know anybody, who actually that I know, that says D12 is wack or anything like that. But anybody that knows anything about the history of D12 knows that we ain't just a motherfuckin' Mickey Mouse group that got together. We were all solo artists before we all came together in one big clique, you know what I'm saying? It was like an artist project. It was like if Toronto started to hook up and say Choclair, Saukrates, and this guy and that guy and that guy form a clique, you know what I'm saying?

**They did.*

Bizarre: So that's what D12 is. That clique like that. All MC's from all parts of town just came out with

D12, and how we've been together for so long, you know what I'm saying? That's how our clique is just on some lyrical shit that's smashing motherfuckers.

Swifty McVay: And never biting their tongue type shit too.

What's up with "Purple Pills" to "Purple Hills"? *What's the deal with that?*

Bizarre: I don't know, man. Ask over here. He knows.

Kuniva: You talking about the single or the album?

The single. Why is it called "Purple Hills"?

Swifty McVay: *"Purple Hills,"* that's the clean version, man.

Kuniva: "Purple Hills" is just basically just having a good time and chillin'. That's the cover up for all the drugs that we take. "Purple Pills" is the actual song where we taking the drugs. [2]

2 * *Saukrates, Choclair, Kardinal Offishall, Jully Black, Solitair, Marvel, and Tara Chase formed The Circle out of the Fresh Arts Movement in 1992.*

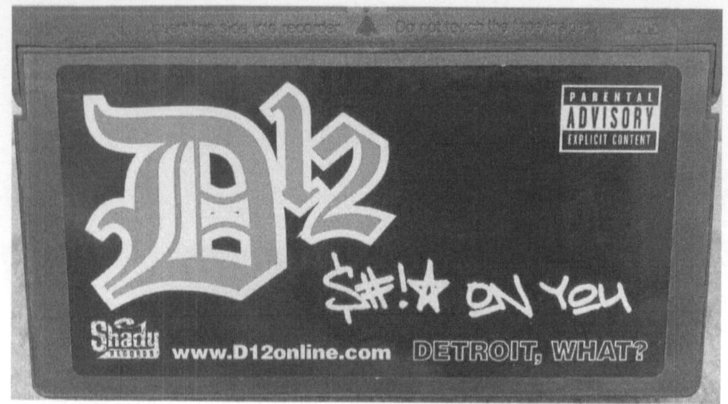

D12 VHS! DETROIT, WHAT?

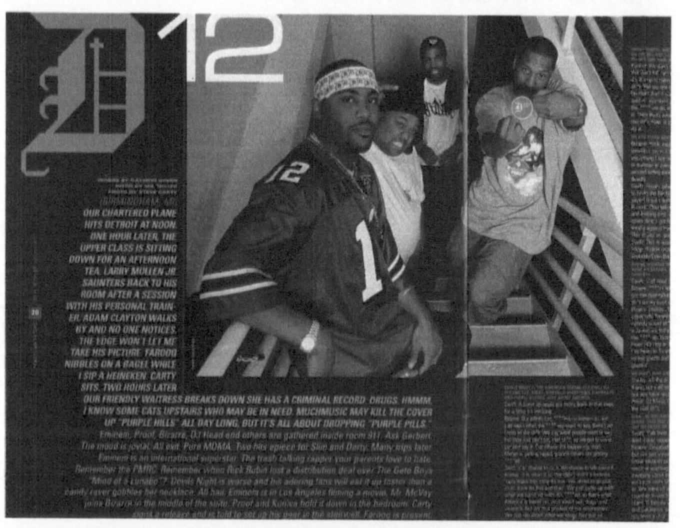

D12

OUR CHARTERED PLANE HITS DETROIT AT NOON. ONE HOUR LATER, THE UPPER CLASS IS SITTING DOWN FOR AN AFTERNOON TEA. LARRY MULLEN JR. SAUNTERS BACK TO HIS ROOM AFTER A SESSION WITH HIS PERSONAL TRAINER. ADAM CLAYTON WALKS BY AND NO ONE NOTICES. THE EDGE WON'T LET ME TAKE HIS PICTURE. FAROOQ NIBBLES ON A BAGEL WHILE I SIP A HEINEKEN. CARTY SITS. TWO HOURS LATER OUR FRIENDLY WAITRESS BREAKS DOWN SHE HAS A CRIMINAL RECORD. DRUGS. HMMM, I KNOW SOME CATS UPSTAIRS WHO MAY BE IN NEED. MUCHMUSIC MAY KILL THE COVER UP "PURPLE HILLS" ALL DAY LONG, BUT IT'S ALL ABOUT DROPPING "PURPLE PILLS."

Eminem, Proof, Bizarre, DJ Head and others are gathered inside room 911. Ask Gerbert. The mood is jovial. All exit. Pure MDMA. Two hits apiece for Slim and Derty. Many trips later Eminem is an international superstar. The trash talking rapper your parents love to hate. Remember the PMRC. Remember when Rick Rubin lost a distribution deal over The Geto Boys "Mind of a Lunatic"? Devils Night is worse and his adoring fans will eat it up faster than a candy raver gobbles her necklace. All hail. Eminem is in Los Angeles filming a movie. Mr. McVay joins Bizarre in the middle of the suite. Proof and Kuniva hold it down in the bedroom. Carty signs a release and is told to set up his gear in the stairwell. Farooq is present.

This is a Four-Star stairwell

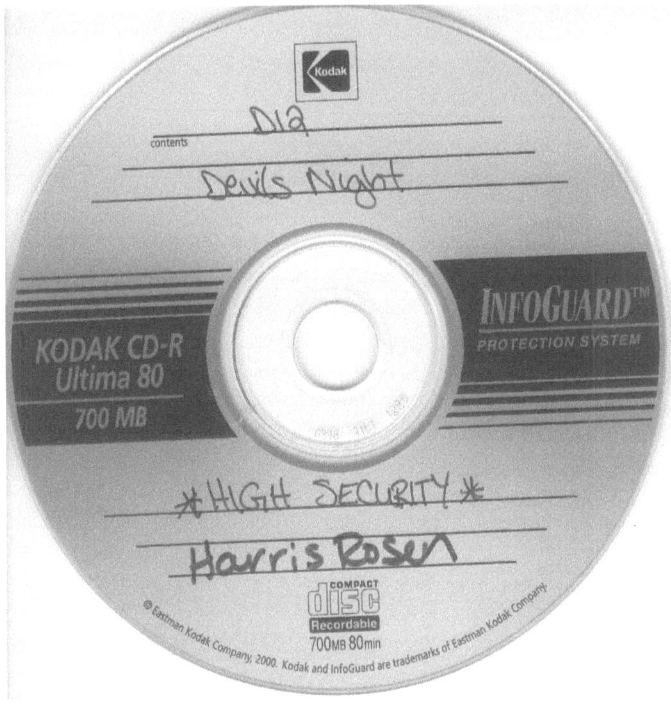

High Security x 2001

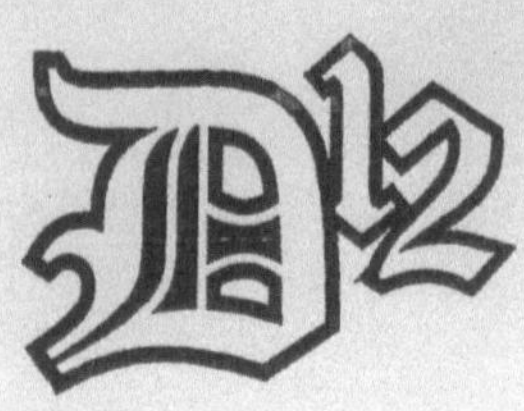

"DEVILS NIGHT"

1. ANOTHER P SERVICE ANNOUNCEMENT	0:49
2. SHIT CAN HAPPEN	4:52
3. PISTOL PISTOL	5:23
4. BIZZARE (SKIT)	1:12
5. NASTY MIND	4:43
6. AIN'T NUTTIN' BUT MUSIC	5:11
7. AMERICAN PSYCHO	4:36
8. THAT'S HOW (SKIT)	0:37
9. THAT'S HOW	4:49
10. PURPLE PILLS	5:05
11. FIGHT MUSIC	4:22
12. INSTIGATOR	4:58
13. PIMP LIKE ME	5:57
14. BLOW MY BUZZ	5:10
15. OBIE TRICE	1:07
16. DEVILS NIGHT	4:19
17. STEVE BERMAN (SKIT)	0:50
18. REVELATION	5:48

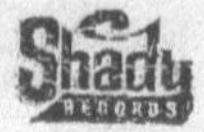

℗© 2001 Interscope Records. For promotional use only. Not for sale.
All rights reserved. Unauthorized duplication is a violation of applicable laws.

This is How We Do It promo duplication x Great White North

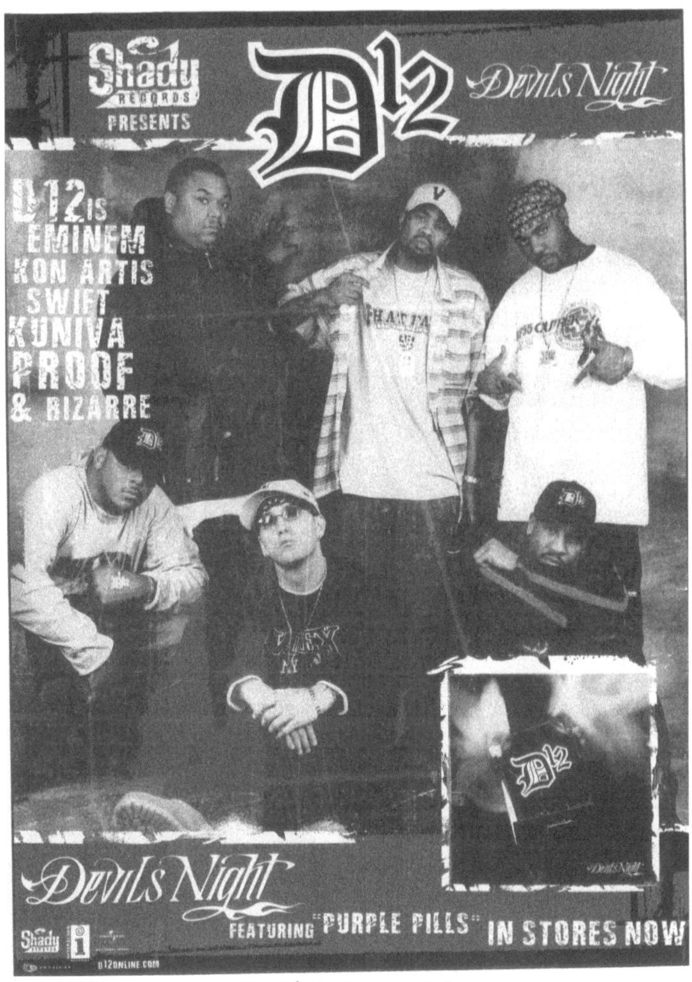

Yeah! Full-page Ad

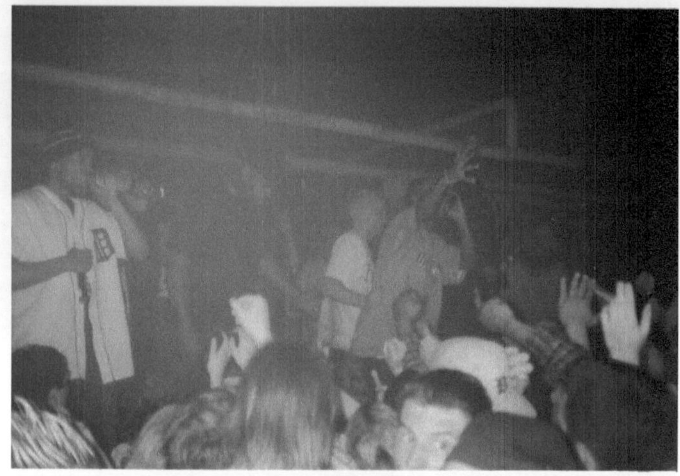

What do you know about Big Proof, Royce da 5'9 and Eminem live in '99?

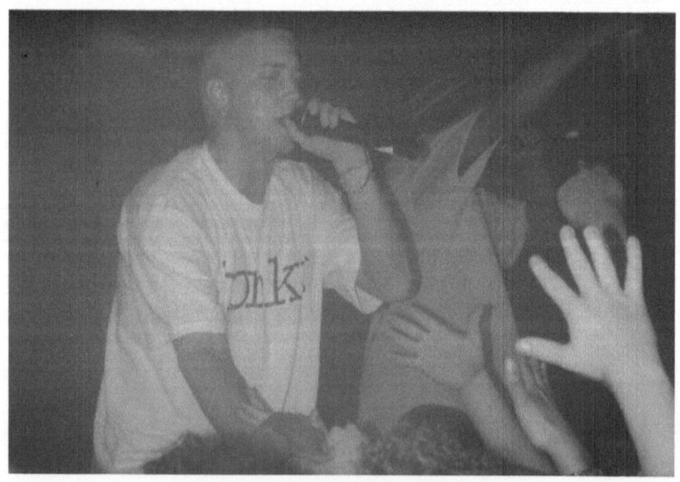

I sure see a lot of honkeys in here

IX

CONTROVERSY

I don't do shock value rap. There's a difference between wanting to shock people and wanting to piss people off. I'm not trying to piss everybody off. I'm trying to piss off people that's uptight; people that's critics; people that don't know about Hip-Hop.
- Eminem

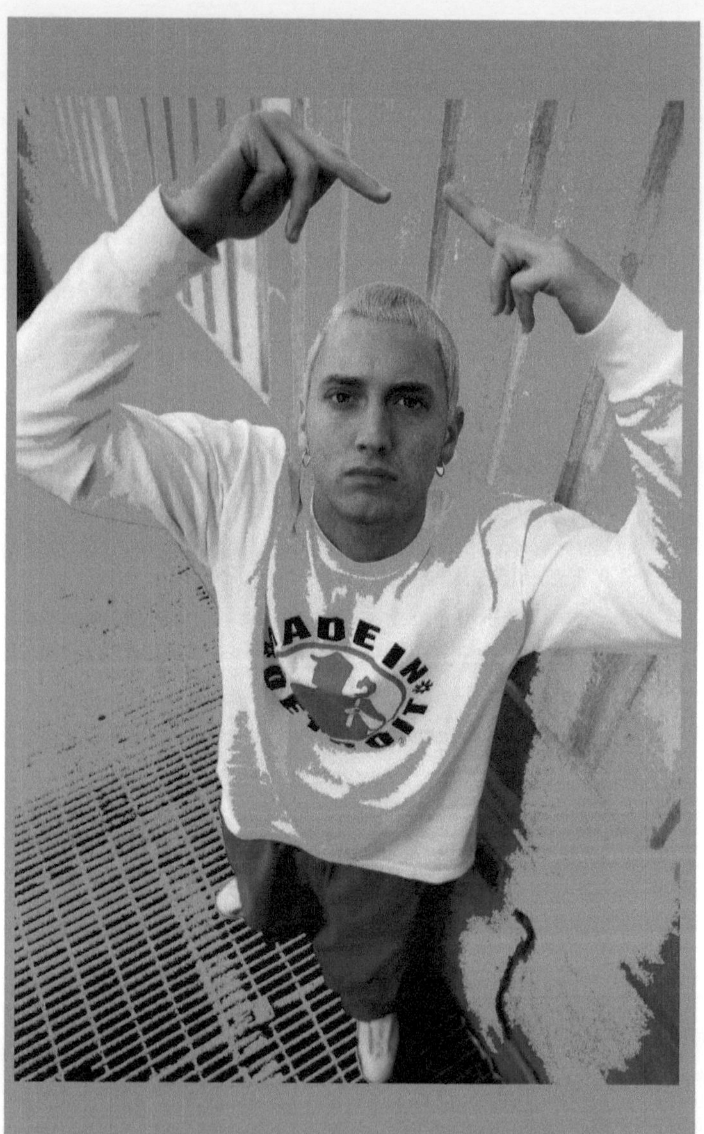

I Don't Do Shock Value Rap

It took less than two weeks for the gospel of *The Slim Shady LP* to spread worldwide. Middle finger extended to the moralistic, Eminem simultaneously enabled a new breed of a Rap fan and polarised purists. The sick, expressive artistry of Broke City Trash Rapper Eminem rapping on guns, knives, rape and murder broadcast to the different brainwaves of a symbiotic army of a lower class that related to his pain. An alternative level of sensibility appealing to indignant youth fed up with the spoon-fed pablum of prevailing media.

Sensing insurgency and unrest, those who did not grow up in the same manner, nor experience similar life situations, began to persecute him. Church, media, and government conscripted to neuter a son went astray. Prevailing leaders of morality who took it upon themselves to censure and censor his transmissions. Eminem branded evil, to be taken down by any means necessary. Every word he uttered placed under the microscope, his every move monitored. Instantaneously, the most scrutinised and debated person in the United States of America.

Eminem didn't invent Horrorcore or the ill lower class

mentality. Everything he wrote, rapped or expressed had been in the mix, in one form or another, before. The dichotomy of caste unmistakable. The elemental distinction of being bound by birth to the white-skinned race. Therefore, by default, his versification evolved contrary to that of the Black people who established the Art Form. This is the domineering world we inhabit.

The lines converged with prudence when it came to acceptance or denial of his substance. A man who refused to bend, break or buckle to the proclaimed moral agenda, Eminem spoke his mind with no regard of consequence. Alternatively decided to spit impassioned lyrics back in their face. Is he a role model? Obviously not.

Eminem detailed and revealed the thought process behind his lyrics and why his fans love him. The role of the bad guy is part of the fucking job.

26

Role Model

Detroit, Michigan

April 4, 1999

Are you a role model?

Eminem: Hell no, I'm not a role model! Fuck no, I ain't-a role model! Do I look like a role model?

A lot of kids look up to you.

Eminem: Do I sound like I'm a role model? A lot of kids look up to me. I'm not asking them to. I'm not telling him to, you know? Regardless.

What do you want someone to get from listening to your album? What are you trying to deliver?

Eminem: Get whatever you want to get out of it. I don't give a fuck what you get out of it. This is my world; I'm putting it out there. I'm expressing my views. Get whatever you want to get out of it, and I don't give a fuck whether you love it or you hate it. I don't give a fuck! I don't give a fuck! I'm putting my shit out; this is how I do it.

27

I'm the Bad Guy

All I have in this world is my balls and my word and I don't break them for no one. Do you understand?
- Tony Montana

Toronto, Ontario
April 10, 1999

The media has branded your Art shock value rap.

Eminem: I don't do shock value rap. There's a difference between wanting to shock people and wanting to piss people off, and I'm not trying to piss everybody off. I'm trying to piss off people that's uptight, people that's critics, people that don't know about Hip-Hop. There's a difference. You can be shocked but not be pissed off - You can be like, *'Oh, my God! I can't believe he said that,'* and not be mad at it. I'm trying to piss them motherfuckers off. I'm trying to say fuck you! I'm trying to say everybody who fucking — I'm trying to piss off the people who don't like Hip-Hop and criticise it, and that's who I'm pissing off. So, I guess I did my fucking job.

Proof: Right. This how fucked up the world done got: In Hip-Hop, the whole idea was to add on to this shit and bring something new to the table, right? That was from the jump.

From Kool Herc.

Proof: Somebody do it, and they make it like, *'Yo, he just crazy,'* because they're so used to everybody sounding like him, or sound like Snoop, or sound like Dre, or sound like this, or sound like that. Man jump in the door, do something new, add-on fresh air, the new vibe in Rap. Now you gotta destroy it, you know what I'm saying? Because of the innovation of it. It's a lot of stuff that - It's been so monotonous that something new comes along they don't know exactly what to call it. He's just having fun with it. So, pissing motherfuckers off and wanting y' all to say some dumb shit.

Eminem:

Spitting in hotels
Pissing in elevators
Punching hookers in the fucking mouth
I'm a mother-fucking rap rebel

The world can suck my dick because I don't give a fuck
Like my middle finger was stuck

It's futuristic stuff like Kool Keith. The subject matters have all been touched before.

> Proof: Right, it's all about the angle and the direction you're taking, totally. People have said ill shit; you know what I'm saying? It ain't that it's in his form of illness, you know what I'm saying?

I spoke with Scarface, and he broke it down. Basically, to breakdown the whole game, it's the delivery, the flow. It's how you're dropping it, what you're saying. The stuff you're talking about is affecting a whole different people than the typical rappers because of your colour is one thing. Not because you're a rapper or white rapper, whatever. It's just affecting different people. Different people are looking at you because of that. You know what I'm trying to say?

> Eminem: Yeah, because there's a lot of motherfuckers. There's a lot of lower-class people in the world, and there's a lot of motherfuckers that have been through a lot of bullshit that can relate to what I'm saying. Obviously, you know what I'm saying? I'm selling records so motherfuckers can relate to what I'm saying. They see; they feel that shit. They're like, *'Oh, I've been through that shit. I know where he's coming from.'* That's why I try to make my shit so visual that you can see it and you can feel it. When

I'm telling a story you can fucking see, you know what I'm saying? And if you've ever been in that same situation, you can relate to it.

Everybody's hated on a bit. Everybody's taken mushrooms, or at least everybody I know. Everybody's done all that shit, and it's -

Eminem: As soon as I come out it's like I invented that shit, I'm the bad guy. I'm the first person who said something about raping a girl on a record, or I'm the first person who's talking about guns. The first person talking about knives, or killing somebody. Ice-T did a song a while back about killing his mother, killing his own fucking mother, you know what I'm saying?! I didn't hear shit about that. I didn't hear anything about that. I don't think — I can't recall hearing shit about that.*

I didn't invent this shit. I didn't fucking invent ill rhyming. I didn't invent this fucking ill, broke, lower-class mentality. I didn't fucking - I didn't invent the shit. I didn't fucking invent it, but I lived it, I seen it. I've done it, and I'm speaking on it. I'm probably taking it a little bit farther than most people have taken it if I'm doing that, you know? And I think I'm taking it in a - I'm taking a humorous approach. It may be vulgar humour, but I'm takin it — I'm just having fun with it, man.

I take things - I sit back, and I watch shit, and I look at the world, and I take things that's fucked up with the world, and I talk about it, you know what I'm saying? I poke fun at it, like, this and this and this and this is wrong with the world. Ain't that fucked up? Let me make a joke about it. You know what I'm saying? Fuck it; we might as well laugh about it. If we don't, we're going to cry about it, so fuck it. Why not have fun with it, man? You don't know how long you're going to be on this fucking planet; you could die right now, you know what I'm sayin'? Nobody knows.

Do you live for today?

Eminem: Definitely live for today. I live for today. I think about the future in the sense of my daughter; you know what I'm saying? I want my daughter to have a future, but I live day by day because I don't know what the fuck is going to happen, man. I've got this status, this certain status now. The public, everybody's watching, you know what I'm saying? And I don't know what the fuck is going to happen. I don't know what's gonna happen.

I talk a lot of shit, you know what I'm saying? And there's going to be motherfuckers out there that's always going to be looking for Eminem, you know what I'm saying? Looking. They want that motherfucker to stop talking shit.

But you don't talk shit. You just speak what's on top of your mind.

Eminem: Yeah. Well, I'm sayin', I come across like — I come across to motherfuckers like — I come across real. I come across like I don't give a fuck about you, who you fucking hang with, what your fucking views are, your opinions. Motherfucker, these are my views! This is the way I see the world, and I'm going to tell it like it is, and I don't give a fuck what you got to say about it. A lot of people respect that attitude. There's a lot of motherfuckers that hate it too. Look what happened to Pac, and look what happened to Biggie, you know what I'm saying? I'm not even trying to compare myself to them, but shit happens, man. Shit happens. We don't fucking know; we don't know. We're not promised tomorrow.[3]

---

[3] ** - Ice-T's Metal band, Body Count released their self-titled debut album on March 31, 1992. A socio-political statement on life in the United States as a Black man. Its focus on racism, drug addiction, and police brutality mixed with tongue-in-cheek over the top madness and anarchy. The album cut Eminem referenced, "Momma's Gotta Die Tonight," surely an influence on the lyrics he penned for "Just The Two Of Us." Wherein, Ice-T set his racist mother on fire and completed the act by hitting her with a Louisville Slugger, carved her up, placed her in Hefty bags, and then took her on vacation around the country in the trunk of his car.*

Slim's claim he heard nothing about that one is odd. Considering, the album contained "Cop Killer." Its lyrical vitriol elicited negative comments from President George H. W. Bush, Vice President Dan Quayle, law enforcement agencies, and other moralistic leaders of society who demanded it is pulled from the album, in spite of the First Amendment.

Sadly, Warner Bros. Records acquiesced following cancelled, and police blockaded Ice-T and Body Count concerts, death threats issued to its executives, and shareholder withdrawals that came close to taking down the Time Warner empire.

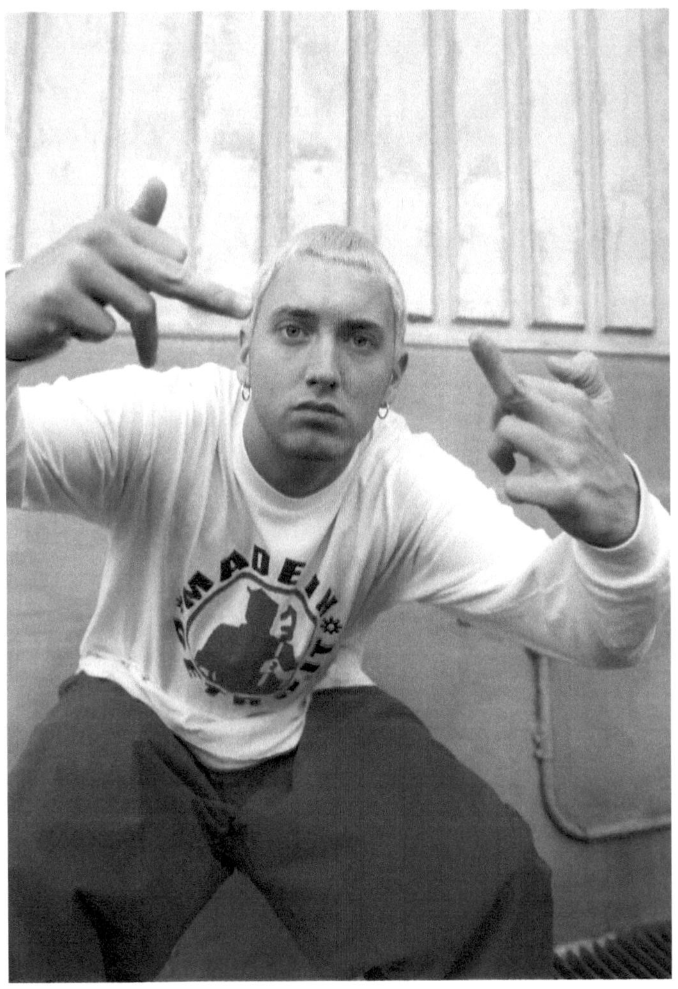

Slim had the middle-finger game on lock since '99

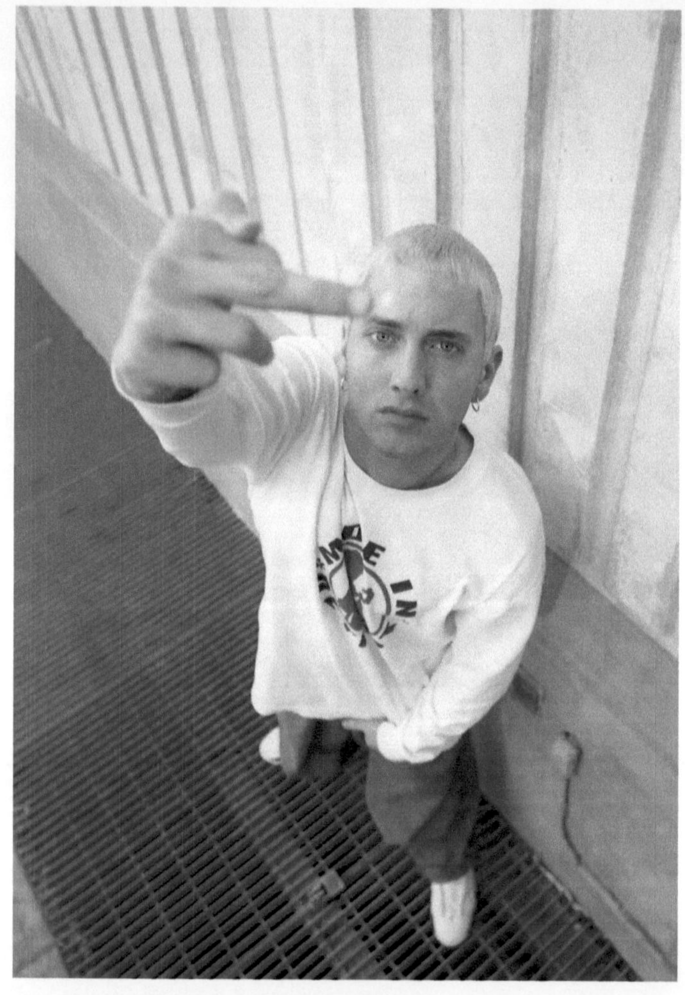

Mirror, Mirror on the Wall, Who's the Fairest of Them All?

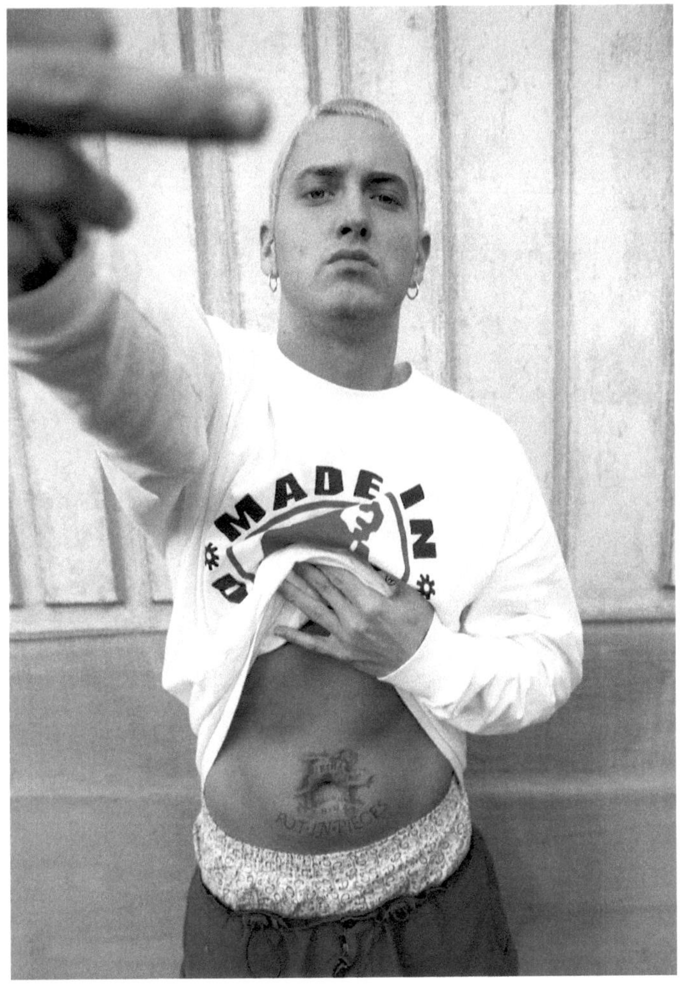

Broke City Trash Rapper book cover photo. Rot In Pieces, Kim!

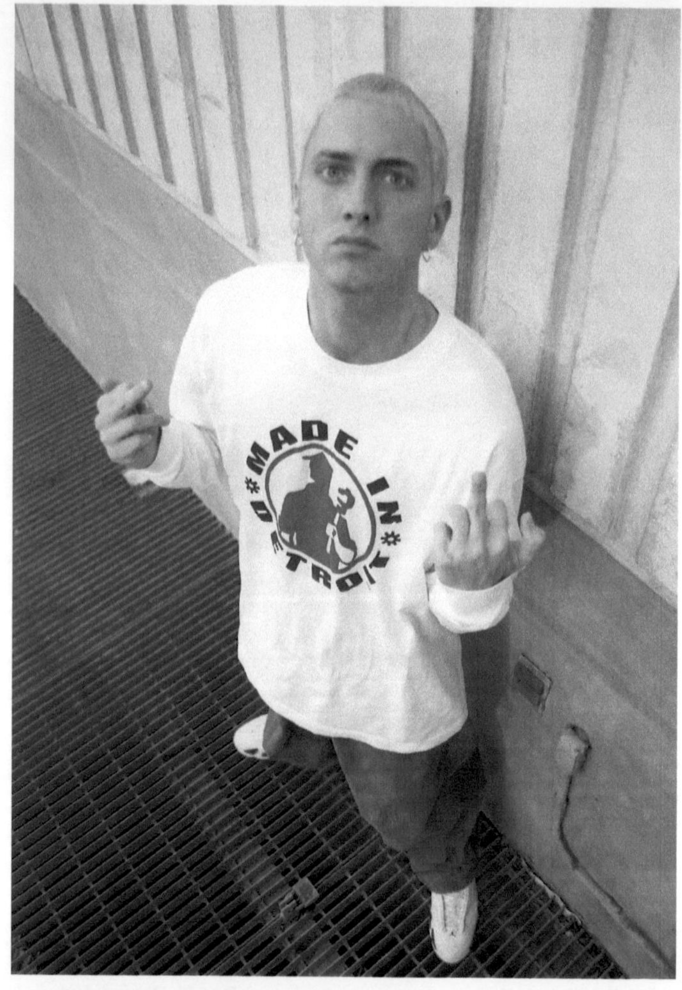

I told that muthafucka I ain't never scared. (east-side!)

IX

SHIT TALK WITH BIZARRE & SWIFTY McVAY

Yeah! We try to go totally against the grain, you know what I'm saying? This is us. This is how we was rapping in the Hip Hop Shop, you know what I'm saying?
- Swifty McVay

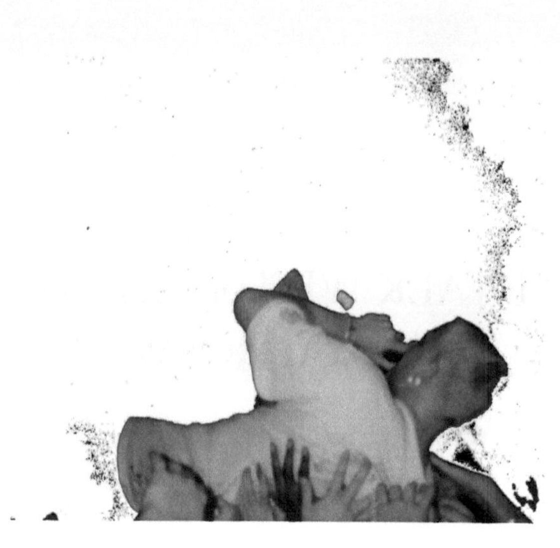

28

Looking For the Coke They Say Bizarre Smokes

The Detroit River separates Detroit, and Windsor, Canada. The cities connected by the 1570 metres Detroit-Windsor tunnel. The second busiest border crossing between the two countries and the crucial commercial, economic engine of the region.

The Hip-Hop communities of Detroit and Toronto share a special relationship. Both cities reared on a steady diet of Dance Music and Hip-Hop. Detroit City as the birthplace of revered Art Form Detroit Techno. Toronto is known for its vibrant underground Dance Music warehouse and club culture and dedicated to all things Dilla.

Bizarre is Bizarre. Co-founder of D12, his grotesque lyrical violations exemplify Horrorcore.Swifty McVay grew up on West 7 Mile, seven miles North of the Detroit River. His name adopted from decorated Persian Gulf War Army Infantry soldier turned radical terrorist, Timothy McVeigh. McVeigh responsible for the terrorist act of the Oklahoma City Bombing, and its toll of 168 dead and 600 injured on

April 19, 1995.

Bizarre and Swifty McVay detailed select extra-curricular tales and the obtuse method behind their own lyrical madness and D12. Supplemented by a few thoughts on Toronto and Canada. Bizarre going the extra bit to offer up lyrics on Canada's infamous border.

29

G-Shit

Bizarre & Swifty McVay

Birmingham, Michigan

May 30, 2001

What happened at your favourite Rave?

Bizarre: Shit, man. We all got high o nitrous balloons and had a good time partying and came outside and somebody's car is in front of ours. So, take these white boys and move somebody's car into they car. It was like moving the car out of the way; shit was crazy, crazy, crazy.

Swifty McVay: Bizarre knows.

Is that where you recruit for your stable?

Bizarre: What's stable?

You said you're a Mack.

Bizarre: Oh, no, man. Nah, Nah. I go to Churches, Churches and old folks homes.

Do you take the Sunday School girls?

Bizarre: No, old people.

Swifty McVay: I mack Churches. I mack elderly people for their bingo money, yeah! (Laughs)

Bizarre: Where's my scratch, bitch?

You gave me your album, the cassette of Attack Of The Weirdos *back in the day. You have always been a character with the same steelo. Now that you're with Em and D12 is getting a big push everybody's going to know who you are and your whole deal. How are you handling that shit? People are expecting you to top yourself. They're expecting you to go into a restaurant and order an ice cream sandwich with shit on it or something. What are people expecting out of you?*

Bizarre: Um, I don't know. I just be me, man. And just by being me something stupid, something crazy comes out. I mean, I just be me, man. Sometimes the shit I do they might think it's bizarre but, you know? It just might be my first time. I don't go out to try to be bizarre. I might be in an interview, and

I might not say a word than just be there saying the same shit. *'Oh Bizarre, you're just sitting there and didn't say shit the whole interview.'* You know what I'm saying? It might be that bizarre. I'm just doing my thing trying to be Bizarre, Bizarre things.

Swifty McVay: G shit.

Swifty McVay.

Swifty McVay: That's me, man.

Are you upset they're letting you live?

Swifty McVay: Man, I'm going to live on and live on. I bet you are wondering about that McVeigh thing too, you know what I'm saying?

Did you take part? Have you ever been to Oklahoma?

Swifty McVay: Man! Hey, I was driving you, you know what I'm saying? But, Nah. That's what that reference is; Swift McVay - I try to blow up this Rap industry. I blow up stadiums, blow up venues. Get it? You know what I'm saying? And when the McVeigh did what he did, not saying what he did was good, but he stepped to the bat. He was in court with a straight face. He didn't feel no - *"I did it, okay."*

You're a man who stands for his convictions.

Swifty McVay: It's like, *"I did it! What's up? Said it, what?"* I mean, hey, you know what I'm saying? He didn't hold anything back. His facial expression was just like, *"Okay, well, you got to kill me, Y'all. Hey, kill me."* Whatever he did, he did for whatever reason he believed in to do it, you know what I'm saying? I stand for what I believe in. The same attitude, you know what I'm saying? Like, you don't stand for anything, you'll fall for anything.

Do you feel the same way, Bizarre? Do you stand behind all your lyrics, proud?

Bizarre: Yeah, man! I stand behind everything I say, or I wouldn't say it, you know what I'm saying? But, I don't want anybody to take everything I say seriously. But, like I said, it's some jokes in there and everything. I don't want anybody going o killing themselves. I don't want anybody killing for it. Just don't take it so seriously.

Swifty McVay: People take it too seriously, man. Trying to bring the fun back into Rap, you know what I'm saying? It ain't nothing but music.

Bizarre: Stop talking about what flavour is my ice and looking nice, and, *'Yo, son, let's shoot dice.'*

Swifty McVay: Yeah, we try to go totally against the grain, you know what I'm saying? This is us. This is how we were rapping in the *Hip Hop Sho*p; you know what I'm saying?

Bizarre: Ain't nobody changed, man.

Swifty McVay: Bizarre come in and be like: I'm shooting up anybody/Even the girl I came with. 'Cause it was just us back then, you know what I'm saying?

Think lyrical. You're working on the next album writing a song about Canada. What are some ill thoughts on Canada?

Bizarre: Canada . . .

Swifty McVay: Y'all need cigarettes with menthol.

Bizarre: Fucking border, border. Shoot, man.
Border got me over talkin' trash
Calling me nigger, sticking shit up my ass
Looking for the coke they say Bizarre smokes.

I don't know, man. Canada's crazy, especially Toronto. You don't even know what race nobody is and shit, man. Like, what is you, dog? *'I'm a Jamaican Indian American,'* you know what I'm saying? Everybody's just like fucked the fuck up. Everybody smoke weed. Everybody loves Hip-Hop in Toronto, but it gets scary, man. I mean, I visit Toronto but like I don't see Y'all ghettos and shit over there. What do y' all think over there is ghetto?

We don't have a ghetto.

Swifty McVay: What is ghetto is all the drugs in the world you can get over there but you can't - Y'all ain't got no Newports. What's up with that? No Newports but you have heroin.

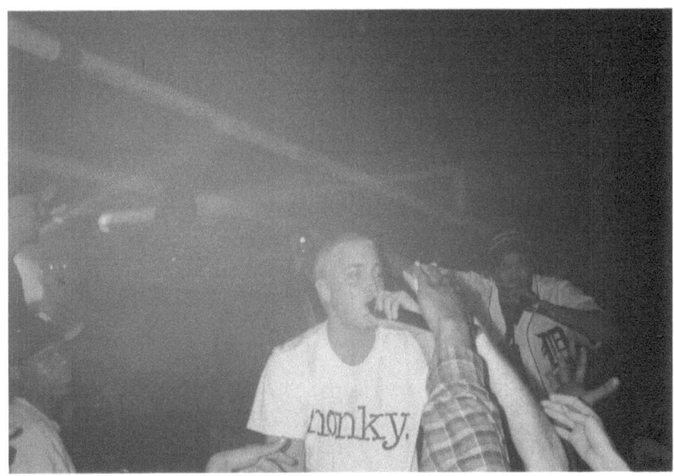

HIStory

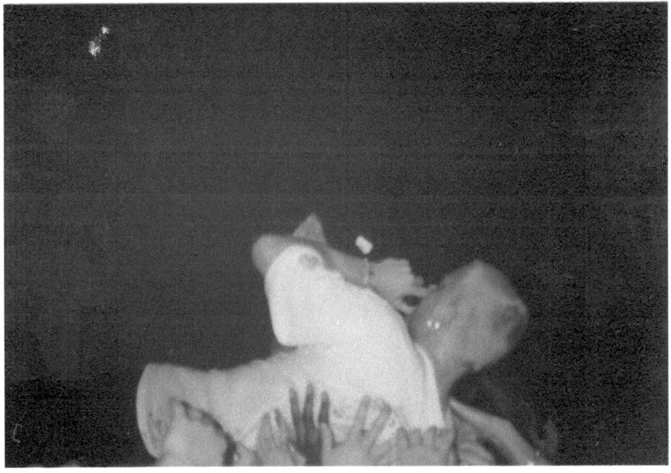

Eminem is for the people

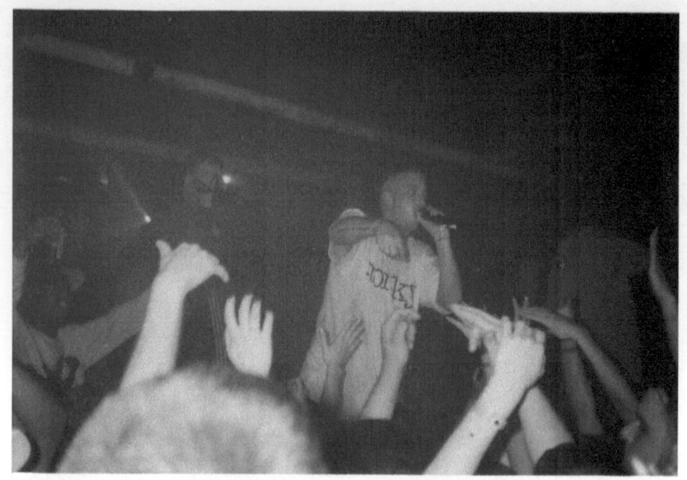

Never call me honky to my face

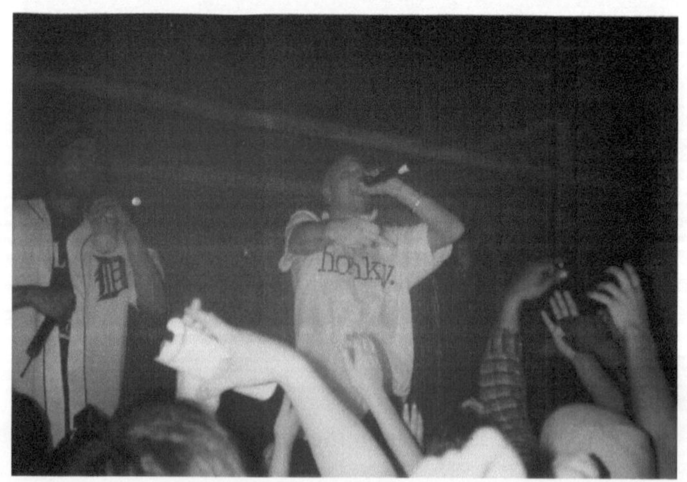

Assassins

X

POLITICS, POLITICS, POLITICS

Who Is Fred Durst?
-Proof

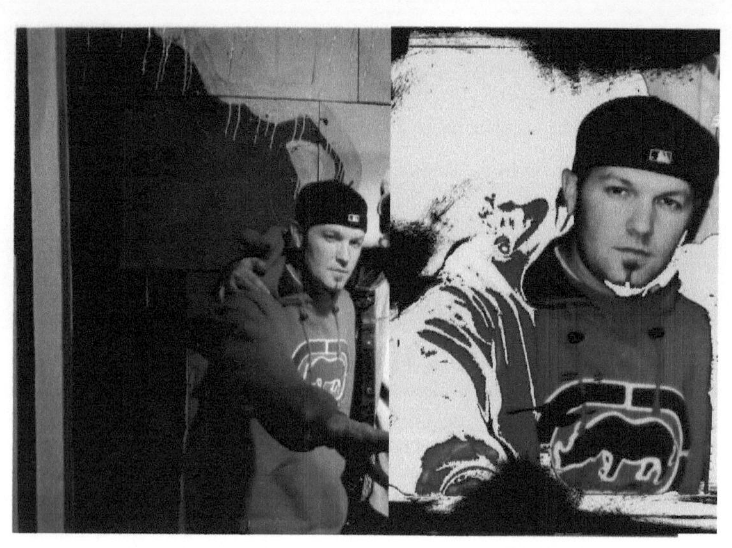

Crucible of War

During the period of this interview, Eminem and D12 were at war with ICP, Cage, Everlast, Dilated Peoples, and Fred Durst and DJ Lethal of Limp Bizkit, at the same time. The root of the war with Everlast dates back to when they briefly crossed paths in a hotel lobby, and Everlast felt disrespected by Slim. Naturally, diss tracks followed.

Everlast the first to bat when he directed a veiled threat at Eminem as one of the featured guest on Dilated Peoples "Ear Drums Pop" Remix - with Planet Asia, Defari, and Phil Da Agony. The song released on Los Angeles Hip-Hop stalwarts Dilated Peoples *The Platform* album on May 23, 2000.

Eminem's vital response "I Remember (Dedication to Whitney Ford)," the B-side of D12's Shady Records debut, "Shit On You." Indeed, my favourite Eminem song for its range of music and determined battle rap lyrics down to its relentless assault of Everlast in the outro.

Round II initiated by Everlast, who summoned the Rap Gods and came with the fluid flow on the poignant "Whitey's Revenge" over Gang Starr's "Suckaz Need Bodyguards." The original known for the manner the legendary group called out secured MC'.

Instinctively, Eminem took offence and planned to clap back. He discussed a new Everlast diss song with D12 and somehow got Fred Durst and DJ Lethal to accept his invitation to participate. Keep in mind, DJ Lethal and Everlast released three albums and one EP, and actively toured together between 1991 and 1996, as two-thirds House of Pain with Danny Boy O'Connor. The group of Los Angeles affiliated Soul Assassins beloved for their brand of Hardcore Hip-Hop, notably arena anthem "Jump Around."

Eminem and Limp Bizkit had worked together in the Spring of 1999. Slim extended an invite to join the band in the studio and feature on a song during the production stage of the multi-platinum *Significant Other* album. The outcome of the session "Turn Me Loose," a play on the Loverboy cock-rock classic, unfortunately, left off the record. The working relationship maintained on the first leg of the inaugural *Anger Management Tour* through the U.S. and Canada, October 19-December 19, 2000.

Hindsight is 20/20. Durst and Lethal likely blinded by Eminem tour magic changed their minds and individually dropped out on the day of the recording session. Eminem stayed the course and went in on Everlast on "Quitter." Then doubled up by extending the song over 2Pac's "Hit 'Em Up" beat to go in on Dilated Peoples and Everlast. The track close to seven minutes with Eminem featured on the intro, five verses, four hooks, two interludes, and the outro. Kon Artis, Kuniva, Proof, and Swifty McVay added individual verses too. "Quitter" released to digital outlets in late November 2000.

The beef between Eminem and Limp Bizkit ignited in December 2000 by DJ Lethal, when, as a guest of *MTV*'s *TRL (Total Request Live)*, he was asked to comment on the beef between Eminem and Everlast. Beginning with the sentiment that they're both men and it will be worked out, he went on to state that if it ever went beyond diss records and turned physical, Everlast would prevail. As a result, tension built when the *Anger Management Tour* travelled overseas for dates in Germany, Norway, Sweden, Netherlands, Belgium, France, and England, from February 2-10, 2001.

In a devious plan to add insult to injury and kick the beef up to the top of the food chain, Slim went all in. He recorded a solo song titled *"Vicious Pussy"* going in on Fred Durst, DJ Lethal, Everlast and Dilated Peoples, and added it to the upcoming D12 album. The power move presented a conundrum for Interscope Records, where Fred Durst worked behind the scenes as acting Senior Vice President. His hands in A&R, marketing, producing and videos. Limp Bizkit earned big money as international sales of *Significant Other* approached 16 million units. Nonetheless, the cult of Eminem fans had blasted *The Marshall Mathers LP* on its way to 32 million units. "Vicious Pussy" retitled "Girls" and included on *Devil's Night* as an unlisted, particular hidden track.

Devils' Night released to the public on June 19, 2001. It debuted at number one on the Billboard Top 200 chart and re-entered the position its third week of release. Moving on to sell 2 million copies in the U.S. and 3 million more internationally. As the album topped the charts, Interscope Records made it official and posted a press release that confirmed Fred Durst as Senior Vice President.

Dilated Peoples had shared a freestyle with Eminem, Aristotle and D12 on the *Sway & Tech Show* and harboured no ill will towards Eminem. When it came to the Everlast verse on the "Ear Drums Pop" Remix, those were his words and not Dilated Peoples. Obviously, Eminem failed to buy-in to that theory and placed their name in his mouth. Dilated Peoples entry to the beef, "Search 4 Bobby Fischer," arguably the hardest Eminem diss, ever. Bobby Fischer, the mercurial Chess Grandmaster, considered the greatest player of all-time, disappeared from public life after he won the *World Chess Championship* in 1972. Primarily controlled by Evidence, with Raaka Iriscience on the brief intro and DJ Babu on the cuts, it artfully expressed their response to the lyrical assaults of "Quitter" and "Girls." The song leaked to the masses in late December 2001.

Eminem did not respond to Dilated Peoples. A short one-liner on "Without Me," the lead single of his third album, *The Eminem Show*, reserved for Limp Bizkit.

Proof, Kuniva, Bizarre and Swifty McVay spoke their piece on the matter and laid down the gauntlet. The drama with Limp Bizkit and the secret hidden track, "Girls" disclosed. The message is understandable and straightforward.

31

Vicious Pussy

Proof & Kuniva

Birmingham, Michigan

May 30, 2001

Let's talk about record company politics.

Kuniva: Ahhh, politics, politics, politics.

My question is this: You guys are on Interscope -

Proof: Are we?

Distributed, same deal; they're catching a cheque.

Proof: We're not even on Shady anymore.

Break it down. What is it?

Proof: We're on Death Row; we signed with Suge.

So, you guys are on Interscope. Your buddy Fred is on Interscope.

Proof: Who?

Fred Durst.

Proof: Who is Fred Durst?

Some fucking guy tries to rap but can't flow.

Kuniva: It sounds familiar, but we don't know the name.

The guy is on Interscope, and apparently, he's a VP. So, was there politics in getting that song released? Did they try and hate on you and say put it on a B-side like "I Remember"? What was the deal with that?

Proof: I mean, I don't know about the politics and all that shit. But it's like, I know Jimmy Iovine, the owner of Interscope over there. He's involved in our project, and he sat down and told us the do's and don'ts, and that song wasn't even one of the concerns. So, I don't think it has - I'm pretty sure it's a political piece, but we don't know about the politics of the piece. Do you know anything about the politics of that piece?

Kuniva: I don't know any politics about it. I just

know it's on the album.

Proof: It's on the album.

Kuniva: It just happened to be on the album, and that's it. We didn't talk to nobody. We just - we don't know about the politics of it, man. I guess they overseen that it was on the album; it's a song.

Proof: "Vicious Pussy"

Kuniva: "Vicious Pussy"

Is that what it's called?

Proof: Hell yeah!

32

Dom DeLuise

Bizarre & Swifty McVay

Birmingham, Michigan

May 30, 2001

What is the deal with "Girls" and Fred Durst? He's a bitch to do that shit to you. What is the politics of that song going on? He's a quote-unquote VP of Interscope, and you guys are distributed through Interscope. Did they try and stop that song coming out? Did they try to stop you guys from talking dirty shit about him?

> Bizarre: Wow! They didn't care too much about it. It got on. They didn't ignore it or whatever, you know what I'm sayin'? Or try to squash the shit.

So that shit is going down? "When I see you I'm swinging." Is Em going to knock out Lethal? Are you guys going to be backing him up? Or, is that all just nonsense?

Bizarre: I don't know, but I think you just got to just look at the history of D12, homie. Read newspapers and magazines.

In other words, you're going to knock them.

Bizarre: That's what you said!

Yeah, you can't say anything incriminating. Paul Rosenberg is a smart guy. If you say it on paper, too. Then they're going to get you. You can get away with saying it on a record because everybody talks shit on record.

Swifty McVay: Exactly.

What's up with that? Everybody's from Detroit; everybody follows through with words and actions.

Bizarre: All I know is that's the kind of city we live in, you know what I'm saying? Before we were rappers. People don't fake beef or don't talk shit, you know what I'm saying? In Detroit; ain't no motherfucker - ain't no dissin' nobody on record from local to anybody, you know? We D12, we're a big group, but we just one of those local rappers out here. They gonna get in our ass ready to fuck us up and beat us up just like we be at they ass ready to fuck them up. We're just on some street made shit, man.

It's like motherfuckers work too hard and put too much time in the studio and effort, you know what

I'm saying? Trying to get they shit pressed up and trying to get deals and let motherfuckers hear their shit, to have some wack motherfucker come spit on they name. When you are dissing a motherfucker you spitting on his credibility, you know what I'm saying? So, you talk about credibility then, you know what I'm saying? You deal with it, you know what I'm saying? I mean, it would be fake. I mean, that's fake as hell if he dissed you on a record and you dissed him on a record, and Y'all see each other you on some, *'Hey man! Blah blah blah, man.'* You're on a record, man! You know what I'm sayin'? Hell, you sittin' there eating ice cream together and some shit?

*WWF shit.**

Bizarre: Yeah, man.

Swifty McVay: I'm saying like that. These my brothers, man. And one of my brothers got hurt, you know what saying?

Bizarre: If you know the band, we don't diss anybody. Motherfuckers diss us first then we just reactions. They try to diss us first.

Swifty McVay: We tell it like it is. We tell it like it is; how it is in this world, you know what I'm saying? And we might joke about it, but we don't diss you unless you diss us, you know what I'm saying? I call

Bizarre Dom DeLuise all day, but, you know what I'm saying.

Bizarre: We ain't stupid, man. We know we can get got just like anybody else, so we just mind our own business. We don't want to be in motherfucking butt-fuck Iowa somewhere, and then here comes fifty dudes rushing the stage beating our ass for no reason.

Are you worried about the lyrics? Some religious person is going to come after you and shoot you?

Swifty McVay: Nah.

Bizarre: Fuck them.

Swifty McVay: Kiss our ass!

Bizarre: I ain't gonna never gonna change.

Swifty McVay: Me neither. We just do what we do, man.

33

Eminem x Everlast & Limp Bizkit Diss Songs

EMINEM X EVERLAST DISS SONGS

"Shit On You"/"I Remember" - D12 b-side - October 2000

"Whitey's Revenge" (Eminem Diss) - Everlast ***Whitey's Ultimate Collection of Rare and Unreleased Tracks*** October 1, 2000

"Quitter" (Everlast Diss) - Eminem featuring D12 - December 2000

EMINEM X LIMP BIZKIT SONGS

"Our House" featuring Fred Durst on the hook, produced by DJ Lethal

January 1999, and released August 28, 2012 on Slaughterhouse ***Welcome to: OUR HOUSE***

"Turn Me Loose" *1999*

"Vicious Pussy" AKA "Girls" - ***Devil's Night*** - June 19, 2001

"Without Me" - ***The Eminem Show*** - May 14, 2002

DILATED PEOPLES x EMINEM DISS SONGS

"Ear Drums Pop" (Remix) - Dilated Peoples ***The Platform*** - May 23, 2000

"Quitter" (Everlast Diss) - Eminem featuring D12 - December 2000

"Vicious Pussy" AKA "Girls" - ***Devil's Night*** - June 19, 2001

"Search for Bobby Fischer" January 2002

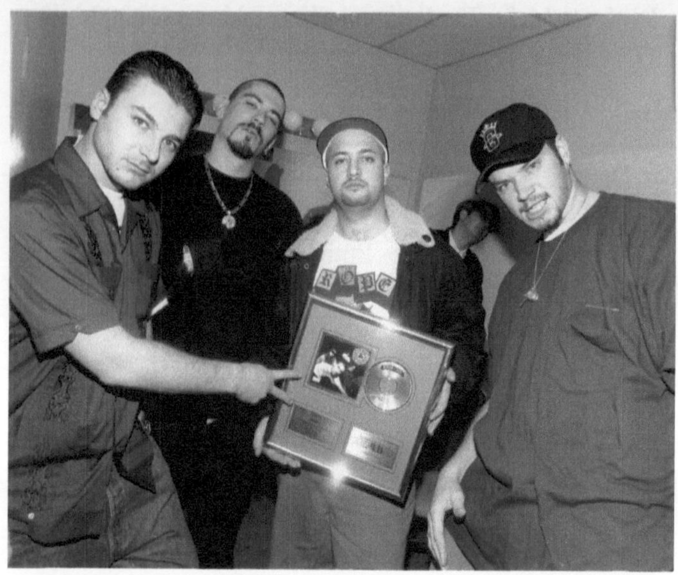

There's Gold in Them Thar Hills! House of Pain's Fine Malt Lyrics Strikes Canadian Gold, 1992

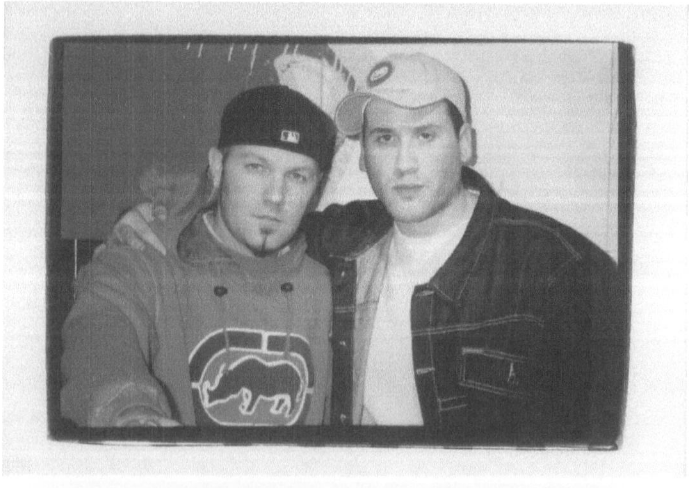

Indeed, I introduced Fred Durst and Marc Ecko @ MAGIC International, 2000

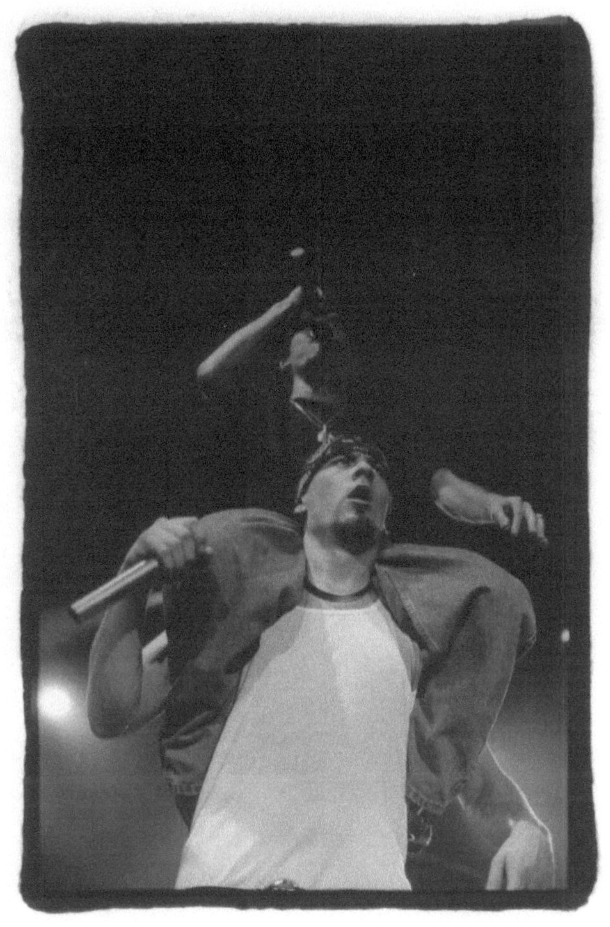

Everlast and Sondoobie Toronto, Canada 1993 by Ed Yee

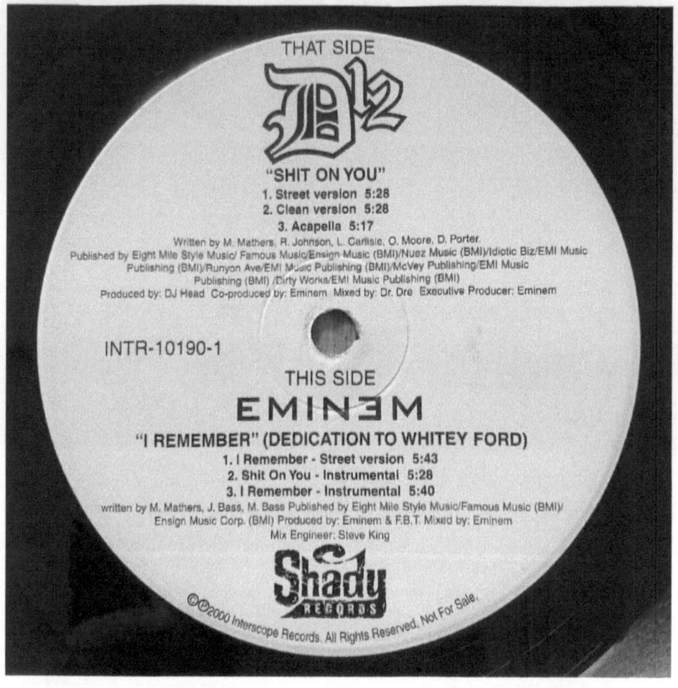

Shady Records first 12" complete with Eminem heat

XI

LIFE IN THE FAST LANE

It's fucking hectic, man. It's hard. I ain't going to lie. There's a lot of bullshit that goes along with being famous, a lot of bullshit.
- Eminem

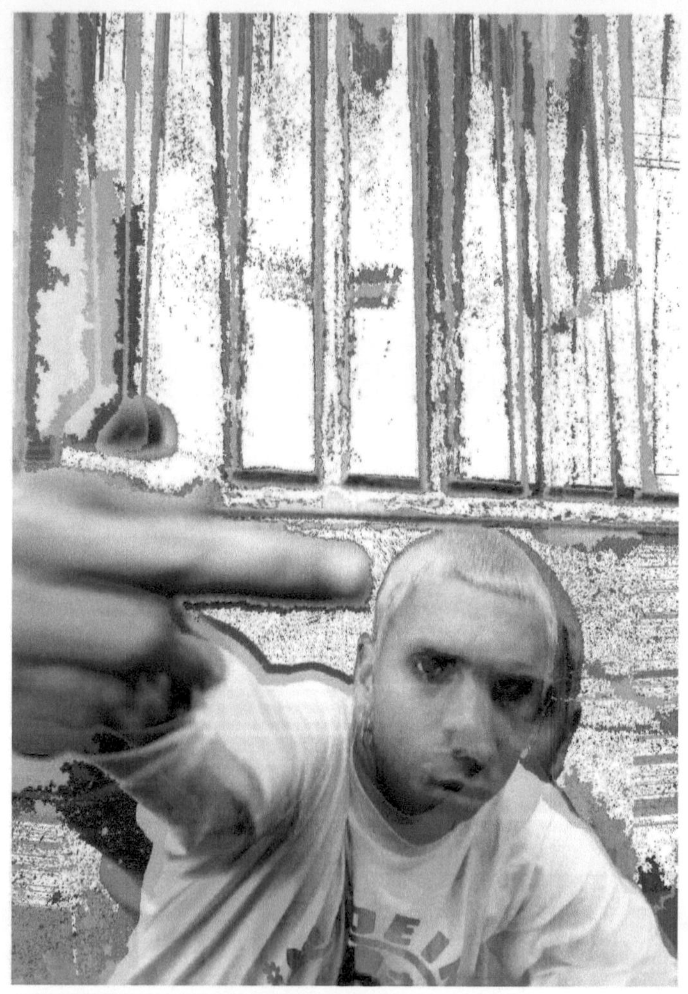

34

Drugs, Sex & Hip-Hop

In April 1999, Eminem stood at the crossroads of life. Antennae to the streets, strapped and ready to blast off. A preternatural urge to live on the edge primed for war. An open book expressed in detail on merciless raps. Detroit City to the max.

The music business had put forth a new beginning, and he was all-in. The advancement of his career paramount. Flights, hotels, shows, and screaming fans. Drugs, sex and Hip-Hop. His fate forever clouded by childhood tribulation and psychosomatic diagnosis.

Everlasting love for his daughter enabled him to keep it together. His mother had relocated, and he took over payments on the trailer, though rarely used it as he toured. Narrow passages of free time at a premium, it's not hard to fathom what happened in-between commitments. Indeed, Slim the predecessor of current individual artists known to encourage illicit drug use.

Eminem spoke on the fundamental changes to his life since the release of *The Slim Shady LP*, and cooly offered a glimpse of the future.

35

Sleep

Toronto, Ontario
April 10, 1999

How has shit changed now that you got loot and you don't have any free time?

> Eminem: As far as like the money goes, it doesn't matter if I have money or not. I ain't got the fucking time to spend it. My life right now is on a schedule, you know what I'm saying? My life is completely fucking controlled right now. It's like, be here, be there, be here, be there, be there. Do this, do that, do this, do that, you know what I'm saying? It's fucking hectic, man. It's hard; I ain't going to lie. There's a lot of bullshit that goes along with being famous, a lot of bullshit.

You told me last week that you're having problems sleeping. How are you dealing with all this shit?

Eminem: The best way I can. What I do is a lot of drugs. [Laughs] Besides that, I got to stay focused, you know what I'm saying? I know what I gotta do, and I just do it. I love Hip-Hop so much that I always seem to fucking muster up energy to keep doing it.

You also told me last week that you only trust your crew and people you roll with.

Eminem: No doubt, that's it.

So, what's going to go on? What will you do once the album's done and you have time off? What's going to go down?

Proof: The second album.

Eminem: Second album, fucking second album.

What else do you want to put in this story? What do you want people to know about you that hasn't gotten out?

Eminem: Nothing that's not on the album. My personal life — Anything I want the public to know I put in my records, pretty much. That's how I do it. Anything that I have got left to say and got left for people to know and I want them to know, I'll tell it on the next album. If I don't catch it on the next album, I'll catch it on the album after that, you know what I'm saying?

Pretty much — my album pretty much tells my

story, and what I'm about, you know what I'm saying? It's pretty self-explanatory. To be honest, people can listen to these interviews – I mean, people can listen to this music, and I shouldn't even have to do any interviews, any press. It's so fucking self-explanatory, you know what I'm saying? It's just like, you know.

Is there anything else?

Eminem: No, that's it. We good.

Proof: No. It gets iller, watch.

What do you say to everybody who just thinks you're a sick fuck?

Eminem: I am a sick fuck. I'm a sick minded fuck, I think. I've got an imagination that's out this world, I think, and I don't know. I just don't - I don't think that — I don't think my brain works like nobody else's, you know what I'm saying? I think I have a different brain. Maybe it's a chemical imbalance or something.

It's weird. I always think that I don't know anybody — 99% of the people I know don't have a 9-to-5 job. Everybody's a character, everybody's doing their own thing and on their vibe, and you're probably the same. You and your whole crew.

Eminem: I'm definitely on my own shit. I live in my own little world. I'm closed out. I'm kind of oblivious to everything else that's around me. I live in my own shit.

Okay, we're going to wrap up. Cool, thank you. Mr Proof -

Proof: Yo!

Anything to say, Sir?

Proof: Yes! Slim Shady is going to make my album dope. He's going to oversee it.

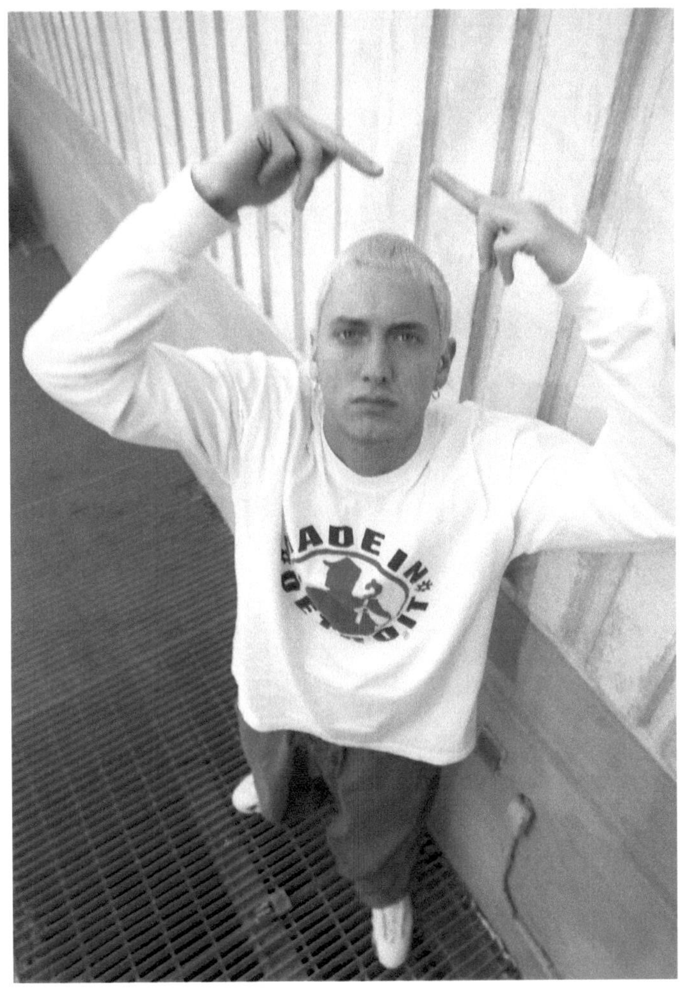

You say we're evil, you say we're lazy

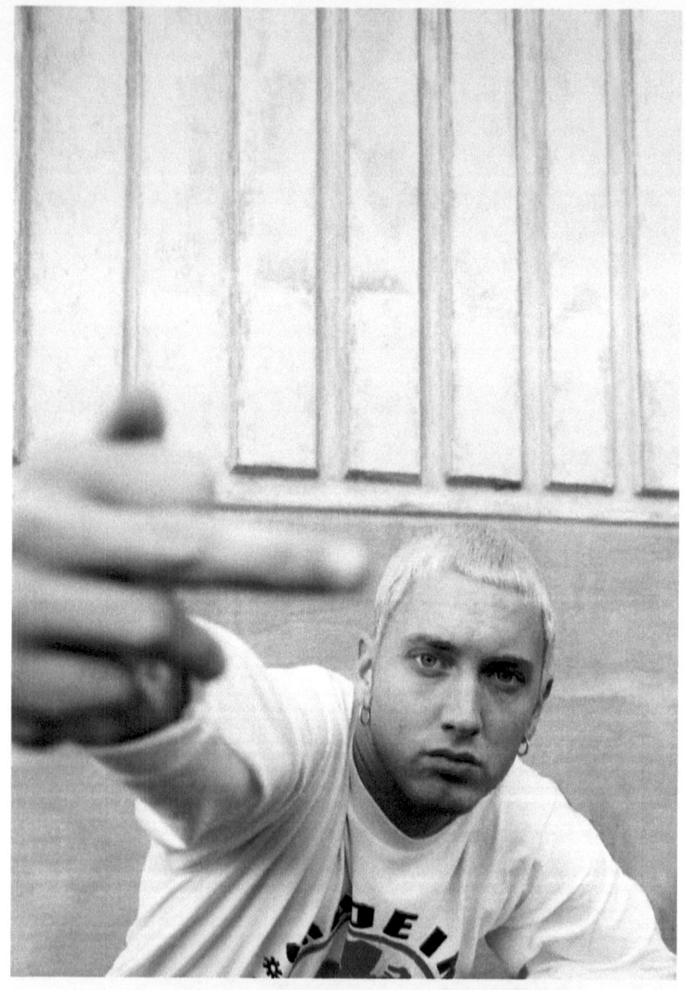

We don't care what you say, FUCK YOU!

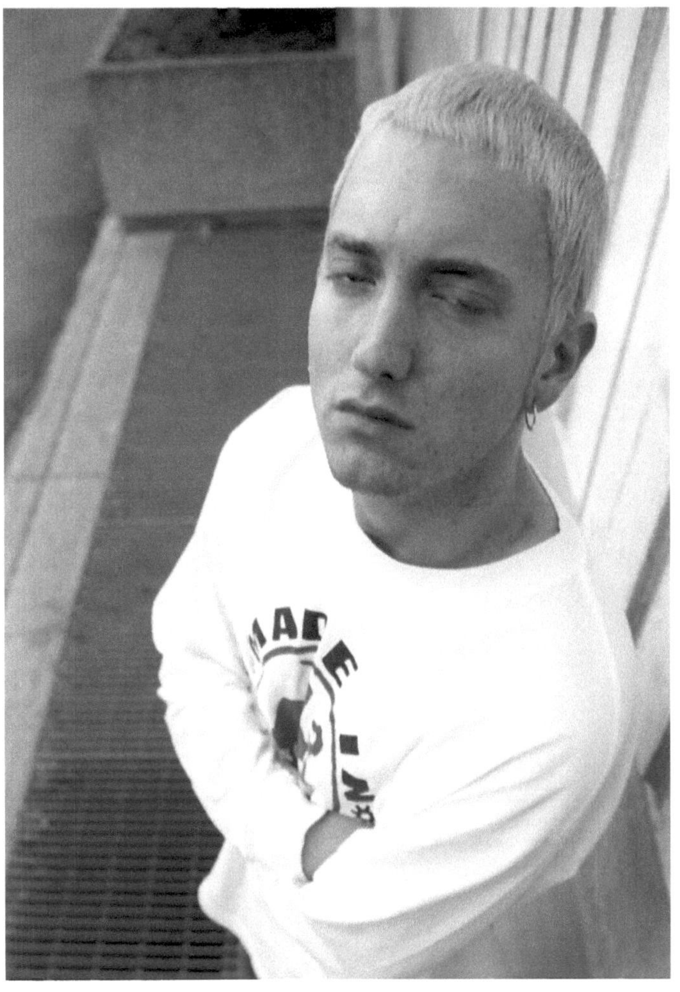

You are getting very sleepy

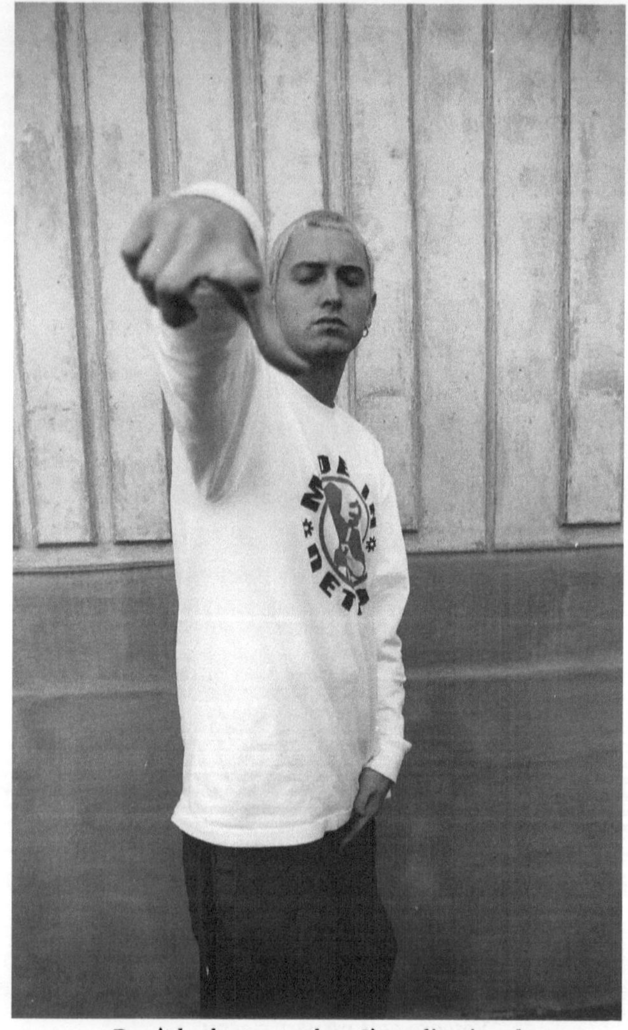

Don't look at me when I'm adjusting deez

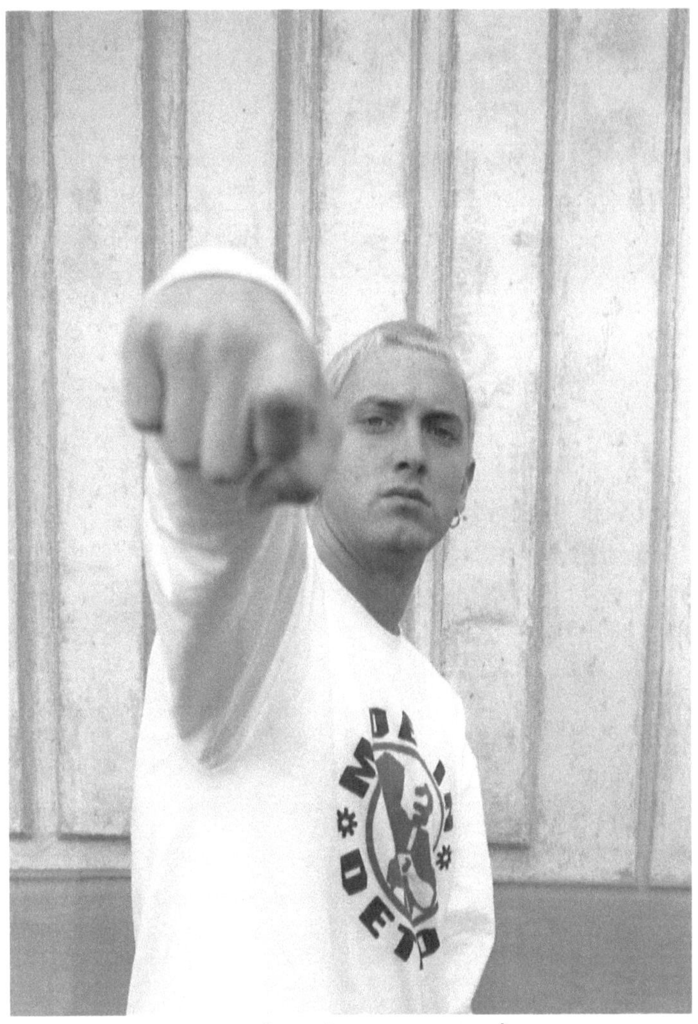

Uncle Eminem Wants You!

XII

FLASHBACK

Matt Sonzala directed the April 4, 1999 Eminem interview.

Ron Boudreau had a photo shoot with Eminem in Toronto on April 10, 1999, and took live shots of his performance at Warped Tour on July 24, 1999.

Gavin Gerbz met with Eminem and Proof inside Room 911 of the Primrose Hotel on April 10, 1999.

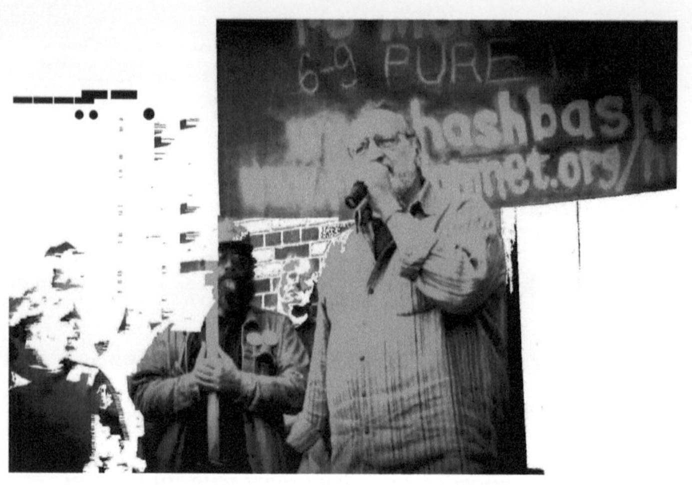
6-9 PURE
hashbas
net.org/

36

Flashback #1: Matt Sonzala's Lamb's Breath

I used to write about rap music for a living. I had a few real jobs, but in my formative years I was mostly temping for various agencies, and then hitting the road in search of new music, and often local, underground stories. My work was published in *The Source, 4080, XXL, Murder Dog* and most of the Rap magazines of the Rap magazine era, and I fought with every editor, all the time.

I wanted to cover the newest up and coming dope music, and really didn't care about the artists standing in the industry, or budgets. I just liked dope shit and loved being the first one to tell people about it

I met Harris Rosen at *Canadian Music Week* in Toronto in 1997. I was out there solo, so I asked a friend I worked with at *4080 Magazine*, Bijan Kazemi, if he knew anyone in Toronto that I should link with. Both for companionship at the event, and well, weed. Bijan gave me phone numbers for Harris Rosen, who had a magazine called *PEACE!*, and Sol Guy who was a burgeoning label executive.

Sol was an incredible help to me on my first night in Toronto. We went to a Reggae club, and he broke down pretty much every detail about what was happening in Canadian Hip-Hop to me. Sol was on his ascent. He literally had the entire Canadian Hip-Hop community in his Rolodex and probably helped 80% of the artists to ever come out of that country. He was and remains to this day, the real deal. He was only in town that night if I remember correctly, so we made sure to spend some time and chop it up. Local Toronto Reggae bands and DJs were performing as we sat and discussed and compared the independent Rap music of the south, I lived in Texas at the time, to the independent artists in the north. He listed name after name after name of people I needed to hear while in Canada. One of those names was Whitey Don. *"The white Reggae artist on Jive?"* I was a bit taken aback. Sol is a tall black man with dreadlocks, and I was thinking to myself *"A real head accepts a white Reggae artist?"*

Admittedly I had liked the song "Article" that Whitey had done with Phife Dawg and Chip Fu, but didn't think a whole lot about him. I had actually written bios for Snow, another white Reggae singer from Toronto, as his manager was one of my early mentors, Steve Salem. Steve was the man behind the success of UTFO, Lisa Lisa, Samantha Fox and so many more artists. I was fortunate to be able to learn from him. I never totally accepted Snow, as I thought "Informer" was a bit cheesy, but his song "Champion Sound" always resonated with me. And I was happy to make money writing anything, even bios on a white Reggae pop star.

Anyway, Sol had to leave, and I decided to stay and keep checking out the Reggae. And also hoped to find some weed.

As I was sitting alone, I looked across the room and saw Whitey Don. Sol told me he was really cool, so I decided to go say hello. I introduced myself as Matt Sonzala from *4080 Magazine*, and it turns out that our Reggae columnist at the time had recently written a very positive review of Whitey's record and he literally welcomed me with open arms. We talked about music, and he introduced me to a guy called Friendlyman, who had agreed to sell me some weed. Now if you know anything about Canadian pot, it is often excellent, and generally quite cheap. Friendlyman pulled out a tissue that was wrapped around some of the ugliest weed I had ever seen in my life, and he charged me $40 for it. He says to me *"It's Lambs Breath, mon."* It was after midnight, I was desperate, so I bought it just to have something to smoke before bed. I rolled a joint of this shit having the lowest expectations ever, and to this day it was some of the most fire marijuana I have ever smoked. It looked like dirt but smelled and tasted like Heaven. This was before hydro weed was everywhere in the states. I was used to smoking dirt weed from Mexico, and this stu looked worse than that, but man, it was incredible. Whitey and I decided to meet the next day, the same day I was going to meet Harris. Actually, I'm pretty sure that Harris was just getting back in town that day, and Sol was leaving that day. It totally worked out. Harris, Whitey and I kicked it all week, and Whitey kicked so much reggae knowledge to me that I discovered a whole new way of looking at music.

I say all of this because I have always been a "keep it real" dude to a fault. I really didn't want much to do with any white rappers, let alone Reggae singers. I even thought the Beastie Boys were super corny when they first came out. Of course, I wasn't living deep in New York when their career was ramping up, so my first sampling of them was "Fight For Your Right To Party," and to me, that was just three frat boys making fun of Hip-Hop. When they first announced that they were coming to my home town on their first headlining tour, I wasn't even going to go. Then I heard "Hold It Now Hit It" and decided that maybe I should give these new rap kids a chance. They were great and were one of the few groups in rap to get better with age, but they still were never really my favourites.

I first heard of Eminem on the *rec.music.hip-hop* Message Board. My friend Robert Gabriel, who also wrote for *4080* told me that I should join this online community where other budding journalists and DJ's and rap nerds would discuss the latest releases. This was before file sharing was a common thing. These were the days when you would wait ten minutes for a photo to load on a website. We were talking about the music online, and often trading tapes through the mail. I had some dope ass tapes that I had compiled over the years, and through this message board community I was able to trade with like-minded heads in Mississippi, New York, Seattle, wherever really. We were a small, but dedicated community.

I don't even remember who it was that sent it to me, but I heard an Eminem freestyle on one of the tapes and was immediately intrigued. People on the message board had posted about this white kid from Detroit and his *Infinite* CD, but I had never heard that and was admittedly prejudiced, so I didn't actively seek it out. Eminem was the first white rapper that I ever accepted o rip. From the first time hearing him, I knew he was the shit. Even 3rd Bass, when they came out, I was like *"Who are these CLOWNS?"* Then I realised that they were dope. It always took time for me to accept the white rappers because it was imperative to me that they were not coming in to take over rap and make it their own like so many white artists did to Rock and Roll. And Jazz. And Blues. Etc. His style and lyrics on that first freestyle – forgive me for not remembering exactly which one it was – were all I needed to hear. Couple that with him being from one of the roughest cities in America, and I was sold. I wanted to hear more. But in the late '90s, when a kid would drop a tape or a CD in Detroit, it wouldn't necessarily make it to Texas. People on the message board were going nuts over the release of the *Slim Shady EP*.

I was on a road trip when it came out, and in every city, I would stop into the independent record shops and ask if they had this release from Eminem. No one did. I passed through Vancouver on that road trip and linked with a dude I met the same week I met Harris at *Canadian Music Week*, DJ Jay Swing. Jay was the DJ for the Rascalz, a dope rap group from Vancouver, and we met up, and um, I was probably asking him to find me some weed. But I also asked him the same question I asked everyone on the road trip, "Do you know where I can get the *Slim Shady EP*?" Turns out he had it. I had a couple of blank *Maxell XLII*'s in the car, and I gave him one, and he made me a dub of the EP and a gang of Eminem radio freestyles I had never heard. For the rest of the trip that is pretty much all my wife and I listened to Eminem. Over and over again. That road trip literally ended with us moving to Chicago. Much closer to Detroit, and the friends I made there were way more in tune with Eminem's underground stu than my people in Texas were. I would tell everyone I knew in the industry that *"this white dude from Detroit is about to take over, I'm serious."* I had no idea that around that time he was in talks with Dr. Dre and indeed was about to catapult over the entire industry with one fell swoop.

Just as this happened, another mentor of mine, Kim Buie, who was thanked by name on the back of the first N.W.A 12", and also the first CIA 12" (instantly making her my hero) introduced me to her roommate at the time, Anna Loynes. Anna Loynes was a publicist who just so happened to be hired to do PR for Eminem just as everything started happening with Dre. Kim knew that I knew a lot about Eminem and that I was writing for a lot of people, so she connected us, and we talked like every day. She told me how she had dyed Em's hair blonde earlier one day and that he was going through a bit of an image makeover. That worried me, but I didn't care, the music was dope, and I knew that whatever he was going to do with Dr. Dre would be amazing.

I told the editor and publisher at *4080* that we needed to put Eminem on the cover, we needed to be first. They both totally scoed at me. *4080* covered all sorts of rap music but was West Coast to the core. To put a white kid from Detroit who almost no one they knew about was just ludicrous. I didn't give up though, I kept pushing and pushing and came up with the idea that if we could get Eminem and Dr. Dre together on the cover, it would be huge. I was close with the publicist, I could make this happen. The publisher Lauchlan McIntyre basically told me that if I could pull that photo o, we could make the Eminem cover story, and we would have been first, way first. Then like, a few days later, *4080* closed down, Lauchlan disappeared, and my idea was a moot point. I was so pissed.

I mentioned earlier that I would fight a lot with my editors, and I said that to say that I never fought with Harris Rosen.

I always enjoyed writing for his *PEACE! Magazine*. He listened to me when I told him about underground shit, and he assigned things to me often that may have been too underground for his other writers. We were friends first and foremost and are until this day. I pitched Eminem pieces to every- one around that time, and no one was hearing me. Maybe they wanted to do it themselves, but honestly, until "My Name Is" blew up, a lot of industry people were sceptical, even with the Dre connect.

As I also mentioned about six times in this piece already, I was always a weed head. And being a weed head, I had always wanted to attend this event called *Hash Bash,* in Ann Arbor, Michigan, just outside Detroit. Living in Chicago in 1999 I was so close I had to go. I called my homeboy Harris in Toronto and told him that he should come as well. I also told my friend Anna that I was going to be in the area in Detroit and if Eminem was around I wanted to meet him, and hopefully do an interview. Turns out he had his homecoming show in Detroit that exact same weekend. I really couldn't believe it. Harris was super sold on spending this huge weekend in Michigan and witnessing history on a weed level and on a rap level, and we made plans to meet up.

The drive would have been only 5 hours or so, but my wife and I decided to fly. This turned out to be the right decision as Eminem and his crew – DJ Head and Proof – were just returning from Europe, and had a layover in Chicago. We were all on the same flight! Eminem sat in first class, but Proof and Head sat in the row directly behind us. I introduced myself to them on the plane, and they introduced me to Eminem in the baggage area. I told Eminem I was going to *Hash Bash* and then coming to interview him before his show. Told him I am a big fan, etc. He really didn't care. Barely even nodded at me. Proof and DJ Head were super cool though.

Anyway, *Hash Bash* was everything I had ever hoped it would be. Thousands of people celebrating marijuana culture and openly predicting a future I literally never thought we would see, legal, medical marijuana. Tommy Chong spoke, and Harris and I stood maybe two meters away from him and all of the other activists and medical patients who spoke that day. When that ended, we stayed at some Motel 6 in Ann Arbor and the next day drove into Detroit. No label was paying for anything, so I booked my wife and me into maybe the sketchiest hotel I ever stayed in. There were signs in the room saying that if anyone knocks on your door to call security immediately. Lock everything up, etc. And it was dirty. But whatever, we were in Detroit and were about to finally see the dude I had been so hyped up about for the past year. While I certainly wasn't going to be first, the hype machine had already started churning, I was going to be early, and that meant a lot to me.

We were instructed to meet Eminem and crew at sound check at the venue at say about 3pm. We drove from the hotel quite far down Mack Avenue, and the whole time I was thinking about the blues songs I had heard reference this street so many times and also thinking about the Big Chief album *Mack Avenue Skull Game*. I was cruising down Mack Avenue, in Detroit, feeling like a boss on my way to a reasonably exclusive Eminem show in his home town. When we pulled up to the "venue", it was an old warehouse. In the middle of nowhere. There was standing water on the floor in front of the stage that had leaked in through the ceiling, there was no sound system in place yet, the site looked like it literally was deserted for years, and probably was. This was rave culture, a culture I honestly didn't know a lot about except I knew that so much House and Techno music came from Detroit, and I felt like I was standing in a historic place. A shithole, but historic nonetheless.

Eminem, DJ Head and Proof all arrived on time for the sound check, and Eminem expressed a bit of concern as he looked around the place, wondering if it even had electricity. The sound system was not in place, so a sound check was impossible at that time. You would think that this would be a great time to do an interview. We were all literally just standing in the street clowning, possibly having some beers, talking shit, but Eminem was not ready to be interviewed. So we waited, and waited, outside some dilapidated building o Mack Avenue in Detroit. A straightforward sound check came and went, and Eminem took o from the venue, driving himself in his SUV, no security. Wonderful. I don't entirely remember what happened between Eminem leaving and his arrival at the site later that night. I just remember tons of kids queueing up, and being happy that we were already inside. It was a proper rave environment.

There were Hip-Hop heads in the place of course, but also loads of white people on drugs. I know the "molly eyes" very well, and there were a lot of people sporting them and stumbling around the dark venue, sometimes falling on the uneven concrete. Harris and I really didn't know anyone there, he may have known of a couple of the DJ's, but I was just there, sitting waiting, getting pissed o as I often would when rappers would make me wait to do an interview. This scenario happened way more often than not, interviews with rappers were seldom done on time. And I have never been a patient person. But I was happy to be in the place at that moment, and will always cherish the experience.

Harris and I were supposed to do separate interviews, and have a proper amount of time to talk to Em. As the night wore on, we were told that we were going to have to do this interview together, press conference style, and I got super pissed o. We sat in a room and waited for Eminem to arrive. When he came in and sat down at the table with us, his attention was about 30% on us and 70% on his friends and the ensuing show. I understood that actually. This show was kind of a big deal, all his friends were there, and it marked his transition from underground rap phenom to one of the most prominent artists in all of music. He was like a ticking time bomb, he knew he was about to explode.

I remember him being antsy and quite short with us. In the intro to this book, Harris says the interview lasted thirteen minutes. My only real memory is that I got to ask him a question I had always wanted to ask him. I wanted to know if he, as a shock rapper from Detroit, had any influence from the shock rockers like Alice Cooper and Iggy Pop, who also came from his home town. I asked, and he merely said *"No."* I said *"Really?"* And he looked at me annoyed and said: *"I said No!"* That's really all I remember. I was pissed, annoyed, disappointed and figured the piece would never happen.

My mood changed when Eminem came on stage, and alongside Proof and Royce da 5'9, he did some freestyles and all the future hits. I knew that I was witnessing history. I knew that I was in a special place. I knew that for every crack in the cement walls that surrounded me, there was a story to be told, and this was one of them. The crowd went crazy. It felt smaller than it was, as I was able to get all the way to the front and take some blurry pictures. Blurry because of the rave style smoke machine, and possibly because I smoked a big joint once the interview was finally done.

Like I said, Eminem was literally the first white rapper that I accepted upon first hearing. I didn't need any rough stories from the streets or anything else to prove to me that he was real. I just thought he was dope and represented Hip-Hop at that moment in history really well. He came out during the period that Pu Daddy had been dominating the radio and video shows with everything he did. Honestly, I'm the type of old head who thinks rap music started going downhill around 1996. There's been plenty of dope stu since, but seeing it in its infancy, and then seeing the beginnings of it being co-opted by literally everyone and swinging way more into a pop direction in those days, I was already starting to become a hater.

I saw Eminem as a guy who actually could come in and help steer the ship in the right direction. Dope lyrics, big attitude, real street smarts, clever song composition, everything was there. I loved that dudes music. But as the albums kept coming, I really lost interest. To me personally, I don't even think that *The Slim Shady LP* entirely stands the test of time. I literally never pull it out and listen to it any- more, and really, I didn't even love his second album. I was happy for his success, but in 2019, I can't really also deal with hearing his voice. And rappers I thought were suckers when they first came out – Beasties, 3rd Bass, Everlast – I still jam to this day. I don't know why. I can't really explain it.

Regardless of how I feel, or felt about the man, his influence is evident in every aspect of Hip-Hop culture to this day.

Countless kids were raised on his music, and for many, he was the first rapper they ever heard. He is as legendary as any other rapper you would want to put the legendary label on, and from day one he did things his way. And I feel honoured to have been able to get a first-hand look at those early days, both through association with his first publicist and for having been in the house for this historic performance.

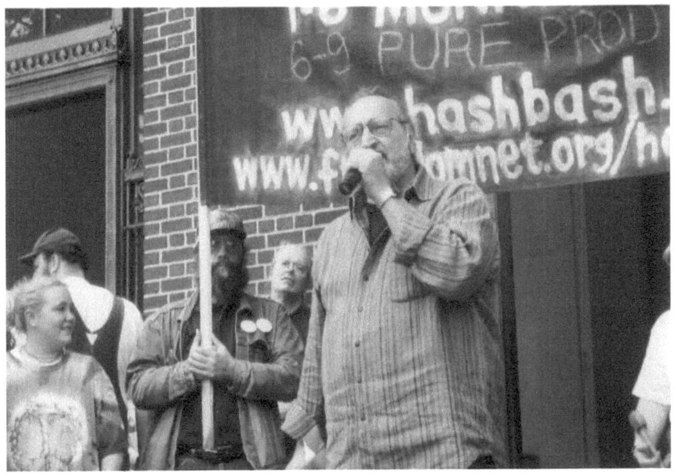

Jack Herer "The Emperor of Hemp" enlightening the masses @ Hash Bash, 1999

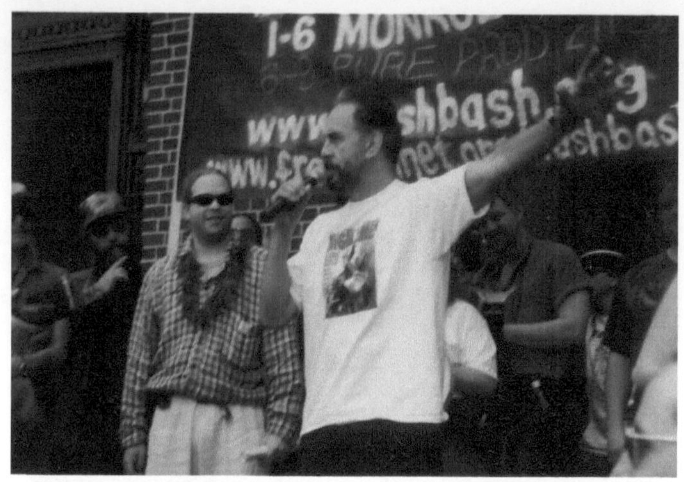

Tommy Chong x Hash Bash, 1999

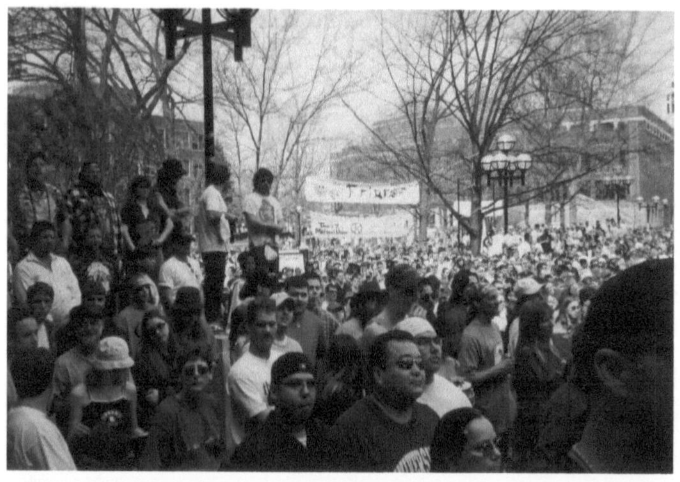

Give me your tired, your poor, your huddled masses yearning to breathe free

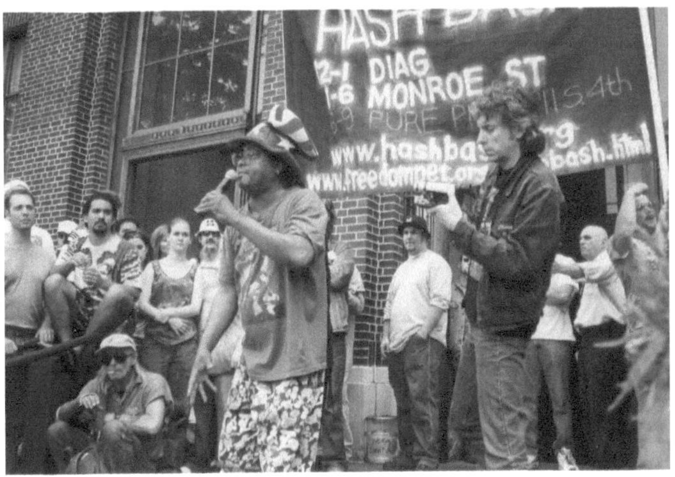

Men, Myths, Legends: Chef Ra and Steven Hagar @ Hash Bash, 1999

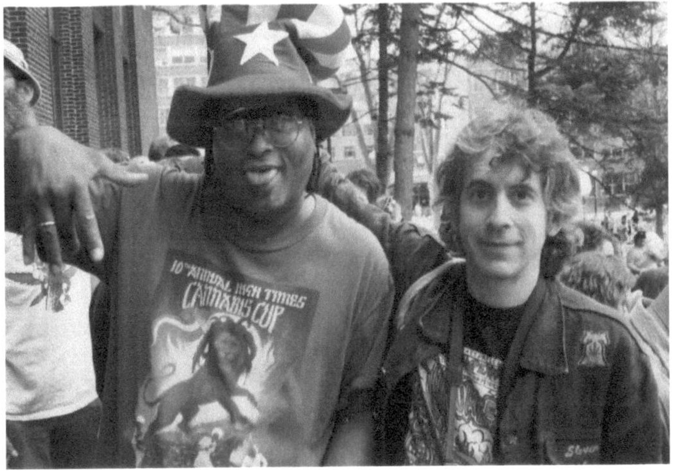

Pot Illuminati?

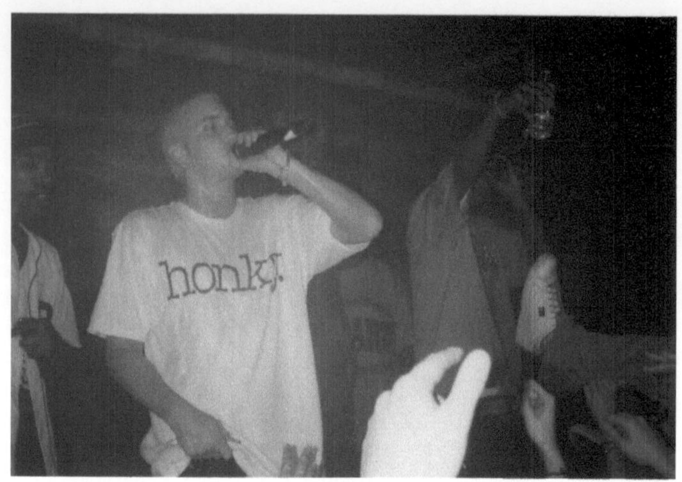

Can I get a hey? (Hey!)

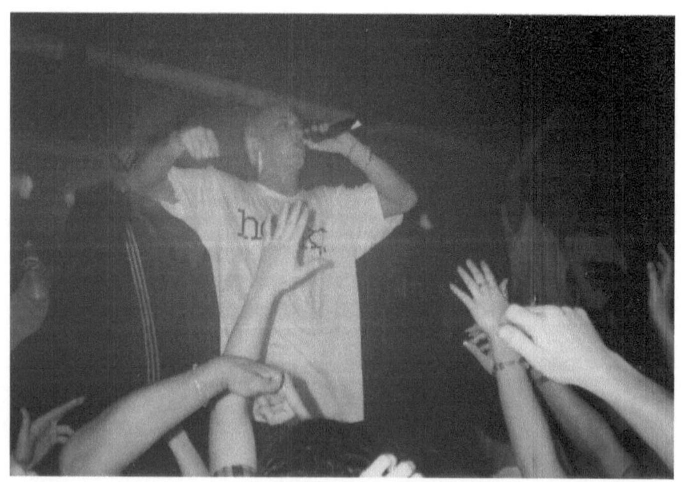

Can I get a yo? (Yo!)

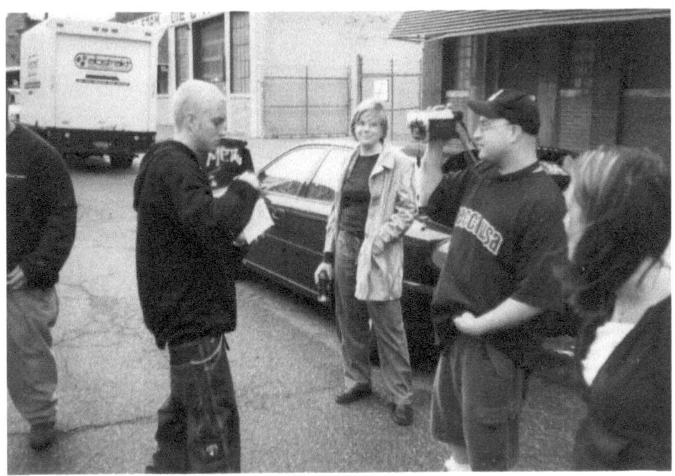

Slim testing some of his notebook treats on the media

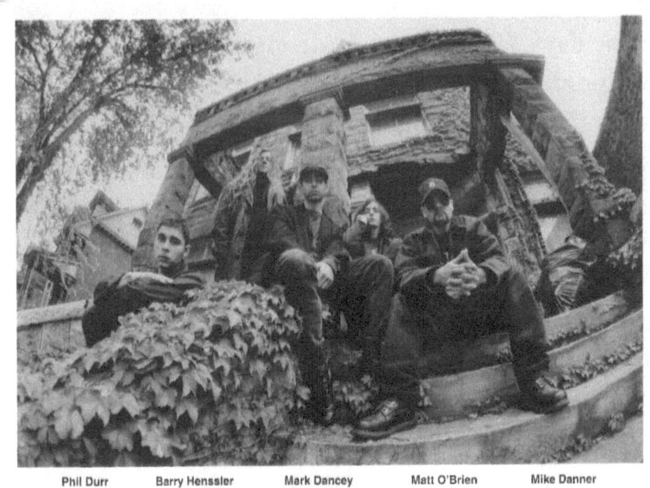

This is Big Chief!

37

Flashback #2: Ron Boudreau and the Melting of Eminem

I was sent an advance copy of *The Slim Shady LP* by Werner Weins of Universal Music Canada in February 1999. I'm a huge Cypress Hill and House of Pain fan at this point. Maybe, Onyx as hardcore as I got in those days. Then, Werner dropped this black CD with Eminem written on it. I popped it in the CD player and instantly knew it would change Hip-Hop, at the least, the modern view of what the Art Form will be. Music seems to get comfortable or reach a certain standard and then someone comes along and redefines it.

There are few times where you hear special music, and you know this is gonna change it. I remember the first time I heard Die Antwoord. There were 100 000 hits on *YouTube,* and one month later it was 10 million, and I had told all my friends this is gonna change everything, again. I saw Eminem doing that before it happened. And it's gonna be controversial because it's a white guy making Black music. Eminem presented something different and new at the same time. I recall trying not to laugh and loving the music.

Playing it for my friends, they were like, *'Holy fuck! I never heard anything like this.!'* Who presents music you can laugh at with a political view and you still go *'Oh, my God!,'* that's brilliant? It needed to be. When you look at it for what it was - oensive. But, if you look at it the way Eminem and Madonna and those kinds of people are, he was just pushing the freedom of expression envelope: *'This is what's in my mind, and you can't do anything about it.'*

I didn't know much about Dr. Dre. I knew Public Enemy, OutKast, M.O.P., and a few other artists we had worked with. Knowing a little bit for me, the white guy Rocker dude, Dr. Dre was part of the Snoop world. Part of that particular era where he was a serious producer. It wasn't like *'Yo, yo, bling bling.'* He was actually trying to make groundbreaking music. Or carving his own niche. That was what Dr. Dre put to that environment. He was a crucial guy going *'Oh, my God, I can do something dierent with Eminem that is groundbreaking.'* The first time I heard it I knew that, too.

I was blown away when Harris asked me to shoot the magazine cover as he was on the point of what was about to break. As opposed to *'Well, this guy was hot five years ago, and I'm lucky to have him on my magazine cover.'* He was the one saying, *'No, I want to put this guy on.'* The same vision Dre had. He wanted to do something dierent. For people to say *'Oh, my God. This is the hottest thing out there, it's Eminem,'* and grab it. I had probably listened to the CD a thousand times 'cause it was so dierent and exciting, and it wasn't the same old blah, blah, blah over, again.

When I got to the photo shoot, I actually remember being a little bit nervous 'cause I also had to shoot the Platinum album presentation with the record company. They were all at the photo shoot watching us; three white guys, Eminem, and a Black guy with dreds. I can't remember who that is. He was pretty smiley that day. It was weird to have the people that generally hired me to do publicity stills. "Hey, this is Bryan Adams and the record company executives with their Gold album." It's a very mechanical shoot, where this was supposed to be capturing what Eminem was all about, and it's kind of hard to do that when you got thirty people standing behind you in a horseshoe going "What do you think?" You got to tune it out. I didn't have a big studio set up. I didn't have this, I didn't have that. I liked the fact it was a down to earth street level photo shoot without going to the typical dirty alley covered in grati or whatever. It was just Eminem on the side of a road, or bottom of a street really, over a storm drain.

Eminem had these big white eyes. It felt like he and I were the only two involved in the photo shoot. I remember standing up on a little pylon planter and shooting down on him and looking over my shoulder. My girlfriend, Werner, and all these other record company people with a look on their faces like, *'The new Great White Hope is here.' 'We've got to see what Harris is breaking with.'* I thought, not only do I want to do the best job I can to make this magazine cover for Harris and Peace! Magazine, but now I got all these record company dudes standing behind me, and I can't really be me.

At the end of the photo shoot, the one time Eminem and I connected, he hugged me. We grabbed each other and shook hands and did a chest hug. He was doing it because I got him through it so quickly. He did pose after pose, and I was ready, on point, the whole time. The photo shoot couldn't have taken more than seven minutes 'cause we only did a roll and a half. It wasn't that much. When I recall that bonding moment we had, it felt like we were the only two that connected. Everybody else was just like *'Well, do you think they got it? Does Eminem look like he's gonna be –'*

Boom! Ninety days later we're at the *Warped Tour.* I got to do the live shoot and shooting live Hip-Hop is so much dierent than live Rock N' Roll. Live Rock N' Roll, they come and stand there and pose for you. Kind of like *'Hi, I got to get in my picture for the magazine.'* Where Eminem was more interested in the crowd and what was going on. To grab a live photo of Eminem was really hard, and when I finally did, I got some shots that I was happy with.

When Harris and I were on the way to shoot Ice-T behind the scenes on the same roll, we walked by Eminem and his crew by the tour bus. I remembered the connection we had at the last photo shoot. He signed five copies of the magazine cover for Harris, and he looked at me like I never existed. I can remember the emotions and the connection that we had for those seven minutes I'm doing the photos. And then the complete realisation of what Eminem had been through in the three to four months when we saw him again, that his mind had melted, which was all made up for when we got to photograph Ice-T.

When Peace! Magazine came out three people were talking about Eminem: *Peace! Magazine*, *Spin Magazine*, and *Rolling Stone* had mentioned something about him. One hundred days later, he's on the cover of everything, everywhere, exploded. That kind of put it in perspective for me. Walking away from where Eminem stood with us with a blank stare, we don't know you guys vibe. He's been through hell and back in three and a half months.

I can't expect everybody to be Sebastian Bach slapping me on the back going *"Hey bud, how is ya doing? Remember the Gasworks days?"* Whereas, Eminem was like I can't remember what happened ten minutes ago because his life was such a whirlwind after that album took o. It didn't make sense to me at the time because that album came only four months before. Guys like Kiss would come back two, three years later and go *"Hey Ron, how you been?"* Or, the guys from Pantera are like *"Ron Boudreau's in the house!"* I just did this first magazine cover of Eminem in the country, and he looks at me like I don't know you. It was weird how you can be so connected with someone, and then he had gone through so much.

I was the only guy that did an Eminem photo shoot. I had magazines calling me left and right up here in Canada asking to use the photos, and I said no, that was an exclusive for *Peace! Magazine.* Only one really cool magazine said if we write a friendly letter to Harris can we get the outtakes for our magazine? I forget the name of the magazine. It was something to do with *Music Express* or one of that spin-o. They got the outtake, and they still got a great cover and a six-page spread inside. It was a good ninety days from street date to street date.

It's interesting how most of my life I worked towards helping individual Rock stars achieve their goals and yet now twenty years later a guy I never hung with who blew me away I'm getting a book cover with him, again. How cool is that? Yet the guys that I worked for and gave my unrelenting dying love mean nothing to me now, or I mean nothing to them. Either way. It was the right time, the right place with the right people, between Harris and Werner. Over the years the reactions of my peers, friends, fans, whatever, they're always in awe of how I shot Eminem before he was huge. Again, right people, right place, right time. Still, to this day, I love showing people my Eminem pictures, every single time. And people look at it and go *'Wow! Is he ever young?'*

Am I surprised now twenty years later that the reference of G.O.A.T is attributed to Eminem? No, not at all. Not many people could change music as quickly and eciently as he did at the time that he did. The music was almost rusted. It seems like there's a new thing that breaks and no matter what happens it gets moulded, and you can tell when a trend is old by seeing old white folks on commercials dropping the mic. *'Bingo!'* - mic drop. *'I'm out of here.'* Okay, time for a new style. Then a guy like Eminem comes along.

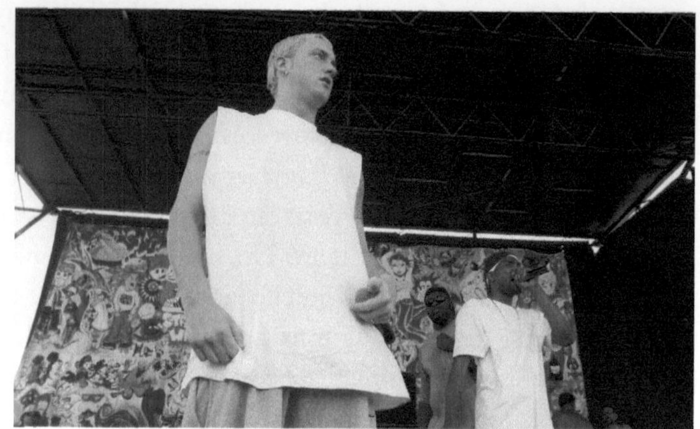

Eminem x Big Proof live in Tha 6 pre-Tha 6 era

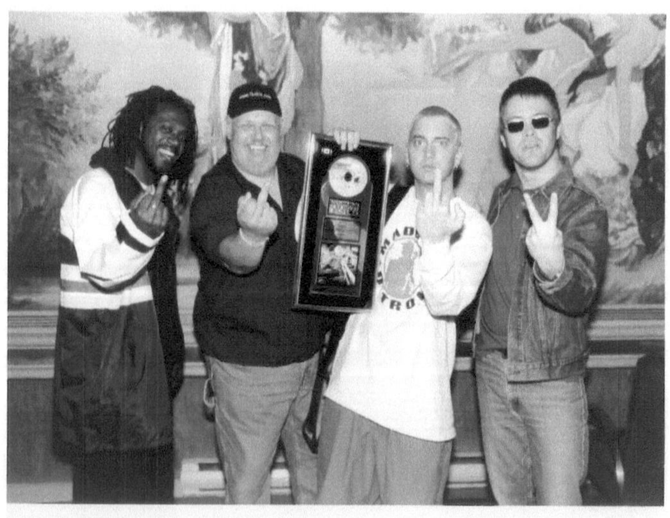

Kevin Barton, Werner Weins, Platinum Award, Middle-Finger Man, Tyson Parker-Gallagher

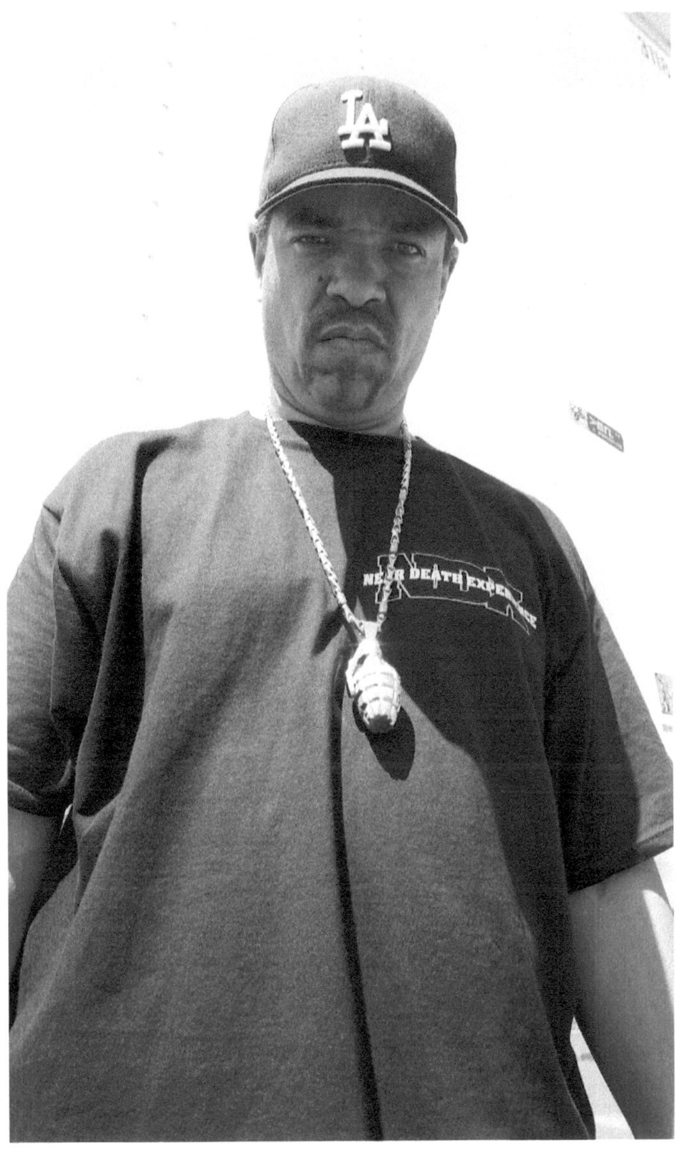

This is MC Ice-Muthafuckin'-T @ The Warped Tour, July 24, 1999

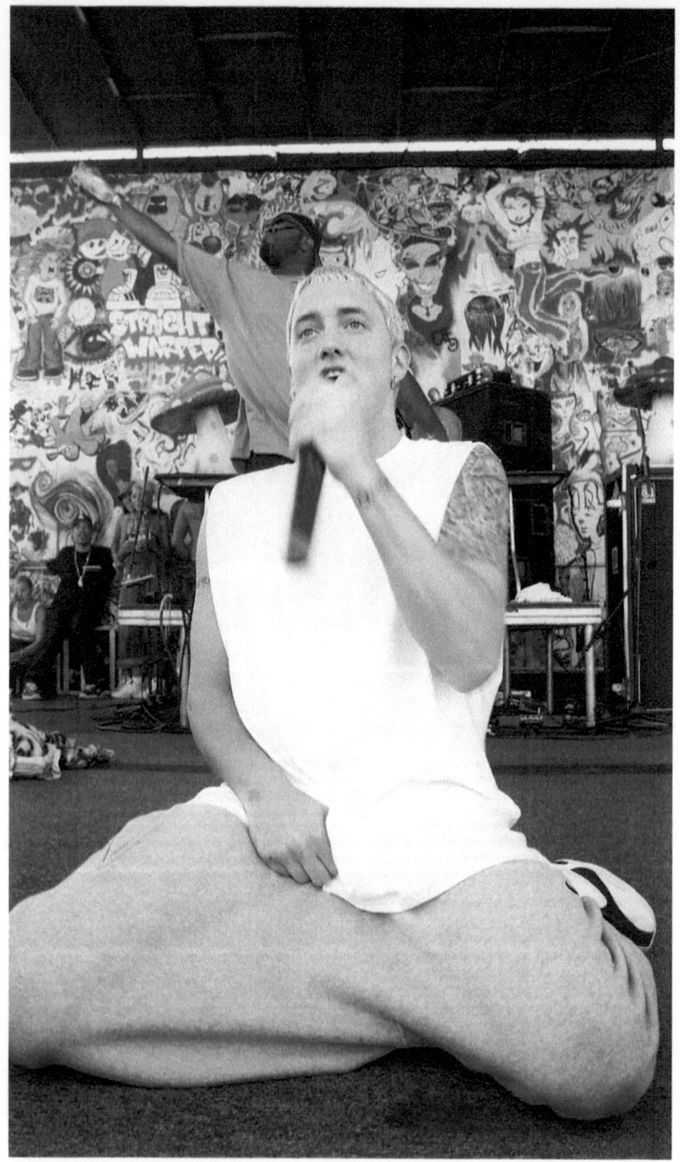

I spy with my little eye, SGT Odafin Tutuola

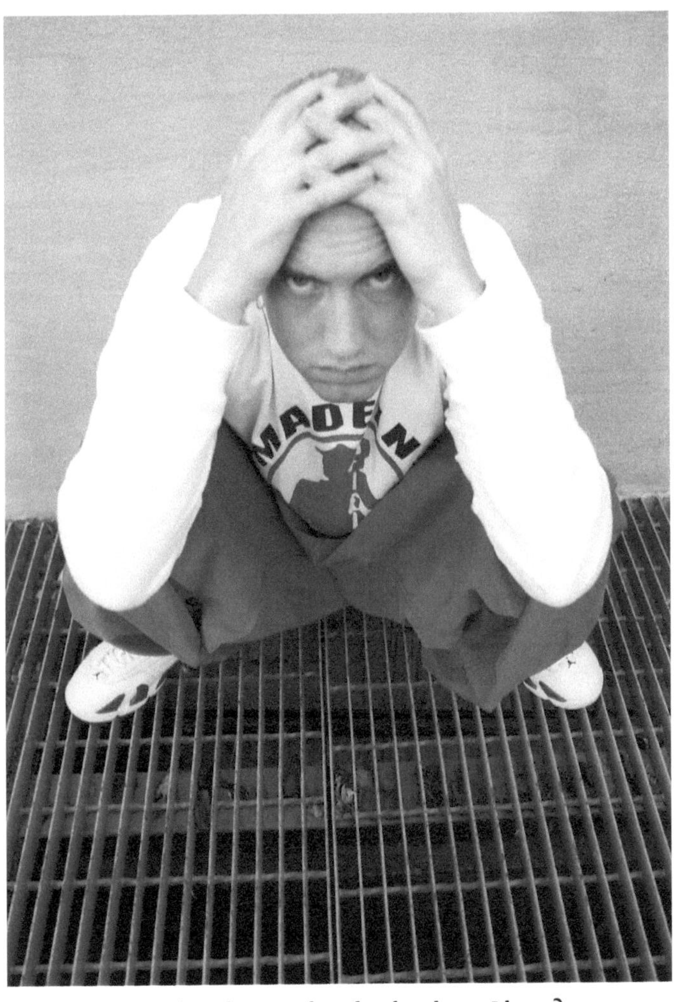

My hand on my head, what have I here?

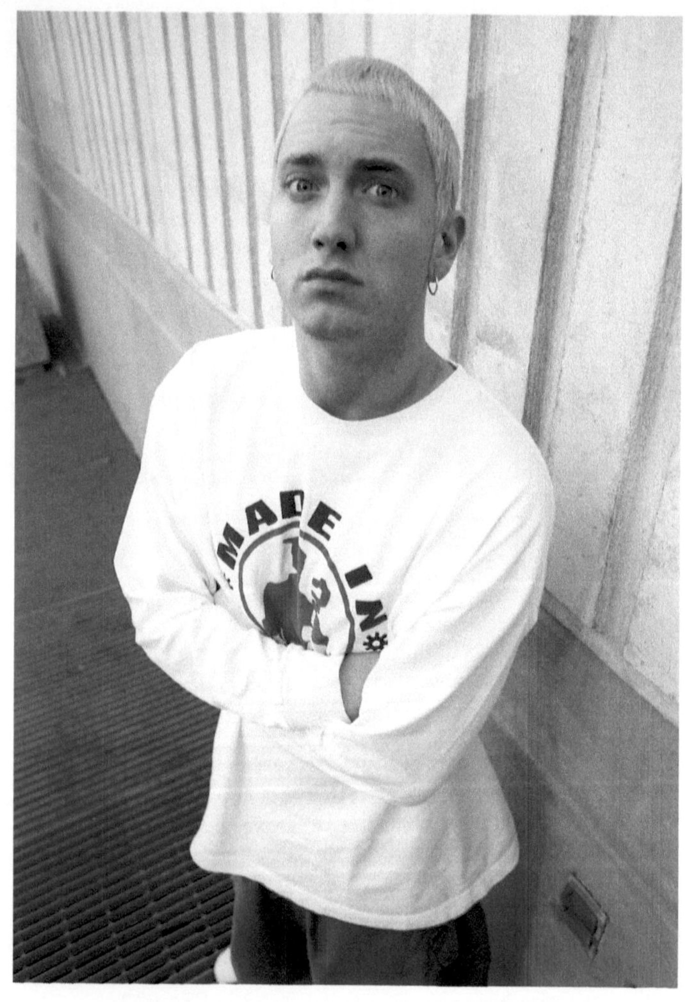

No one knows what it's like to be the Bad Man

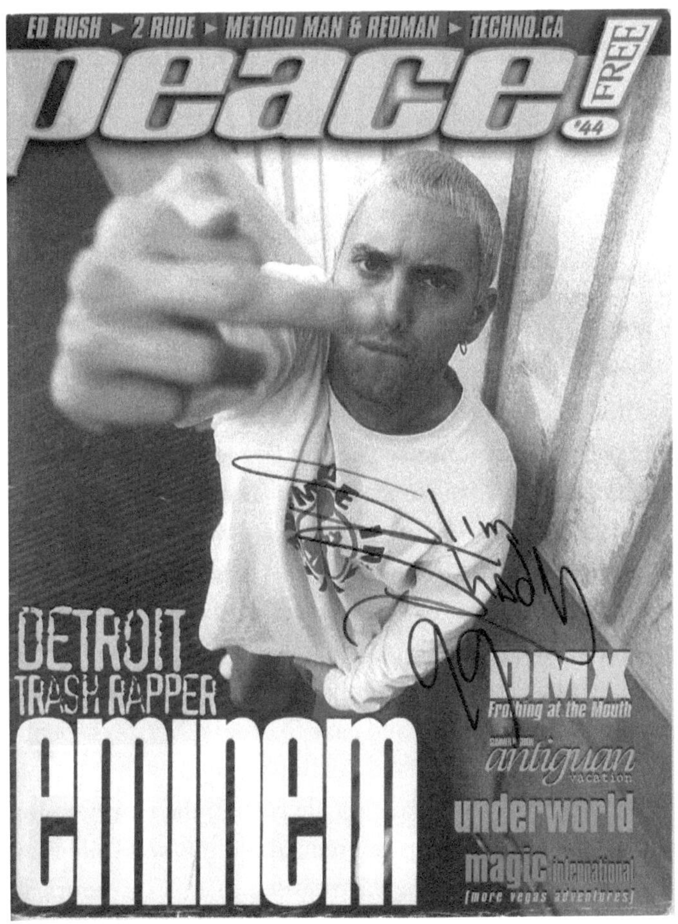

Aussie Aussie Aussie, Oi Oi Oi

Flashback #3: Gavin Gerbz & Mr. Heller

Eminem's appetite for pills is notorious. *Relapse* and *Recovery* fact, not fiction. Despite the Vicodin art on *The Slim Shady LP* CD label, back in the Spring of 1999, few outside of his immediate crew knew that Eminem ate them daily and flourished. Up in the Great White North for his first Canadian concert no different. Still, I was surprised when Proof pulled me aside after the interview and whispered a particular request in my ear: ecstasy - two pills for him and two pills for Eminem. Okay.

When one is immersed in the downtown scene of any city, drugs are omnipresent and easy to access. My days spent in abandoned warehouses and fields fascinated by the deep bass of speaker stacks and dancing cherubs in the rearview, long gone. Proof's request presented a dilemma, so I called for a guide. The zodiac of the day pointed to an after-hours den three floors above a pool hall awash with private elevator, door sta, surveillance cameras, and reinforced metal doors. Fermé.

The designated guide redirected to a loft that bordered lower Parkdale. The district rife with crime, drugs, prostitution, the mentally ill, and rooming houses populated by disenfranchised members of society on government assistance. Once, the month-long refuge of James Earl Ray immediately after he assassinated Martin Luther King Jr. There is no waiting for the man. Reverence and respect for the guide connected the dots with open arms. Nothing to hide, believe what I say. The unusual request met with ease. The contents of the bag 100% MDMA. The caveat communicated to ensure the recipients are prepared for the ride. Why do you think they call it dope?

* * *

Back in 1999, I got a call from my man, Harris Rosen. I co-owned Toronto's internationally known Dance Music club, *Industry*, and contributed updates on DJs who played at the club and what remained of the Rave scene to the magazine. Harris had interviewed Dr. Dre's new rapper, this white kid from Detroit, Eminem. At the time I had no idea who he was as I had not seen the "My Name Is" video. Still, I had heard about a young white rapper coming up.

> *"Do you want to come and check him out? He's playing at The Opera House."*
>
> *"Yeah, that's cool. I ain't got nothing to do before the club opens."*
>
> *"Be at The Primrose 7:30 p.m."*

The Primrose Hotel is situated around the corner from the besmirched *'Hooker Harvey's.'* Harvey's a fast-food chain known for flame-grilled hamburgers, hot dogs, and its half-french-fries-half-onion rings box of Frings. The seedy area and particular location a bustling stop for street walkers, pimps, fiends, and those seeking snacks.

I was surprised that the label put the kid up there, but he was on the way up, so you got to start somewhere. I met Harris and the guide in the lobby. I hadn't been in that place for a long time. It was super seedy, and I just wanted to get upstairs. We jumped on the elevator, and I asked him what floor. Harris hit nine on the greasy elevator board, and we began the ascent. As soon as the door opened we heard music, the floor was jumping o.

We spotted Bizarre and assumed he was Slim's security. We hailed him up, said we're looking for Eminem, and he pointed down the hall. We turned and bounced down the corridor past rooms 901, 903, 905, 907 and 909, to face Room 911. I was like, *"Damn! That's the emergency room,"* and the door was open! Eminem stood at the opposite end of the room facing the mirror. He noticed us, and a magnificent smirk surfaced as he made his approach while excitedly calling out for Proof.

"Yo! What's up? Did you hook it up? You hook it up?"

I didn't know what he was talking about. I thought he was doing an interview. The guide stared him down and solemnly spoke.

"Yeah, yeah. I got 'em, I got 'em."

That was enough for Eminem to race to the door and jump out in the hall.

"Proof, Proof! Get in here, get in here! Proof!"

Next thing you know, Proof was in the emergency room. Then, the guide reached into his pocket and pulled out four Blue Jays: blue MDMA pills. At the time they were the rage in the scene. I knew a few of those from the party scene. There were Red Rockets and Blue Jays. I knew they were right. I was surprised because this was 7:30 at night and I didn't know what the hell was going on, but, these kids were talking about E's. I knew they were rappers. I didn't think they knew about ecstasy.

Eminem asked what they were and had a stunned look on his face when the guide told him they were pure MDMA. He and Proof stared at the bag in silence and exchanged knowing glances. The excitement was palpable. Next thing you know, Eminem grabbed two and handed the bag to Proof. They just smashed those things right at the same time. I was like *"Yeah! You just hit two – You gonna do that right now and go perform?"* Eminem looked at me, nodded and said, *"Every night."* Damn! Right then and there I knew I had to go to the show. I wanted to see how the fuck someone was gonna snap o two pills and then just go rip up a crowd.

On the way back to the elevator, Bizarre slipped Harris a copy of his tape, *Attack of the Weirdos.* The first song is called "Rap Guys." Harris popped it in the car cassette deck and turned up the system. What is up with Bizarre?

Sure enough, we got to *The Opera House,* and the place was going o. There was like 700-800 kids in there acting crazy. The lights were dimmed, and it was on. Eminem jumped out, and stage dived into the crowd. Then, he gets back onstage and pours two bottles of water over his head. Harris told me the song is called "Brain Damage." Shit was popping off. I was like, holy shit, an AK47 just set o in *The Opera House!*The place went bananas, and as I was jumping all over the room, I lost my keys. The second set in two weeks. It was an electrifying experience. I walked out of there, and I knew who the fuck Eminem was. That's what's up.

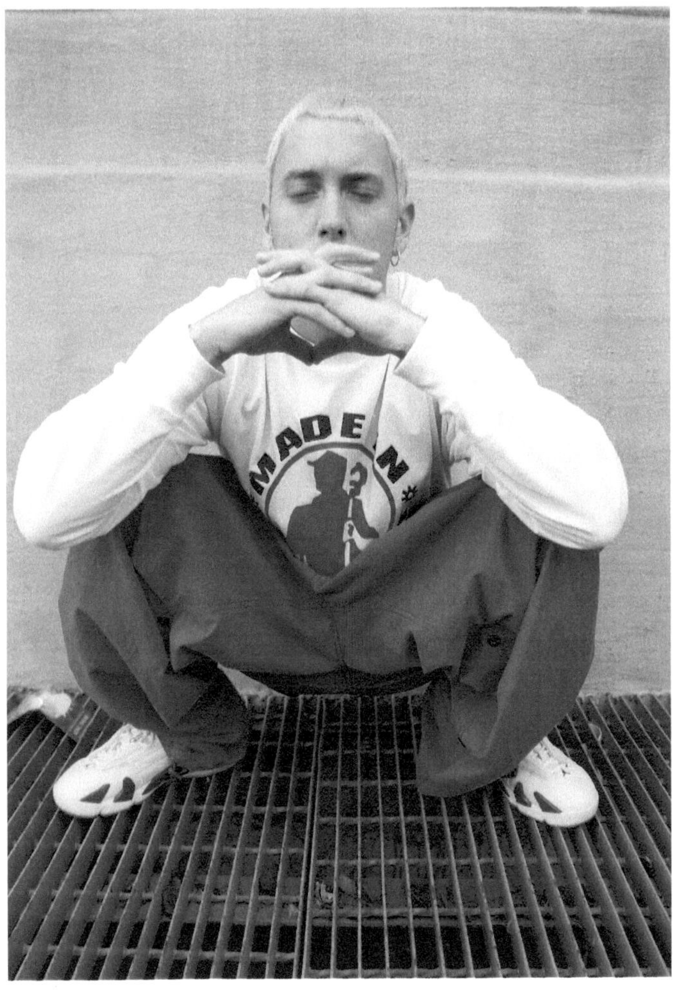

To engage in contemplation or reflection

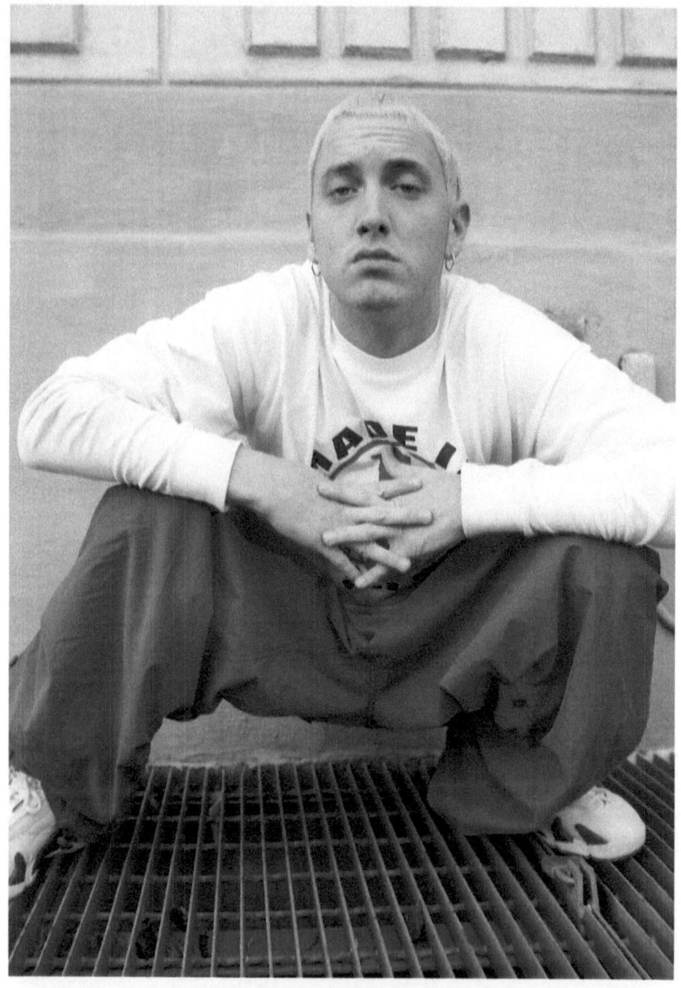

All I've got now in my defence is my innocence. I've been hypnotised

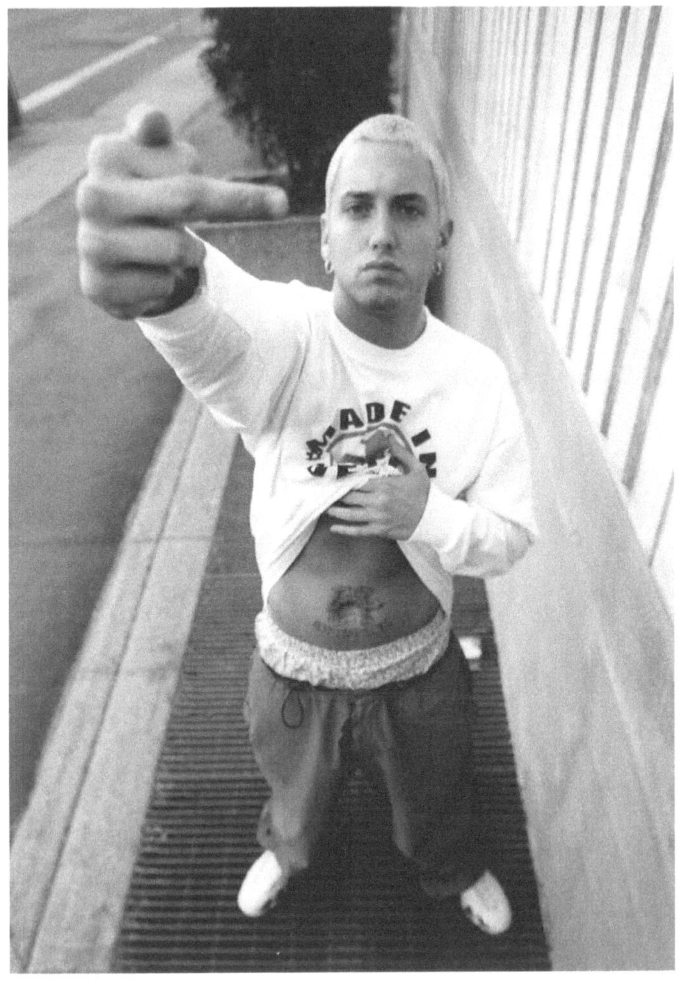

The Valedictorian of Middle-Finger U

XIII

CODA

DeShaun Dupree Holton, aka P, Big Proof, Proof & Derty Harry, got murdered at the CCC Club on 8 Mile Road, at 4:30 a.m. on April 11, 2006, at the age of 32.

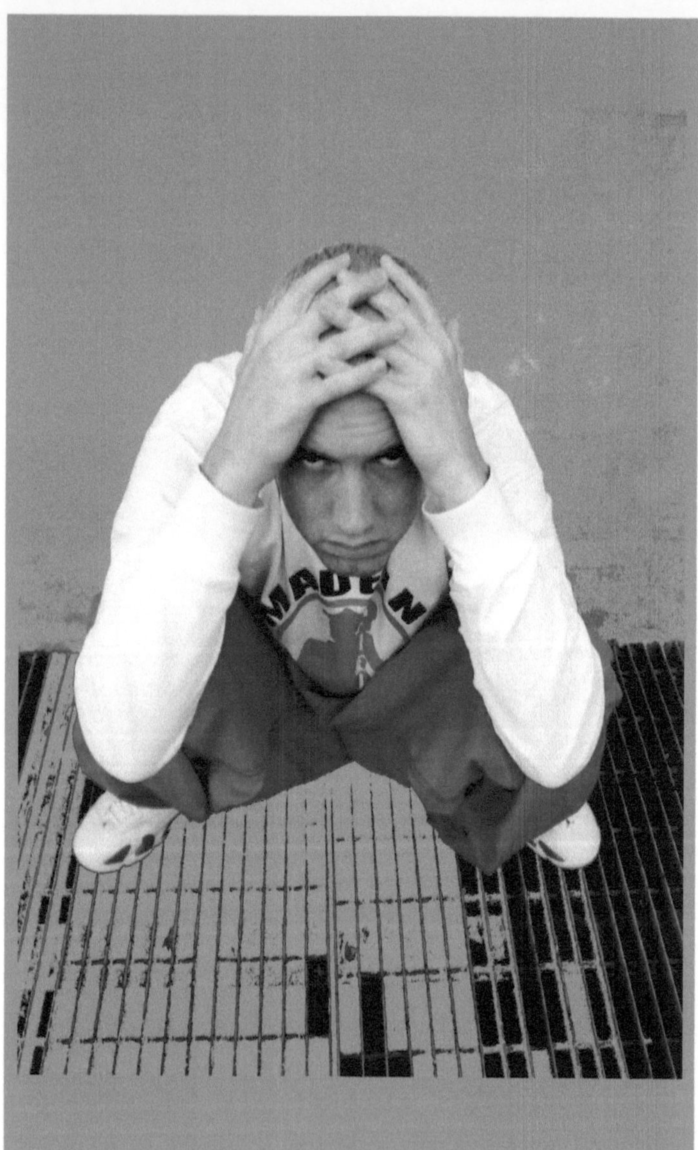

39

Postscript

DeShaun Dupree Holton, aka P, Big Proof, Proof & Derty Harry, got murdered at the *CCC Club* on 8 Mile Road, at 4:30 a.m. on April 11, 2006, at the age of 32. Several accounts made the rounds and depicted what happened. The agreed facts it stemmed from a game of Billiards; the club cleared out as Proof lay dead on the floor. His body stripped of money and jewels and discarded out the back door.

Proof and Desert Storm veteran Keith Bender got into a heated argument. The Bouncer, Bender's cousin, Mario Etheridge, fired one warning shot. Proof responded by shooting Bender in the head. Etheridge spontaneously responded by firing four rounds into Proof; two to the head and two to the chest. In another account, Etheridge fired two warning shots. Proof responded by shooting a slug into the ceiling, Bender attacked Proof, and Etheridge shot and killed both in the ensuing commotion. Other portrayals indicated gunshots by several CCC Club patrons. Etheridge fired two shots into the ceiling and Proof shot Bender; Etheridge fired warning shots as Proof and Bender continued to fight.

The Detroit Police and *Detroit Free Press* framed the story as a "Thug Rapper" killing a war veteran. The narrative that both Proof and Etheridge entered the club not in possession of a gun, and each grabbed a firearm during the melee. Proof pistol-whipped Bender, and then shot him in the face and threatened to do it again. Etheridge responded and shot Proof once in the back of the head and twice in his back. Mario Etheridge turned himself into the Detroit Police, who charged him with two counts of possessing and discharging a weapon without a license. Etheridge pleaded not guilty, sentenced to time served and a $2000.00 fine for weapons violations. He became a free man on October 26, 2006, and a new season of violent Detroit murders ensued.

The death of Proof occurred in the worst period of Eminem's life. The demand for his time and the associated pressure of living as Eminem caused him to hit a wall as the *Anger Management 3 Tour* came to a halt in Detroit on August 13, 2005. Forthwith, ten European dates set for the next month were cancelled. Slim hospitalised on August 18, 2005, and placed in rehab for six weeks to face his addiction to sleeping medication, Ambien; *Shady Records* artist and friend, Obie Trice faced death on New Year's Eve 2005. Trice targeted on the Detroit expressway by a barrage of hollow-point bullets that entered his Range Rover. Two shots connected, precisely one to the dome where it remains to the day; He remarried Kimberly Anne Scott two weeks later on January 14, 2006. Sadly, the joy turned to pain when the marriage ended in divorce after 82 days; His estranged mother, Deborah Nelson Mathers continued to suer from Munchausen Syndrome, drug addiction, and breast lymphoma.

The cumulative damage precipitated a relapse of significant consequence. Slim absorbed up 100 Valium and Vicodin pills daily to mollify his sorrows, and the opioids served to produce a life of mental anguish and isolation. Shady Records satiated the masses concerned for the health of Slim and delivered *Curtain Call: The Hits* for Holiday season 2005, and *Eminem Presents: The Re-Up* one year later for Holiday 2006.

Eminem briefly resurfaced on September 12, 2007, to address rumours circulated by Shady Records artists that he was in the studio recording. He armed a state of limbo with no set date on new music and established that he went through personal things and felt good. An inevitable Methadone overdose equal to four bags of heroin transpired two months later in November 2007. Eminem rushed to the hospital within hours of losing his life as his vital organs began to shut down.

Slim marked his return from the shadow of death with a performance at Ernst Happel Stadion in Austria on January 8, 2008.

The long-anticipated *Relapse* album, his first in five years, released on May 15, 2009. *Relapse* entered the Billboard Top 200 at #1 and became the best-selling Hip-Hop album of the year. He performed eight dates with two shows in England and six in the U.S., including *Jimmy Kimmel Live* and the *American Music Awards*. *Relapse: Refill* discharged on December 21, 2009, with seven more songs.

Relapse the recipient of the 2010 Grammy Award for Best Rap Album. Back in the groove, Eminem showed no signs of letting up when *Recovery* dropped on June 10, 2010. The album entered the Billboard Top 200 at #1 and held the spot for seven consecutive weeks becoming the top-selling international album of 2010. He performed fifteen times with dates in France, England, U.S., Switzerland, Scotland, Ireland, and Brazil.

"Not Afraid" the recipient of the 2011 Best Rap Solo Performance Grammy, and *Recovery*, the recipient of the 2011 Grammy Award *for* Best Rap Album and Album of the Year. Eminem continued to make up for the lost time and joined forces with Royce da 5'9 for the long-awaited return of Bad Meet Evil. The nine-song EP, *Hell: The Seque*l delightfully served to the masses on June 14, 2011. He performed eleven times beginning with the *43rd Annual Grammy Awards* on February 23, and select dates in the U.S., Canada, England, Northern Ireland, and Australia.

Eminem performed four dates in 2012. A cool-guy showcase in Austin for *SXSW*, and overseas in Japan, South Korea, and the rich-guy exhibition at the *Formula 1 Abu Dhabi Grand Prix*.

The Marshall Mathers LP 2 released on November 5, 2013. It debuted at #1 on the *Billboard Top 200* and became the second-best selling album of the year. He performed ten shows with dates in the U.S., Belgium, Ireland, Scotland, France, and England.

Slim performed twenty-three concerts over 2014. Seventeen solo shows in the U.S. and Canada, and overseas on the *Rapture 2014 Tour* in South Africa, Australia, and New Zealand. Six of the performances in U.S. stadiums as co-headliner with Rihanna. The release of *Shady XV* - a double-disc tribute to *Shady Records* fifteen releases - November 24, 2014.

"The Monster" featuring Rihanna, the recipient of the 2015

Best Rap/Sung Collaboration Grammy and *The Marshall Mathers LP 2* the recipient of the 2015 Grammy Award for Best Rap Album. *The Ocial Eminem Box Set* issued on March 12, 2015. Eminem, the Executive

Producer of the *Southpaw* soundtrack and creator of its lead single, "Phenomenal," released on June 2, 2015. Slim active behind the scenes and in the studio also recorded "Best Friend" with Yelawolf, and finally matched up with TechN9ine and Krizz Kaliko to record "Speedom (Worldwide Choppers 2)." The lone live date a promotional performance at the YouTube Space in New York City on September 1.

D12 released *The Devil's Night Mixtape,* Hosted By DJ WHOOkid as a free download on Hallow's Eve, October 30, 2015. Missing in action on its first iteration, Eminem responded to the outcry of fans and quickly recorded "Devils Night Intro" for its *Reloaded* re-release.

2016 delivered performances on three *Lollapalooza* dates; Brazil on March 12, Argentina on March 18, and Chile on March 19. The "Kill For You" single with singer, songwriter Skylar Grey came on September 23, 2016. "Campaign Speech" marked Slim's return to the freestyle world. The eight-minute socio-political thriller released on the eve of the third Presidential debate, less than three weeks before the election on October 19, 2016. The twentieth anniversary of the *Infinite* album celebrated in digital on his VEVO channel.

Eminem continued to record in 2017. "No Favors" with Big Sean is a Detroit City aural treat The storied *BET Awards* "The Storm" freestyle, masked as a cypher in an underground parking lot, focused on the 45th President of the United States and gun control. He performed six times with four dates in England, one in Scotland, and on *Saturday Night Live* in New

York City. Eminem's 8th consecutive Billboard #1 album, the maligned *Revival* released December 15, 2017.

"The River" featuring Ed Sheeran set o 2018 in proper form with over 60 million views of its video. Fueled by anger brought on by the poor reception to *Revival, Kamikaze* came without warning on August 31, 2018. It is the 9th consecutive Eminem album to debut at #1 on the Billboard Top 200, and the best-selling album of 2018. He performed eighteen times throughout the year with dates in the U.S., Norway, Sweden, Denmark, Switzerland, Italy, Germany, Netherlands, and England.

February 15, 2019, Slim performe d a one-o show at Aloha Stadium in Honolulu, Hawaii. The short five-dat e *Rapture 2019 Tour* - February 20 - March 2 - his long-awaited return to Australia for four stadium shows and a stop at Westpac Stadium in Wellington, New Zealand. February 23, 2019, marked the 20th anniversar y of *The Slim Shady LP*. Its *Expande d Editio n* reissu e include d acapellas , instrumental s and radio edits.

Eminem is the most successful artist to debut after 1983 and the most successful rapper of all-time. He has sold 97 million studio albums, including 8 Mile, 14.4 million physical singles, 18 838 000 compilation albums, and 197 million downloads. With the addition of 17 200 199 801 audio streams and 22 726 962 356 video streams. D12 has sold 8 450 000 albums. (chartmasters.org)

Eminem profoundly declared his withdrawal from D12 on the Kamikaze album's "Stepping Stone."

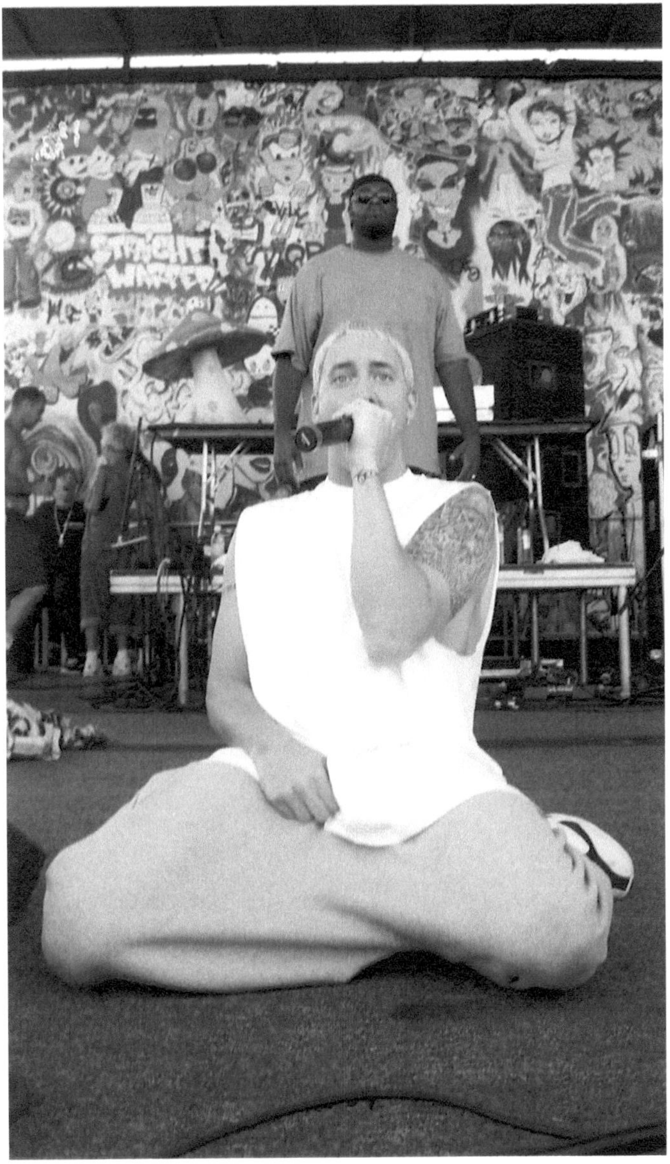

Go Chubby Boy, make tha block hot. Go Chubby Boy, make her pussy pop

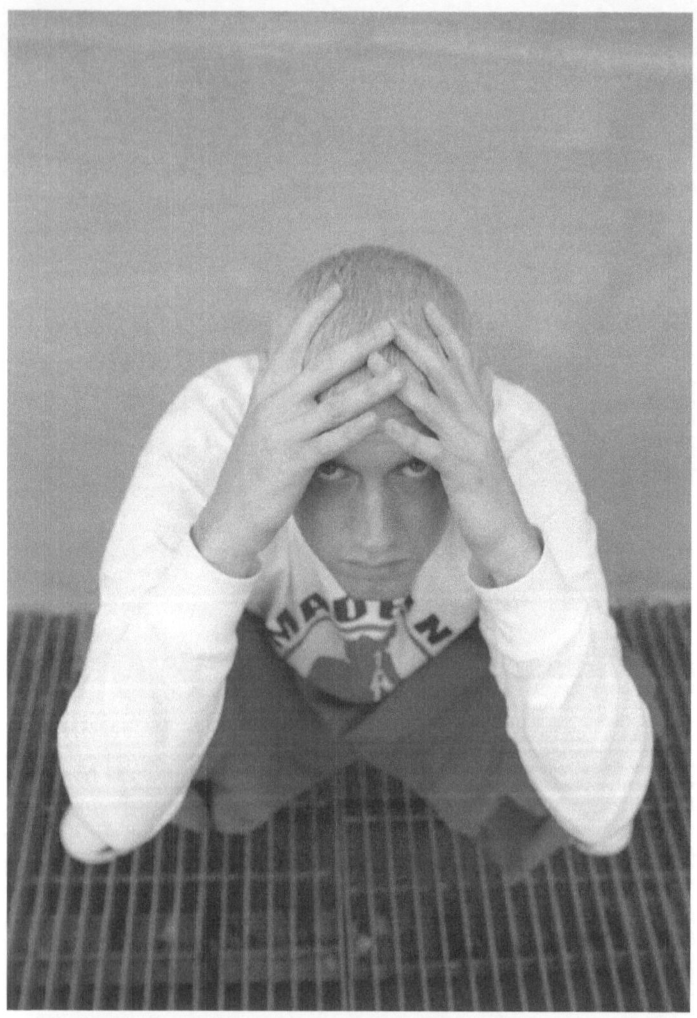

I got so much trouble on my mind. Refuse to lose. Here's your ticket.

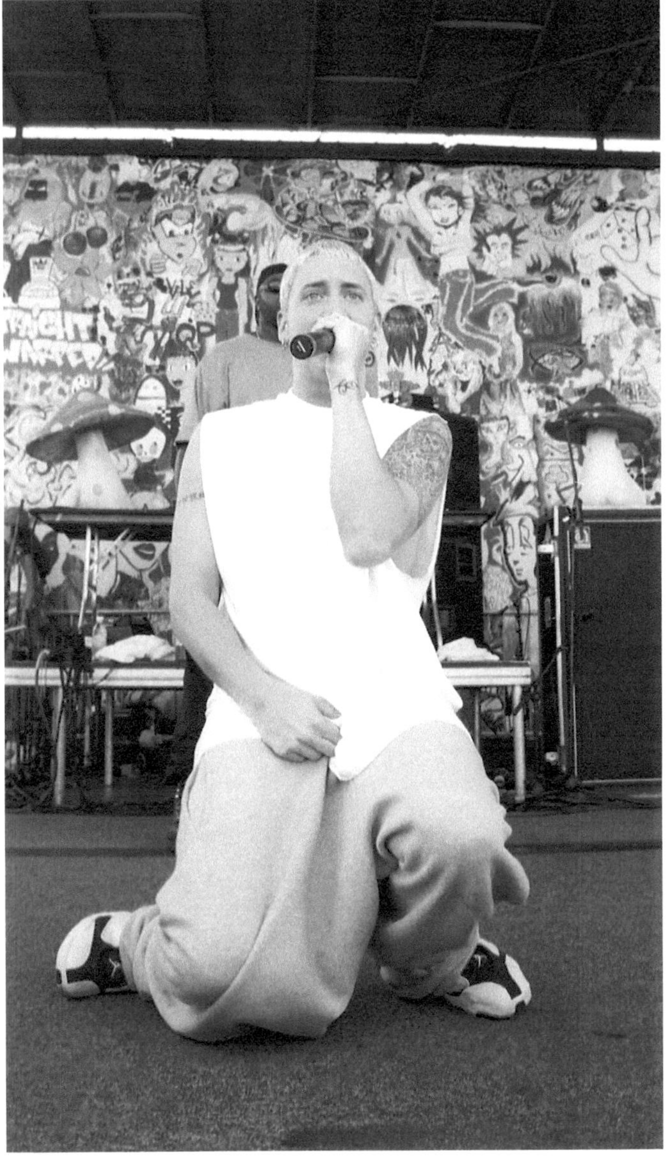

What's better on a hot summer day than baggy track pants and J's?

XIV

1999 SHOWS

A list of every show and city Eminem performed live in 1999.

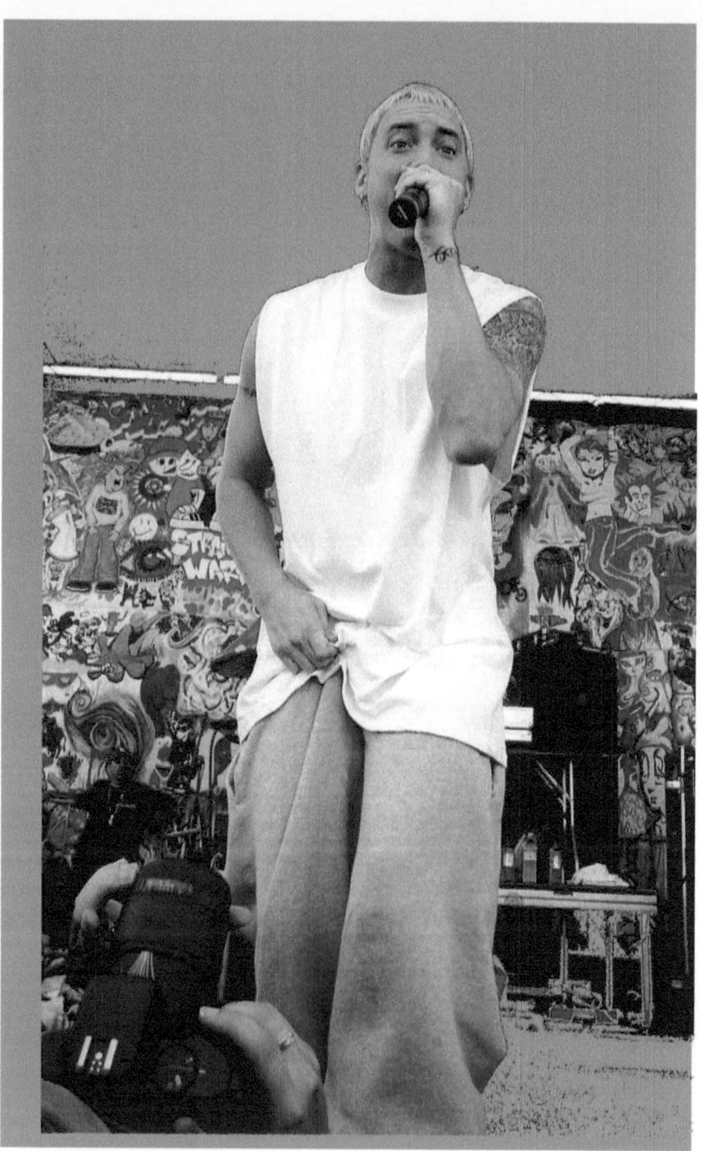

40

1999 DATES & THE SLIM SHADY LP TOUR

January 9 – Tramps, New York, NY

February 16 – The Middle East Downstairs, Cambridge, MA
February 22 – House of Blues, West Hollywood, CA

March 5 - The Lane, Staten Island, NY
March 29 – Subterania, London, UK

April 3 – Mack & Bellevue, Detroit, MI
April 7 – House of Blues, Chicago, IL
April 8 – The Odeon, Cleveland, OH
April 9 – Metropol, Pittsburgh, PA
April 10 – The Opera House, Toronto, ON
April 11 – Le Studio, Montreal, QC
April 13 – Conte Forum, Chestnut Hill, MA
April 14 – The Palladium, Worcester, MA
April 15 – Hammerstein Ballroom, New York, NY
April 16 – John Hopkins University – Shriver Hall, Balti-

more, MD
April 18 – Nation, Washington, DC
April 20 – House of Blues, North Myrtle Beach, SC
April 21 – Tabernacle, Atlanta, GA
April 22 - House of Blues, lake Buena Vista, FL
April 23 – Cameo Theatre, Miami, FL
April 25 - Janus Landing, S. Petersburgh, FL
April 27 – House of Blues, New Orleans, LA
April 30 – Albuquerque, N

May 2 – Summit Music Hall, Denver, CO
May 4 – Club Rio, Tempe, AZ
May 5 – House of Blues, Las Vegas, NV
May 8 – House of Blues, West Hollywood, CA
May 8 – House of Blues, West Hollywood, CA
May 9 – The Fillmore, San Francisco, CA
May 11 – Roseland Theatre, Portland, OR
May 12 – The Rage, Vancouver, BC
May 13 – Showbox, Seattle, WA
May 16 – First Avenue, Minneapolis, MN
May 17 – Liberty Hall, Lawrence, KS
May 19 – The Rave, Milwaukee, WI
May 21 – Van Andel Arena, Grand Rapids, MI
May 22 – Cincinnati, OH
May 23 – State Theatre, Detroit, MI

June 26 – Astro Arena, Houston, TX
*June 27 – Artist Square, Dallas, TX
*June 29 – Celebrity Theatre, Phoenix, AZ

*July 2 – Orange Pavillion, National Orange Show Event

Centre, San Bernardino, CA

*July 7 – Thunderbird Stadium, Vancouver, BC

*July 8 – Kingdome, Seattle, WA

*July 9 – Kingdome, Seattle, WA

*July 10 – Utah State Fair Park, Salt Lake City, UT

*July 14 – New World Music Theatre, Tinley Park, IL

*July 16 – Randall's Island Park, Randall's Island, NY

*July 17 – Three County Fairgrounds, Northampton, MA

*July 18 – Stone Pony Lot, Asbury Park, NJ

*July 23 – Parc des Iles, Montreal, QC

*July 24 – The Docks, Toronto, ON

July 25 – Phoenix Plaza Amphitheater, Pontiac, MI

July 27 – Robert F. Kennedy Memorial Stadium, Washington, DC

July 28 – House of Blues, North Myrtle Beach, SC

*July 29 – Lakewood Amphitheatre, Atlanta, GA

*July 31 – Pompano Beach Amphitheatre, Pompano Beach, FL

September 9 – MTV Video Music Awards – The Metropolitan Opera, New York, NY

September 10 – Universal Amphitheatre, Universal City CA

September 11 – Tampa, FL

September 18 – Pic-a-Chic Farms, Bloomington, IN

October 25 – Rockefeller, Music Hall, Oslo, Norway

October 26 – Cirkus, Stockholm, Sweden

October 27 – Columbiahalle, Berlin, Germany

October 29 – AJZ Talschock, Chemnitz, Germany

October 30 – Planet Music, Vienna, Austria

October 31 – Muathalle, Munich, Germany

November 2 – LKA Longhorn, Stuttgart, Germany
November 3 – X-tra, Zurich, Switzerland
November 4 – Capitol, Oenbach, Germny
November 6 – Live Music Hall, Cologne, Germany
November 7 – Manchester Academy 1, Manchester, UK
November 8 – Astoria Theatre, London, UK
November 9 – Astoria Theatre, London, UK
November 10 – Barrowland, Glasgow, Scotland
November 12 – Melkweg The Max, Amsterdam, Holland
November 14 - Vega, Copenhagen, Denmark
November 16 – Kulturbolaget, Malmo, Sweden
November 17 – Grosse Freiheit, Hamburg, Germany
November 26 – Royal Oak Music Theatre, Royal Oak, MI

December 13 – Downtown Royal Oak, Royal Oak, MI

***Warped Tour**

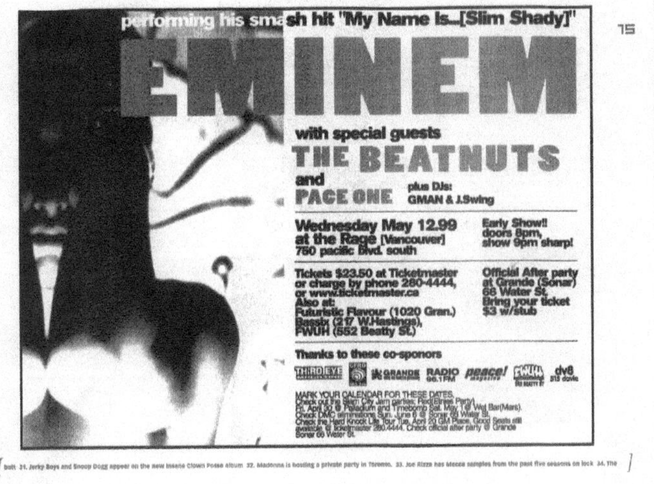

Performing his smash hit "My Name Is" in VanCity, 1999

Harris Rosen

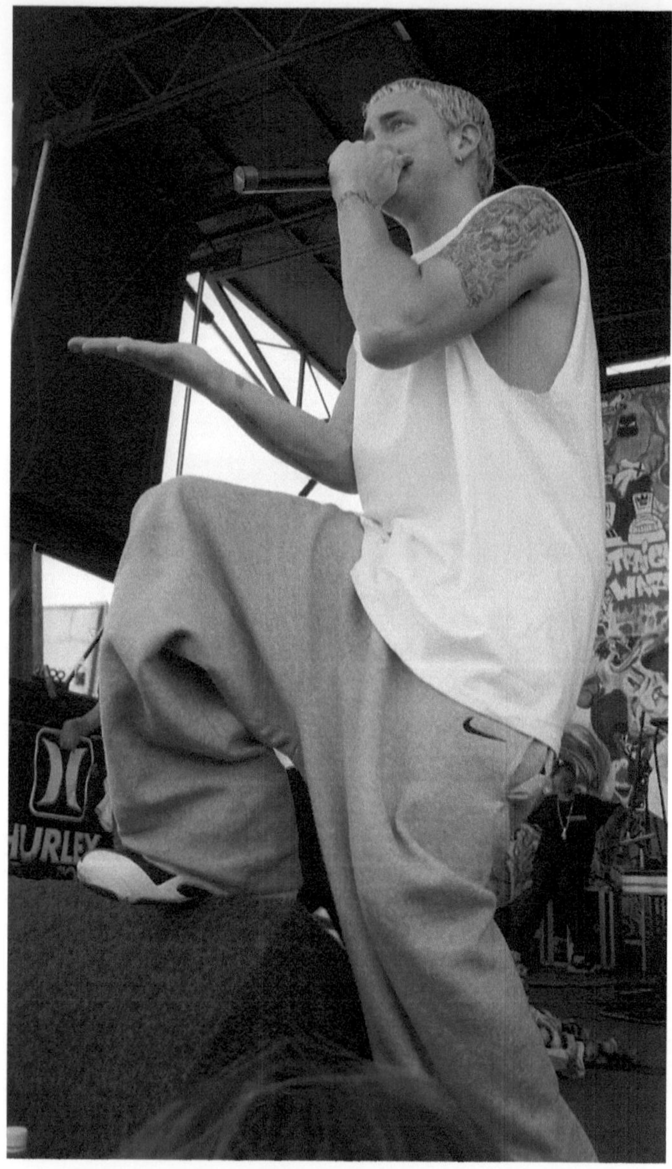

Friends, Romans, countrymen, lend me your ears

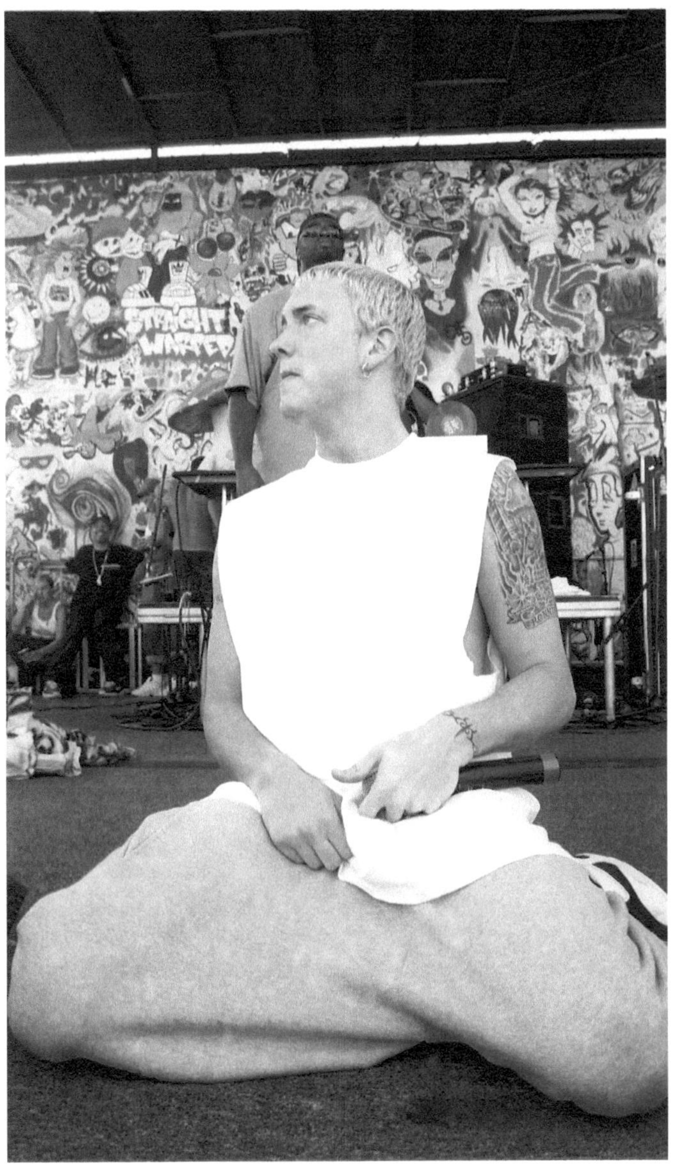

Straight Warped. Salute to Kevin Lyman.

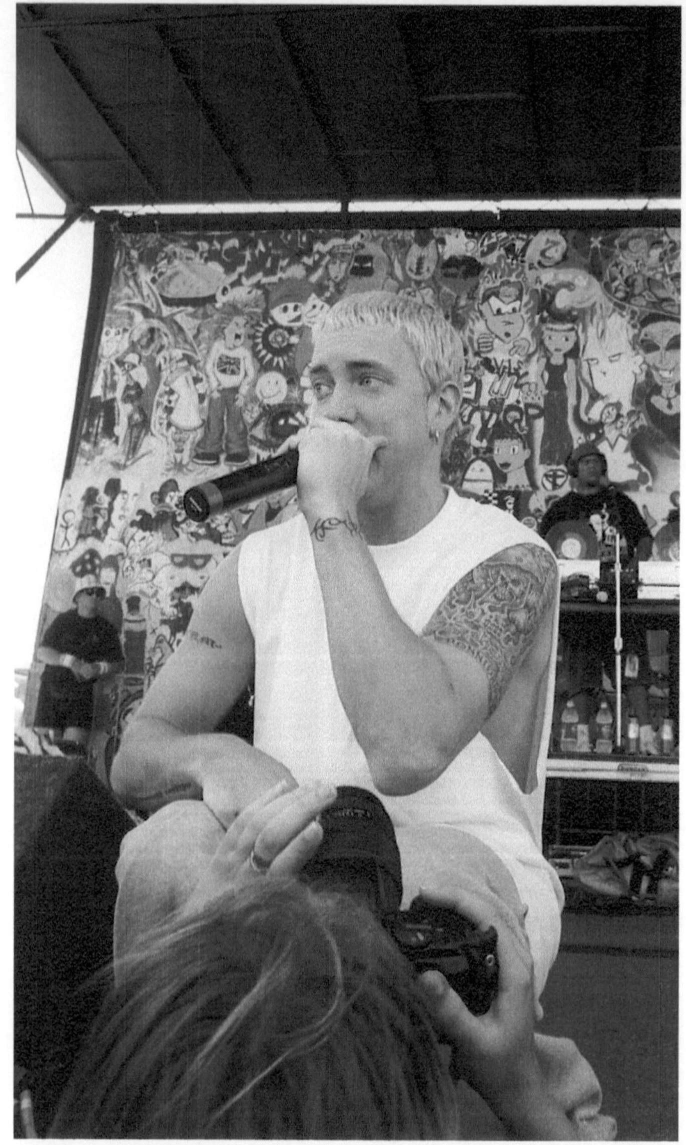

Up close and personal, getting nuff attention

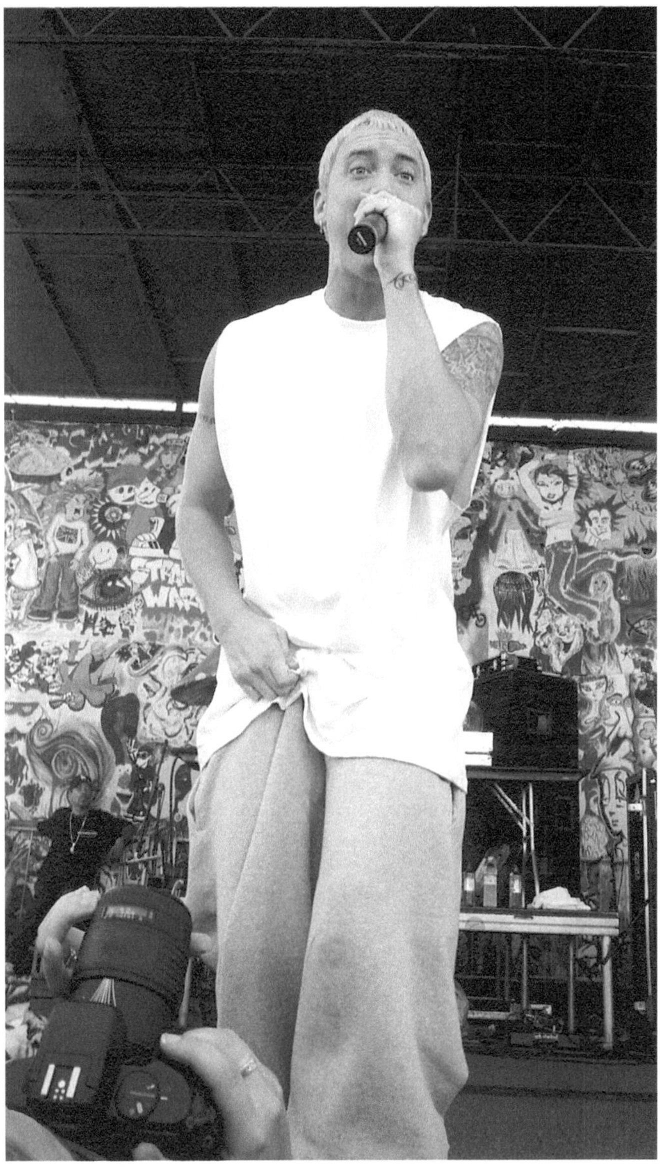

You're emotion in motion, my magical potion

XV

DISCOGRAPHY

Albums, Singles, and Featured Artist music

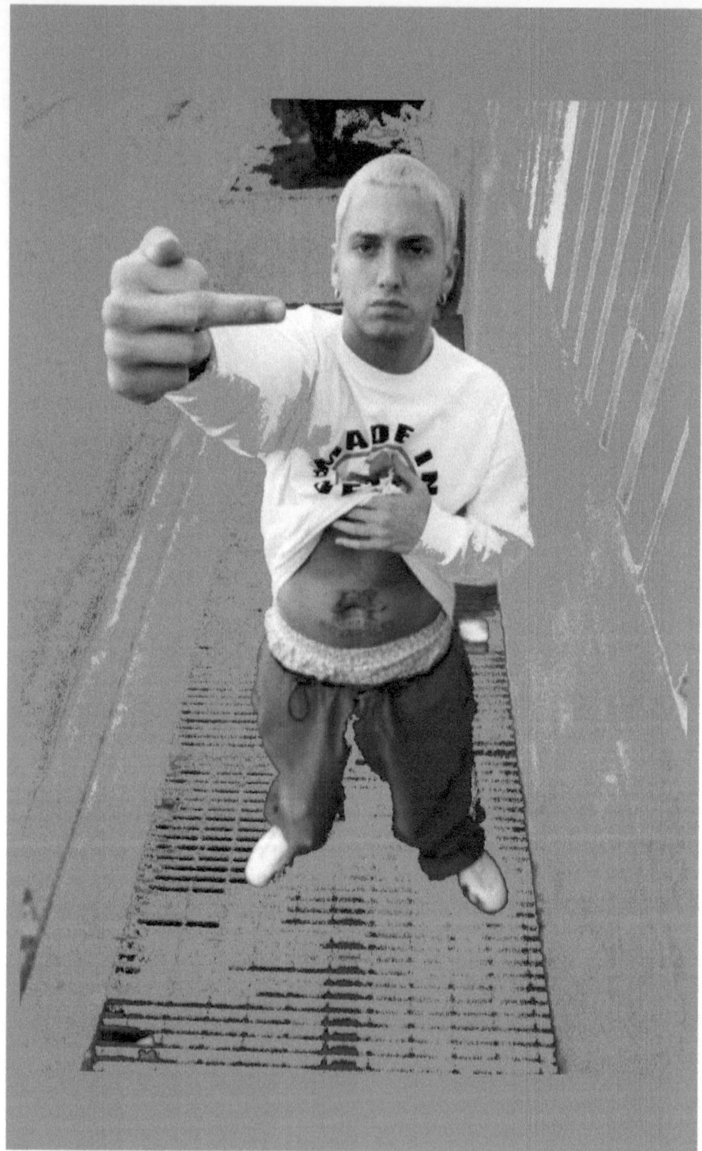

41

Albums

Eminem

Infinite - November 12, 1996
The Slim Shady EP - December 10, 1997
The Slim Shady LP - February 23, 1999
The Marshall Mathers LP - May 23, 2000
The Eminem Show - May 21, 2002
Music From And Inspired By The Motion Picture 8 Mile - October 29, 2002
Straight From The Lab - November 7, 2003
The Singles - December 23, 2003
Encore - November 12, 2004
Curtain Call: The Hits - December 6, 2005
Eminem Presents: The Re-Up - December 5, 2006
Relapse - May 19, 2009
Relapse: Refill - December 21, 2009
Recovery - June 21, 2010
The Marshall Mathers LP 2 - November 5, 2013

Revival – December 15, 2017
Kamikaze – August 31, 2018

D12

Devil's Night - June 19, 2001
D12 World - April 27, 2004

Bad Meets Evil

Hell: The Sequel EP - June 14, 2011

42

Singles

1997

"Just Don't Give A Fuck" - September 23, 1997 (Web Entertainment)

1999

"My Name Is" - January 25, 1999

"Role Model" - May 26, 1999

"Guilty Conscience" featuring Dr. Dre – June 8, 1999

"Any Man (Fucking Crazy)" ***Soundbombing II*** (Rawkus Records)

"Bad Influence" - November 2, 1999 ***End of Day***s soundtrack

2000

"The Real Slim Shady" - April 15, 2000
"Spread It Out" - August 26, 2000 (Yosumi)
"The Way I Am" - September 7, 2000
"Stan" - November 21, 2000

2001

"I'm Back" - April 3, 2001
"Bitch Please II" (featuring Dr. Dre, Snoop Dogg, Xzibit, Nate Dogg) promo only

2002

"Without Me" - May 14, 2002
"Cleanin' Out My Closet" - July 16, 2002
"Lose Yourself" - October 28, 2002
"'Til I Collapse" (featuring Nate Dogg) promo only

2003

"Superman" (featuring Dina Rae) - January 27, 2003
"Sing for the Moment" - February 25, 2003
"Business" - July 22, 2003

2004

"Just Lose It" - September 28, 2004
"Mosh" - October 26, 2004
"Encore" (featuring Dr. Dre & 50 Cent) - November 9, 2004

2005

"Like Toy Soldiers" - January 24, 2005
"Mockingbird" - April 25, 2005
"Ass Like That" - June 7, 2005
"When I'm Gone" - December 6, 2005

2006

"Shake That" (featuring Nate Dogg) - January 17, 2006
"You Don't Know" (featuring 50 Cent, Lloyd Banks and Ca$his) November 7, 2006

2007

"Jimmy Crack Corn" (featuring 50 Cent) - March 6, 2007

2009

"Crack A Bottle" (featuring Dr. Dre & 50 Cent) - February 2, 2009
"We Made You" - April 7, 2009
"3 A.M." - April 23, 2009
"Old Time's Sake" (featuring Dr. Dre) - May 15, 2009 promo only
"Beautiful" - August 11, 2009
"Hell Breaks Loose" (featuring Dr. Dre) - December 15, 2009
"Elevator" - December 15, 2009
"Music Box" - December 21, 2009 digital only

2010

"Not Afraid" - April 29, 2010

"Love The Way You Lie" (featuring Rihanna) - June 25, 2010

"No Love" (featuring Lil Wayne) - October 5, 2010

2011

"Space Bound" - June 18, 2011

2013

"Berzerk"- August 25, 2013

"Survival" - October 8, 2013

"Rap God" - October 15, 2013

"The Monster" (featuring Rihanna) - October 29, 2013

2014

"Headlights" (featuring Nate Ruess) - February 5, 2014

"Guts Over Fear" (featuring Sia) - August 25, 2014

"Detroit VS Everybody" (featuring Royce da 5"9, Big Sean, Danny Brown, Dej Loaf & Trick-Trick) - November 11, 2014

2015

"Phenomenal" - June 2, 2015 ***Southpaw*** soundtrack

"Kings Never Die" (featuring Gwen Stefani)- July 10, 2015 ***Southpaw*** soundtrack

2016

"Campaign Speech" - October 19, 2016 digital only

"Infinite" (F.B.T. Remix) November 17, 2016 (Web Entertainment/Bass Brothers) digital only

2017

"Walk On Water" (featuring Beyonce) – November 10, 2017

"Untouchable" - December 8, 2017 digital only

"River" (featuring Ed Sheeran) – December 15, 2017

2018

"Chloraseptic" (Remix) (featuring 2 Chainz & PHresher) January 8, 2018 digital only

"Nowhere Fast" (featuring Kehlani)– March 27, 2018

"Fall" - September 4, 2018 digital only

"KILLSHOT" - September 14, 2018 digital only

"Venom" - September 21, 2018 digital only

"Lucky You" (featuring Joyner Lucas) - November 30, 2018

* * *

Bad Meets Evil

"Nuttin' To Do" / "ScaryMovies" - 1998 (Game Recordings)

"Lighters" (featuring Bruno Mars) - June 11, 2011

"Fast Lane" - June 14, 2011

D12

"Shit On You" - December 5, 2000

"Purple Pills" - June 5, 2001

"Blow My Buzz" 2001

"Ain't Nothin' But Music" - October 2, 2001 (France and Belgium)

"Fight Music" - October 2, 2001

"911" (with Gorillaz) – December 7, 2001

"My Band" - March 14, 2004

"How Come" - June 6, 2004

43

Featured Artist Singles

1998

"We Shine" with Da Ruckus 1998

1999

"Dead Wrong" with Notorious B.I.G. - October 26, 1999
"Shady Vs. Stretch" with Stretch Armstrong 1999
"What's the Dierence" with Dr. Dre and Xzibit – November 16, 1999

2000

"Forgot About Dre" with Dr. Dre - January 29, 2000

2002

"Rock City" with Royce da 5"9 - January 5, 2002

"Hellbound" (H&H Remix) with J-Black & Masta Ace - April 22, 2002

"Rap Name" with Obie Trice - October 22, 2002

"Love Me" with Obie Trice and 50 Cent - October 29, 2002

2003

"You Must Be Crazy" with DJ Rectangle, Hot Karl & Dree

"Patiently Waiting" with 50 Cent – February 6, 2003

"Hail Mary" with 50 Cent & Busta Rhymes – April 15, 2003

2004

"One Day At A Time" (Em's Version) with Tupac featuring Outlawz - March 22, 2004

2005

"Drama Setter" with Tony Yayo & Obie Trice - June 28, 2005

"Welcome 2 Detroit" with Trick-Trick - October 11, 2005

2006

"Smack That" with Akon - September 25, 2006

2007

"Touchdown" with T.I. - July 3, 2007

"Peep Show" with 50 Cent– September 11, 2007

2009

"Forever" with Drake, Kanye West and Lil Wayne - August 27, 2009

"Drop The World" with Lil Wayne – December 28, 2009

2010

"Airplanes (Part II)" with B.o.B. and Hayley Williams - April 13, 2010

"Roman's Revenge" with Nicki Minaj - October 30, 2010

"Love The Way Your Lie PT II" with Rihanna – November 12, 2010

2011

"That's All She Wrote" with T.I. - January 11, 2011

"I Need A Doctor" with Dr. Dre and Skylar Grey - February 1, 2011

"Writer's Block" with Royce da 5"9 - March 29, 2011

2012

"Throw That" with Slaughterhouse - August 21, 2012

."Numb" with Rihanna - November 19, 2012

"My Life" with 50 Cent and Adam Levine - November 26,

2012

"C'Mon Let Me Ride" with Skylar Grey - December 11, 2012

2014

"Calm Down" with Busta Rhymes - July 1, 2014

"Twerk Dat Pop Dat" with Trick-Trick and Royce da 5'9 - July 5, 2014

2015

"Best Friend" with Yelawolf - April 14, 2015

"The Hills" with The Weeknd - October 10, 2015

"Speedom (Worldwide Choppers 2)" with TechN9ne & Krizz Kaliko - May 4, 2015

"Medicine Man" with Dr. Dre, Candice Pillay and Anderson.Paak

2016

"Kill For You" with Skylar Grey - September 23, 2016

2017

"No Favors" with Big Sean – February 3, 2017

"Calm Down" with Busta Rhymes – April 22, 2017

"Revenge" with Pink – October 13, 2017

2018

"Caterpillar" with Royce Da 5'9 and King Green – May 3, 2018

"Majesty" with Nicki Minaj and Labrinth – August 10, 2018

2019

"Rainy Days" with Boogie – January 25, 2019

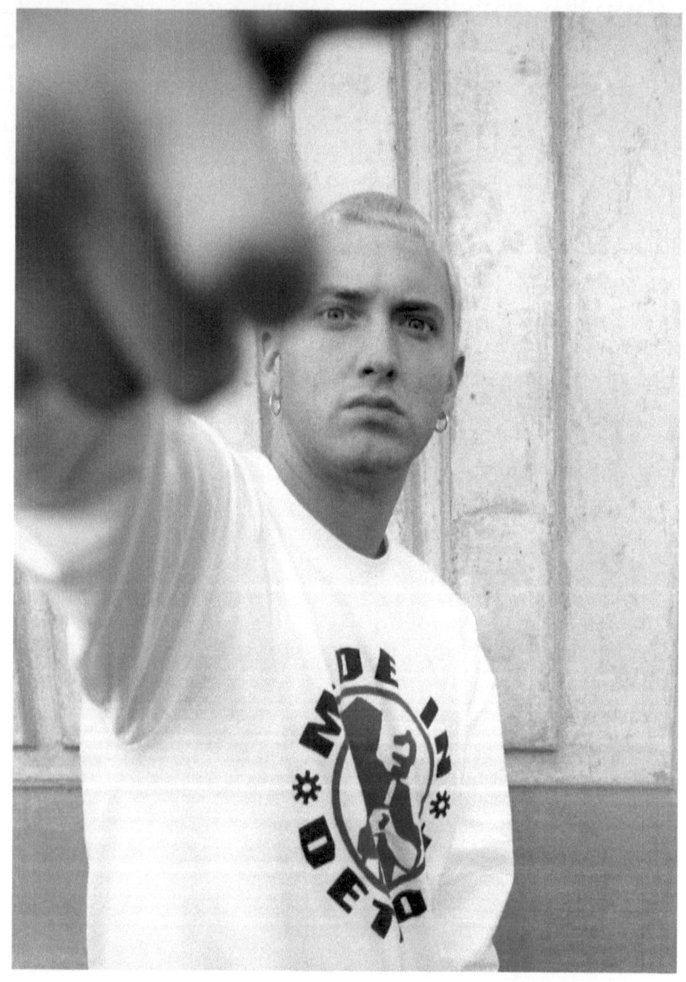

Last shot sure killed me. Pour another drink.

Acknowledgments

Thank you, those who inspired me behind the scenes to produce this book. I appreciate your support, friendship, guidance, and understanding.

Matt Sonzala - it is twenty-two years since we met up here in Toronto, Canada, during *Canadian Music Week*. I do not keep in contact with many people, yet, you and I have managed to maintain over two decades of friendship. Indeed, this speaks to you being one of the real ones, which is rare in this life. For an American citizen living in Texas, your dedication to the *Trailer Park Boys*, *FUBAR*, and *Creemore Springs* is legendary. I hope to see you and your daughters up here for many summers to come, and that one day you realise the dream of becoming a Canadian citizen. Thank you for the behind the scenes photos of our day at *Hash Bash* and the Eminem rave in downtown Detroit. The Flashback you wrote inspired more than words can say.

I am grateful to Ron Boudreau for digging in his storage tubs to unearth long-forgotten negatives from our April 10, 1999 photo shoot and the summer '99 instalment of the *Warped Tour*. The trust you showed by permitting me to scan them speaks volumes. Indeed, we have come a long way from the days of *Rock 'N Roll Heaven* in the late '80s to now.

To Gavin Gerbz, well, we did it, again. Another one of our infamous missions has come to light. Thank you for the detailed recollection, and a special salute to the one they call Grayson.

To Toronto Wayne, Wayne O'Brien, the courses and meetings have already enabled hundreds to utilise the internal tools proven to make them flourish in life. I look forward to the continued build of our efforts.

Salute to Eon Jr., CEO, The K, Moosh, Freebird & Nic, Eric Wilson, Dr. David Esho, Dr. S., YellowCardFeChatBack crew, Walter and Scadding Court Community Centre, Hone Fitness, Grandma Shirley and Auntie Krystal, Rob Harris, William J. Genereux, Phil Demetro, Gabo, Whitey Don, Brett Lightstone, Dennis Garces, & Original Kid Rock.

Respect to the legions of international Slim Shady fans. This one is for you!

Limited Edition Giclée Prints

Photos featured in this book are available to order as 11 x 14 & 16 x 20 Giclée prints signed by the photographer.

This offer is exclusive to The Real Eminem.

Email info@behindthemusictales.com for details.

Review Request

Please share your opinion of this book with a rating and review wherever you got it. I appreciate all of your feedback, and I love hearing what you have to say.

Thank you!

Who is Harris Rosen?

Father. Son. Brother.

HARRIS ROSEN was born and lives in Toronto, Canada. He is the author of ten Behind The Music Tales books. For twenty years, he self-published the national lifestyle magazine Peace!

Rosen compiled an authentic archive of audio, images and videos interviewing hundreds of composers, artists, actors, and athletes in the midst of a whirlwind of musical and cultural revolutions that occurred throughout the '90s and 2000s.

Harris Rosen is the co-founder of Canada's largest ADHD community. Through community, compassion and connection, the program facilitates free courses and meetings that simplify how to apply the fundamental internal tools to thrive in life.

adhdtoronto.com
twitter.com/mrheller1
instagram.com/behindthemusictales
facebook.com/behindthemusictales
behindthemusictales.com

Praise for Harris Rosen

"This guy! I plead the fifth. This guy is nuts."
 - **Eminem**

"Dope questions, man. Very insightful, very thoughtful."
 - **GURU (GangStarr)**

"You like a Psychiatrist or some shit? This shit is just coming out but go ahead."
 - **Mary J. Blige**

"Definitely a real interview! Digging deep up in there, man. Not afraid to ask questions!"
 - **K-Ci Hailey (Jodeci)**

"The Wizard asked me for a copy of your magazine."
 -**Guy-Manuel de Homem-Christo (Daft Punk)**

"You didn't wear your glasses, and you haven't carried your hearing aid. What else is wrong with you?"
 - **Bushwick Bill (Geto Boys)**

"Peace and blessing, Brother Harris. Thank you for inspiring my words. Keep 'yo balance."
 - **Erykah Badu**

"Can I see that pen?"

-Bobby Brown

"What else do you want to know? Talk to me."

- Aaliyah

Free Book

Download New York State of Mind 1.0 FREE!

There are hundreds of interviews and dozens of Behind The Music Tales series books to follow. That's why I am giving you a copy of New York State of Mind 1.0 for FREE!

Get exclusive 1992 and 1993 interviews with Tragedy Khadafi, Brand Nubian, and Pete Rock & C.L. Smooth FREE!

Enter your email to download the book for free. Get the newsletter with updates on new releases, exclusive images, and original audio. Be eligible for free advance copies of upcoming books. You can opt out at any time.

http://eepurl.com/ckHZdb

ADULT ADHD BEHAVIOURS

- A lack of organization
- Usually interrupting others
- Fidgeting
- Easily distracted by others and sound
- Problems starting task
- Unfinished projects
- Inability to follow instructions
- Difficulty learning new things
- Lack of esteem
- Argumentative behaviours with authority figures
- Hot temper
- Trouble coping with stress
- Frequent mood swings
- Sharing inappropriate information
- Easily bored, daydreaming and zoning out
- Difficulty following one thought
- Unable to control impulsive behaviours

THERE IS NO MAGIC PILL

90% OF ADHD IS UNRECOGNISED, UNTREATED OR MISDIAGNOSED

ADHD medication provides cognitive function, the ability to focus and learn. The combination of the correct medication with psycho-educational courses are proven to facilitate change.

It is your duty to self to discover, learn, develop and practice internal wellness techniques to thrive in life. The power to manifest wellness is paramount to your lifestyle.

WHAT IS IN YOUR WELLNESS TOOLBOX?

- Sleep for a minimum of 7 hours daily
- Drink a minimum of 2L water daily & eat a healthy diet
- Exercise to block stress, improve memory, sleep and mood
- Meditate to significantly reduce negative triggers and balance your thoughts
- Get out in the community, go for a walk and avoid isolation
- Identify and pursue your passion
- Be compassionate, express gratitude and practice empathy

www.ingramcontent.com/pod-product-compliance
Ingram Content Group UK Ltd.
Pitfield, Milton Keynes, MK11 3LW, UK
UKHW040022200726
13854UKWH00001B/313